Selling Your Home in 45 Days or Less

Selling Your Home in 45 Days or Less

A Guaranteed Guide to a quick sale in any market

CHARLES T. ADKINS

Printed in the United States of America

First Printing, 2013

Design and typesetting by Kachergis Book Design

ISBN: 978-0-9887931-0-1

This book is dedicated to:

My mother, Carol, who taught me faith and the value of hard work and was and is always there for me,

Wanda Smith, longtime Realtor, who had the common touch and encouraged me to enter into the business of selling real estate,

Dan Cottingham, friend and mentor, who understands real estate like no one else I have met and is always willing to share,

My family and friends who have encouraged me along the way, and

My wife, Melinda, who understands and loves people and is my best friend and partner in all things.

Contents

Selling Your Home in 45 Days or Less

Introduction

YES, IT IS POSSIBLE and even probable to sell your home within the next 45 days!

After the downturn in real estate in 2008, many sellers became discouraged. They read the newspapers and turn on the local news and the messages they receive are less than optimistic. I am here to tell you that your home, any home, can be sold in the next 45 days. Here is the basic premise for accomplishing that task.

To achieve what many people will tell you cannot be done—that is, to have your home under contract and sold in the next 45 days—you will use a basic plan that involves the following steps:

1. Understanding how a buyer will look at and assess the condition of your home and what you must do to get your home in excellent condition for the buyers to view.
2. Becoming a student and then a master of real estate concepts, terms and contracts. In other words, you must know and understand the rules of the game.
3. Staging your home and property to their fullest potential.
4. Choosing the correct team to help you implement your plan for completely conditioning, staging and marketing your home.

I have spent many evenings over the last 20 years sitting at kitchen tables talking to sellers about their homes. After a brief tour and some discussion about structural improvements that have been made, I talk with the owners about their motivations for selling and their price expectations. At some point during the conversation—typically when I am in the middle of my listing presentation—the inevitable statement pops up. "I am not going to give this house away," I am usually told, regardless of what neighborhood, demographic, age group, or socio-economic class with which I am working. Man, woman, married couple, family…it does not matter who is behind the words, but they are bound to come out at every single listing appointment.

The idea of not "giving away" a home is downright pervasive to a home seller and understandably so. For many individuals and couples, a home represents the bulk of their investment portfolios and their life savings. All of that money is wrapped up into a single, neat package called a home. That is a tough pill to swallow when it comes time to sell, particularly when the expectations of the seller do not match market realities.

You may think you "gave it away" but you may have won after all

Cynthia and Sam had purchased a home at the peak of the market in late 2006. There were life changes, first twins, then the loss of a job that led to their decision to sell the home and rent for a few years. They were motivated sellers. Sam had a good friend Tom who was a Realtor who prepared a CMA and looked hard at the supply of homes on the market. The supply was growing each month at a time when buyers were becoming ever more scarce. It was obvious they would have to put the home on the market at a price less than they had paid. When the first offer came in, it was lower than the asking price, but Tom negotiated on their behalf and the home was eventually sold for a price of 11% lower than they had paid. Both Cynthia and Sam were understandably upset with their first real estate venture ending in a loss. But after another five years had passed, the home sold again, this time for 25% under the amount they had accepted. It was only then that they both thought themselves to be fortunate to have listened to Tom.

No one wants to give away their life savings; no one wants to give away their most valuable asset. Complicating the challenge is the fact that most homeowners are also psychologically attached to their homes. Maybe their children were born there and took their first steps in the backyard. Maybe a deceased parent or spouse spent time at the dwelling, which represents happy memories and good times. Regardless of the individual situation, there are always ties that bind us to our homes.

And now it is time to move onto another place; perhaps downsizing is the goal. This is a typical motive for empty nesters that no longer need five bedrooms and three bathrooms to accommodate their family size. The kids are off at college (and commanding a new chunk of the checkbook!) and maintaining so many square feet is no longer necessary or practical. Maybe it is a job transfer to a new city or perhaps it is time to "move up" into that new neighborhood that you have had your eye on for years. No matter what is driving you to sell, it is clearly time to move on and put yourself in the seller's seat.

At the center of that decision is a key ingredient: your home's sales price. In the real estate industry we use a term "Fair Market Value" or simply, FMV, to pinpoint the amount of money a buyer will be willing to pay for a specific property.

Now, FMV sometimes loses its "true meaning" in the real world. For example, the buyer may be *willing* but not *able* to buy. Let's say she really wants a home, but cannot afford one right now due to a poor credit score. She is holding her "prequalification" letter from a lender, but the amount she can actually afford to borrow is not accurately reflected in that letter. In another situation, the seller may be *willing* to sell but unable to do so because of a significant financial lien against the property (which would have to paid off before the property could be transferred to a new owner).

What does it mean? FMV is the amount of money that a ready, willing, able, knowledgeable, and unpressured buyer will pay to a ready, willing and able, knowledgeable and unpressured seller.

In today's market, the issue of financing is often the deal breaker between a "willing, ready, and able" buyer and a seller. Perhaps the applicant gave the lender or mortgage broker incomplete or false information that was in turn used to generate the prequalification letter. At some point during the approval process all of that information must be verified. When the red flags go up, the buyer's chances of getting financing go down.

More commonly, a buyer will make an offer on a house and attach a legitimate prequalification letter to the bid. Once the offer has been successfully negotiated and accepted by the seller, the buyer learns that because he has not been on the job long enough—or, perhaps that monetary gift he was expecting to receive will be delayed indefinitely—he is no longer qualified for the mortgage amount. Self-employment, the lack of down payment funds, and other obstacles are also fairly common during this stage, and they make that ready, willing, and able buyer that much more elusive.

These scenarios can be difficult for a seller to digest, particularly when he or she is expecting to close on a $200,000 transaction and move to a new neighborhood, city or state. The seller does not remember, nor does he really care, that the on-target offer was generated by someone who was unqualified to purchase their home. Somehow, that $200,000 number stays in the seller's mind as a benchmark. That number simply *has* to be attained because he already had an offer for that amount. It is a milestone that must be reached, at least in his mind.

Now, getting back to the definition of FMV. It is important to note that it is not always the buyer who is at fault when a deal falls apart. Mr. Smith (the seller) prices his home at $200,000 and Mr. Brown (the buyer) enters into a contract with him to buy the home at that price. Mr. Smith has not disclosed that he owes $220,000 on his mortgage. At closing, Mr. Smith must bring a substantial amount of money to the table—money that he does not have. He is not eligible for a short sale (selling it for less than the mortgage balance and settling up with his lender for the lesser amount). In this example the seller clearly does not fit into the "ready, willing, and able" definition. He is not financially able to perform at the contracted price AND he is probably pressured by circumstance to have entered into the contract in the first place—not to mention the legal implications and possible action against seller and agent.

At the very least, the buyer will remember that the contract price was $200,000. Again this becomes the benchmark in the buyer's mind for what he perceives to be the value of the home. After all, he had this home under contract at this price, regardless of whether this was the FMV for the home...or not.

∿

Here's a simple example of how seller misrepresentation can derail a deal: A seller, Mr. Smith, went under contract to sell his home to a buyer, Mr. Brown. Smith represented when building the home he had sealed the outside of the basement wall and had a French drain extended around the perimeter of the home. However, when it rained for a prolonged period, the basement leaked profusely. The seller had further tried to seal the inside of the basement wall to hide the intrusion. The buyer brought a home inspector and a general contractor to the home and offered to pay to have the drainage system checked in a small area from the outside of the home. As it turned out, the wall had not been sealed and there was no French drain in place. The seller had misrepresented (i.e., lied) about what had been done to prevent water from entering the basement. Although this deal ultimately closed, the seller (under threat of lawsuit) had to perform the waterproofing and drainage that he said had been done. This was a case of intentional misrepresentation.

In another sale, the seller stated to the buyers that, to his knowledge, the crawl space beneath the home was dry and that it had always been dry. A licensed home inspector and a general contractor found that the wooden band sill on which the home rested had areas where the moisture exceeded 20%. The wood was, in essence, rotting away in those areas and had to be replaced.

The sale went through, but the repair negotiations stated that the seller caused the damaged band sill to be replaced. In this case, the seller had been told that the crawl space was dry when he purchased the home several years earlier and he had never entered the crawl space and did not know about the problem with water and dampness that caused the wooden members to rot. This was a case of non-intentional or negligent misrepresentation.

∽

In both of these cases, however, the outcome was the same. One seller had lied and the other simply did not know, but both sellers had to make the repairs to the damaged areas. Both had to pay top dollar to finish the projects within a short time frame and both projects were completed in a situation of duress. In a later chapter we will explain the benefit of having a pre-inspection done and how this would have probably saved both of these sellers a great deal of money.

As you can see, both buyer and seller hold important positions when it comes to being ready, willing, and able to complete a real estate transaction. This is important to note as you strive to sell your home within 45 days.

I Do Not Want to Give It Away!

Since the economic downturn of 2008, homes across many geographic markets have lost value and the market is only now beginning to find a bottom. That means appreciation is still in the future for many homeowners in states like California, Florida, Nevada, and even North Carolina, all of which felt the strong "highs" of the boom times and the resultant "drop" during the recession.

Here's a tip: Across most U.S. markets, home appreciation is *still in the future.* You can use this to your advantage as a homeowner. Most buyers believe that they are getting a good deal on a home and cling to this belief steadfastly. If you or your agent can show why this neighborhood and in particular this home may well appreciate in the near future, a buyer may be more likely to purchase and perhaps pay a price closer to what you the seller have in mind.

Meeting seller pricing expectations right now is a challenge. Many sellers are holding onto appraised home values that were valid several years ago when the real estate market was booming. In 2007, for example, some areas of the country were experiencing home appreciation rates in the double digits. The guy down the street sold his property for *twice what he paid for it just two years earlier!* And across town, new condos were selling for *30 percent more than any other multi-unit property in town!* Things were booming, properties were being flipped, and most of us never had heard of terms like "distressed" and/or "short sale," and "foreclosure" was a term that was rarely heard.

Then the economic downturn happened. Homeowners came back down to reality. Markets that experienced the most significant jumps were hit hardest as home prices retreated to early-2000 levels. Home equity levels plunged, distressed properties flooded the market, and a buyer's market went into full force.

With those realities in mind, it is important to note that what your home was worth in early-2000 does not matter. And what it was worth during the worst of the economic recession makes no difference either. What *does* matter is how much it is worth today. To most effectively manage your pricing expectations you will have to come to grips with this reality:

> ⌒ What your property was worth in the distant past *is not an indicator* of what it is worth today. (And by "distant" I mean three to six months ago.) Sometimes when a seller pulls out and refers to an appraisal that was done two years prior, I have to explain to him that it is no longer a valid estimate of the home's value. It is an entirely different market and financial landscape than it was two years ago. Whenever a "distressed" property has sold in the nearby area, it has affected the value of this seller's home by a small degree. There are certain areas where that price erosion has been substantial.

Now, being a homeowner myself, I know that sellers are subjective when it comes to their homes. In most cases they are both emotionally-bound and psychologically-bound to the property and to the investment that they have in it. They naturally want to get the absolute best return for that investment and for the years of effort that they have put into maintaining, upgrading, cleaning, and caring for the home and the surrounding property.

I cannot argue with that logic, but I can try to help sellers take an objective look at the property in question. Using the "walk a mile in their shoes" philosophy, I encourage sellers to look at their homes through the eyes of a relocating buyer. That person is coming into the market and looking at all of the properties for sale within specific price points, that are within certain geographic regions, and that possess the desired features and amenities. With listing inventories as high as they are right now, the options from which buyers have to choose are great (unless, of course, his or her parameters are extremely specific, in which case the options may be fewer).

Just the Facts: Buyers will *always* buy the better-conditioned and better-priced homes in a particular market.

Now, in order to sell a home to this buyer, your home must be in near-perfect condition and priced competitively with the other homes on the market. The operative word here is "condition"—which has replaced "location" as the mantra for real estate. That's right, location, location, location is out the window and the new mantras are condition, condition, condition and price, price, price.

The Commoditization of Real Estate

As you ponder the pricing issue and apply it to your own situation, remember that homes have become like commodities in a sense. Google Maps can help put this fact into perspective. Use the application to take a view from outer space and then zoom into a particular neighborhood. Now zoom out to where you can see perhaps 50 or so homes. Look at them closely. Just how different are they? From your bird's eye view they appear to be about the same size, right? Without looking at every home's interior you know that each one includes a kitchen, a place to eat meals, a room or two to sit and talk or read or watch a movie. Each one has sleeping quarters for three or four, maybe more, a bathroom or two, and somewhere to park a car.

Your home is just one of those millions of homes that have similar, basic features. Now, I am sure some of you are probably thinking, "Wait a minute, my home is historic and very different than those other properties!" That may be true, but remember that yours is not the only historic home for sale right now. Nor is it the only waterfront property or penthouse suite. No matter how seemingly unique your home is, I can probably find one just like it in your market or somewhere in the U.S. (There are exceptions to every rule but I will stand by this statement that, 99% of the time, real estate *is* a commodity business.)

Acknowledging the fact that your home will be up for sale in a highly commoditized marketplace will go a long way in ensuring a successful sales process.

Real Estate Versus Gold

A friend of mine decided to invest money in gold over the last several years. Gold has been touted by many as a hedge against inflation and he decided to make the plunge. First he bought several ounces at

$1,600 per ounce. Then the price went higher and he bought more at $1,800. Finally he bought several ounces at $1,900.

The gold market was skyrocketing for a while, but then it fell back down to around $1,650. Gold prices fluctuate just like home prices and all commodity prices do. They go up and then they fall back down to earth. Everyone wishes that real estate values would continue to climb like they did during the decades leading up to the 2008 market drop. These are just wishes, unfortunately, because no one is willing to pay 2007 prices for property—at least not at the time of this writing—just like no one is going to pay my friend $1,900 for an ounce of gold. Maybe they will pay that price sometime in the future. Just as in the future the home you are selling may be worth what you hoped it was worth but in many instances, sellers are tied to a vision of what the home was worth in the past, not what it is worth today. It is the hard truth in our free-market economy where prices are largely determined by what *buyers are willing to pay for the goods.*

By now you have probably figured out why statements like, "I'm not going to give this home away," are irrelevant in today's real estate market. My gold-buying friend certainly would not be able to get away with that philosophy in the current market where gold is selling for $200–$300 less than what he paid for it. If he wants to sell, he does so at the price that buyers are ready, willing, and able to pay. In this sense, homes are no different than gold, cars, a 2x4 piece of lumber from a home improvement store, or a gallon of milk from the grocery story. There is a fair market value for each of these items and to get that price, each commodity must be in peak condition and priced at market value (or perhaps a small amount under market value).

You *Can* Sell Your Home in 45 Days or Less

This book was built on a foundation that I have developed and honed over nearly three decades, during which time I have sold over 1,000 homes. Along the way I learned that the mechanics behind the home-selling process is nearly identical across all transactions. Sure there are minor nuances that impact and change the shape of those transactions as they make their way to closing tables across the country but the common elements remain the same regardless of the individual deal.

My goal with this book is straightforward: I want to help you sell your home within 45 days, in any market. That is the amount of time it takes to handle the following basic steps:

* Evaluate the condition of a home and look at it objectively from the eyes of a buyer
* Make possible repairs and updates that make financial sense
* Choose an agent and a team of professionals that come recommended and that have a track record of experience and honest dealings
* Price the home correctly, ensuring that it conforms to the pricing of other sold comparable properties and to those currently on the market for sale
* Have the home staged by a professional and accredited home stager and understand the home staging process
* Market the home to the ready, willing and able, knowledgeable and unpressured buyers in the marketplace
* Negotiate the contract with the help and advice of your real estate consultant
* Negotiate the repairs again, with the help of your Realtor or other real estate consultant
* Receive notification of loan approval of the buyer and other information relating to the closing
* Close the property, making sure the deed is recorded and receive the proceeds from the sale

All of this can and should happen within 45 days. Technically, the home is not sold until it has reached settlement (closing) and has been recorded at the Register of Deeds or the Recording Agency in your state. Those finishing details could take time beyond the negotiation of repairs and notification of loan approval. The majority of transactions are considered to be "under contract" when all of the involved parties are waiting for the attorney, lender, or another party to schedule the closing and prepare the final loan package.

There are always reasons why a seller may not close until a specific date (such as the time it will take for his new home to be constructed and habitable) and a buyer may not want to close until a certain date (if she has 90 days before her company relocates her, for instance). Those reasons are beyond the scope of this book.

My aim is to simply set you on a path that gets to you to the point where your transaction is 99 percent complete, the loan has been approved for the buyer, there is a large amount of non-refundable earnest money protecting your interest and you, my friend, are simply awaiting the actual closing date. Yes, deals can unravel for a multitude of reasons but there are financial safeguards that can be put in place that will help cushion the blow and a sufficient amount of earnest money forfeited to you will certainly help. If that rare event happens, deposit the check, lift your head up, get out this book and start over.

This book will give you a complete understanding of the home-selling process plus all of the terms, conditions, challenges, and scenarios that you may encounter during the 45-day period. Throughout the chapters, which are organized chronologically for easy reference (from the initial "why am I selling my home?" assessment to the purchase of your next home and everything in between), you will be introduced to three major themes. These themes control the sale of your home, and they are:

* The condition of the home: This is a key element since there are many homes on the market for sale. Buyers obviously gravitate to homes that are in the best condition, all other things being equal.
* The price: You will learn a lot about this very important factor. The price is truly not based on what the seller needs but rather on what other comparable homes have been bringing.
* The marketing: Doing everything it takes to find the perfect buyer and to make that *perfect* buyer aware of your home.

Consider this book your ultimate selling guidebook. Read through it, refer to it regularly, and share it with your friends and family. It is unlike anything else available on the market today because it is built around 30 years of experience buying and selling homes in both boom and bust markets. Use the information and knowledge that you learn from it to ensure the smooth sale of your home within 45 days.

In the first chapter we will look at how to develop your game plan, review some key market terminology, and learn which renovations and repairs will pay off when it comes time to sell. If you are ready to start learning, just turn the page.

PART ONE

The Nuts and Bolts

CHAPTER 1

Developing Your Game Plan

∾ Give me six hours to chop down a tree
and I will spend the first four sharpening
the axe.

—ABRAHAM LINCOLN

EVERY SUCCESSFUL VENTURE starts with a game plan. Some of these plans are formal and others are scribbled on cocktail napkins. Regardless of the format, the end goal for your game plan should be to sell your home within 45 days. Sounds aggressive, right? Maybe other agents told you that it could not be done, particularly in today's market where buyers hold most of the cards and many sellers are offering rock-bottom prices on distressed properties.

The good news is that selling a home within 45 days **can be done in any market conditions.** You simply need to follow the advice in this book, price your home correctly, and maintain a positive attitude throughout the entire process. I have been in the business for a long time and believe me, 45 days is not a pipedream—it is a reality.

Kick off the home-selling process with a solid game plan and you will be getting into the market well armed and ready to sell. You will also have a head start over those sellers who take a more laid-back approach to the market. This is extremely important in today's real estate market, which is characterized by high housing inventory levels and tightened lending standards, the latter of which has reduced the number of qualified buyers who are ready, willing, and able to purchase homes.

My goal is to help you develop a game plan for getting your home on the market as quickly and painlessly as possible and then getting it *off* the market within 45 days. The first step will be to prepare your home for its big debut on the market.

Preparing Your Home For Sale

The first step on your 45-day journey will be to take a good, hard, long look at your home and figure out what you need to do to get it ready to sell. Put yourself in the shoes of a buyer who is entering your home for the first time: What stands out when you look around at the home? What are the great aspects of the home?

What are its weak points? Which of those weak points can be fixed, and which are just inherent qualities of the property? Take the time to get out and look closely at the competing properties. Most sellers never do this and do not understand that this can be a powerful insight into what the buyer expects for his money. When viewing competing properties, look closely at the kitchens and bathrooms, at floor coverings, at appliances, at paint colors and condition.

Assessing and comparing your property will also help you review your budget and figure out which of the renovations will actually pay off (and which ones are just cosmetic but not integral to the sales price of your home). Now, it is important to note that not all renovations pay off for sellers.

According to *Remodeling Magazine's* 2011 annual survey, steel entry-door replacements are the sole renovations that definitely boost home value enough to recoup 100 percent of costs. That does not mean other renovations will not help you fetch a higher price for your home. According to *Remodeling Magazine*, renovations that impact "curb appeal" (that first impression that buyers get when they pull up to a home) are worth their salt.

Replacing a home's lighting fixtures recoups over 70 percent of the money you spend for the project, for example, while exterior siding replacement recoups over 80 percent of the cost. Finally, the magazine reports that the typical kitchen (replacing cabinets, flooring, appliances, and counters), master suite, deck, or bathroom overhaul recouped about 60 percent of the cost. Keep these numbers in mind as you ponder any major renovations. Keep in mind that a $3,000 remodel of a 30-year-old bathroom may only net the seller $1,800 in returns. An unsightly and dated bathroom may be the very reason that a buyer asks for $3,000+ in concessions on asking price. Knowing the value that buyers place on various improvements should be the bailiwick of your real estate agent or broker. Lean on them to provide their best opinion of what should be remedied or added.

As you will read later in this book, sometimes a good cleaning, a purging of clutter and furniture, and a few coats of paint can do the trick when it comes to creating a show-ready home. Other properties will need the help of a professional stager, a strategy that you will read about later in this book.

Five Tips for Saving on Renovations

Do-it-yourself. You may already have the knowledge and skill to paint or lay tile in a bathroom or kitchen. Home Depot offers classes on many do-it-yourself projects and the savings can be substantial. A recent quote to paint the interior of a home was $3,200. The actual cost of materials was just under $600. This is quite a savings by using your time and labor. Just remember that there are items where for safety reasons or code requirements it is better to use a licensed contractor.

Saving on sales taxes. Some states and localities have sales tax holidays and some retailers will pay part or all of the sales tax.

Asking for a discount. Most prices offered by contractors are negotiable. Establish your budget and define the job clearly for the contractor. Hopefully, he will work with you to accomplish your project. Sometimes items may be left to you to do it yourself. Also ask if offering to pay cash makes any difference in the pricing. On average it will make you an additional 4%–8%.

Shopping online. Usually if you search long enough, you can find rock bottom pricing on tile, paint, faucets, light fixtures and appliances. Be sure to understand the shipping costs and return policies. Try to get a written quote online if possible.

Comparison shopping and price matching. Many businesses will do what they can to keep your business. If you find it for less at another retailer or sometimes even online, many will match the price. Some will even knock off an additional 10% if you find the same item elsewhere for less.

Again, the best thing you can do at this stage of the game is to think like a buyer. Focus on the kitchen and the common spaces (like screened-in patios) where people will gather and enjoy their homes. Curb appeal is as important as ever, and cleanliness goes a long way in creating a property to which buyers will gravitate.

Here's a Tip: Look at maintenance costs separately from renovations when budgeting for the sale preparation phase. Routine maintenance that you should have been doing anyway (like replacing any dead landscaping and corroded gutters at regular intervals) does not constitute a renovation nor should that be seen as reasons to increase the home's asking price.

Supply and Demand

The last time you had to deal with the economic concept of supply and demand may have been in high school when your economics teacher preached the principle to you. Maybe you had a little extra education on the topic in college or perhaps you are a business owner or financier who grapples with it on a daily basis. A fairly simple concept, the law of supply and demand is based on the fact that a market surplus of a specific product combined with fewer buyers (those "demanding" it) will result in a lower price. The opposite is also true: if the product is scarce and a lot of buyers want it, the price will be higher.

Applying the law of supply and demand to the real estate market is pretty easy: when there are ample buyers and few properties, prices go up. When the tables turn, prices go down. We saw this firsthand in many U.S. states in the early-2000s when the real estate market was in its heyday. Armed with low interest and no-money-down mortgages, buyers went on a tear, purchasing anything and everything that appeared on the market. Viral in nature, the fire was fanned by high property appreciation rates and a large number of first-time buyers making their way into the market. More homes were purchased during this period than at any other time in our history.

To understand the current state of affairs in the housing industry, one has to look at the factors that contributed to the sub-prime mortgage crisis in the late 2000s.

Homeownership had been rising steadily since World War II and peaked in 2004, when 69% of all Americans were homeowners. Part of the problem was that government policies were engineered under a number of agencies to provide a combination of easy money and low interest rates. It was the stated goal of the Department of Housing and Urban Development and two nominally private government sponsored enterprises, Fannie Mae and Freddie Mac, that home ownership reach three out of four or 75% of Americans. The Community Reinvestment Act, first passed by the 95th United States Congress and signed into law by President Jimmy Carter in 1977 and later strengthened under President Clinton's administration, made widespread homeownership its goal.

The Federal Reserve System

Also known as the Federal Reserve, this is the privately owned banking system that is responsible for monetary policy. Its objectives are to insure maximum employment, stable prices and moderate long-term interest rates. As the central bank, the Fed sets the rates and protects against bank panics. The rate at which the Fed loans money to the rest of the private banking system determines the rate at which you may borrow for a mortgage.

The underlying problem was that as the standards were relaxed, more and more people were qualifying to receive loans with little or no money down and with incomes that could scarcely be justified by their ability to pay. All of this led to the home-buying frenzy of the early-2000s. The banks and the government-sponsored enterprises bundled all of these dubious mortgages into packages that were then peddled to unsuspecting investors worldwide.

The problem came of course when the Federal Reserve decided to raise interest rates and all of a sudden the artificially qualified buyer/homeowners were unable to make their monthly payments. As more and more homeowners defaulted, the bundled securities were no longer able to meet their obligations. The entire system came to a halt and this precipitated the Great Recession and we are still feeling the effects. Although there is enough blame to go around, many fingers were pointed at Andrew Cuomo who as Secretary of the Department of Housing and Urban Development (HUD) took a great role in the aggressive policies by HUD to raise the percentage of homeowner-ship by minorities. In fact he boasted about it, stating his initiatives as crusades for social and racial justice.

Over the next several years the fallout was particularly difficult. By September 2008, the average home price had dropped 20% from its peak in 2006. As of March 2008, nearly 9 million borrowers or 11% of all homeowners had negative equity in their homes (meaning that they were worth less than what was owed). That number is believed to have risen to around 25% in 2011 and in an April 2012 Gallup poll, 43% said that the home they lived in was worth less than what they paid.

Think about that for a moment: Four out of ten homes may have negative equity. The life savings of many Americans decimated since much of their net worth was in the value of the home, which now had dropped significantly.

However the crisis happened and whomever you may want to blame, one thing is certain: this event changed the housing market for the five years that have elapsed since then and policies have been reformulated and put into place that affect all Americans, homeowners, renters, and borrowers alike. It has affected our banks, our borrowing ability, our cost of goods and our jobs.

It is safe to say we have been operating in a true buyer's market. Put simply, that means that qualified buyers have held the cards and have called the shots. But the market is changing as it always does. As available properties decrease and buyer demand increases it will again become a sellers market. There is a natural ebb and flow to supply and demand. That is why pricing your home correctly, preparing your home for showings, and working with real estate professionals is more important than ever to getting your home sold within 45 days.

Absorption Rates

Another important measure that you should be looking at as a seller is the absorption rate, or the rate at which homes are selling within a specific geographic region. Real estate absorption rates factor in three key points: a specific time frame (one month, three months, etc.); the number of homes sold within that time frame; and the number of active listings that are currently for sale.

Your real estate agent will be able to tell you what the current absorption rate is for your area. You will use that number to figure out how the market is trending in terms of a buyer's market versus a seller's market and supply and demand. It is important to remember that the absorption rate correlates to the number of days on the market. Many homes have been on the market for an excessive number of days and many times it is difficult to determine exactly how long a particular home has been on the market.

Your real estate agent should be able to help you understand both absorption rate and a true count of days on the market for both the sold comps used as well as the competing homes in the area. The longer a home is on the market, the more it is perceived as a "problem" by buyers and their agents and/or there may be a distressed situation. Ultimately, homes that have been on the market for too long a time end up selling at a lower than market value.

Want Versus Need

There is a difference between *wanting* to sell and *needing* to sell. It is important to make this distinction *before* you get too far into the sales process. Here are some of the questions you should ask yourself:

* Why do I want to sell my property?
  * If the answer is that you need to sell it, due to divorce, a job relocation, etc., then you can skip the next few questions.
* What are the benefits of owning this property?
* What are the downsides of owning this property?
* What will I miss about this property and will I be able to replace those things in a new home?
* What am I experiencing personally or professionally that lends itself to a home sale?
* Am I truly committed to selling this home within 45 days and for the highest possible market price?

Answering these questions honestly right now will not only help you truly determine if now is the time to sell, but it will also provide you with some of the tools that you will need to deal with the inevitable market forces with which you are going to deal. Kind of like the

1990s ads touted, "This is not your father's Oldsmobile," this is *not* the same market in which you may have bought and/or sold homes just 10 years ago. Things have changed.

Here are three very important changes that will impact your 45-day plan:

1. **The distressed market is flooded.** You have probably noticed the many short sale signs in your region and the many foreclosure notices posted in your local newspaper. Perhaps a friend, family member, or co-worker has been impacted by this trend and has lost a home to foreclosure or sold one for less than what was owed on it (a short sale—which we will discuss in depth later in this book). These distressed properties are the bane of "traditional" sellers who are trying to get the highest possible price for their homes and within the shortest amount of time. To attain this goal, homeowners have to compete with short sales that are priced 10–20 percent lower than traditional properties (or, in the case of foreclosures, as high as 30 percent). This is a challenge. Throw in the fact that the economic recession turned many of us into bargain hunters and the situation is even further exacerbated. The good news is that banks are starting to realize that they can get more out of these properties and that they do not have to offer them as fire sales. Also, by preparing your home for the market, staging it properly and pricing it correctly, you can rise above the distressed mass and find ready, willing, and able buyers.

2. **Average depreciation has been high since 2007.** Today's sellers have to come to grips with the fact that they are not going to get the same price for their homes that Joe Smith down the street got in 2006. In fact, depending on when they purchased their homes, sellers may not reap the high monetary rewards from the sale. This is just a market factor that cannot be avoided, regardless of how beautiful, updated, and well positioned your home is. Nationwide, on average, prices in 2012 are at about 2004 levels. Managing your own pricing expectations is very important and your agent can help you wrap your mind around the current depreciation levels and how they have affected your home's value.

3. **It is not location, location, location. It is condition, condition, condition and price, price, price.** The old adage that the location of a property was its top selling factor was thrown out the window a few years ago. Today's magical combination is a market-ready home that is in good condition and priced right. Homes are selling within 45 days when they are priced right for today's market. Some are even getting multiple offers and occasionally full price. This is a shift from the location, location, location mentality that prevailed in the 1990s and early 2000s. With prices on homes continuing to level off in many markets, it is more important than ever to present a complete package that is priced correctly.

As you can see, there are some serious market forces at work right now. None of these challenges are insurmountable, but they all need to be factored into your 45-day sale plan. Ignore the laws of supply and demand, or refuse to price your home at a level that the market will bear, and your home may end up languishing on the Multiple Listing Service (MLS) for months or even years.

Understanding Contingency Contracts

Before we move onto the next chapter and start building your professional selling team, let's look at another important factor that comes up during the typical real estate sale: contingency contracts. In most cases, a contingency will be inserted into a contract with the idea that "something else" has to happen before the deal can close. If that "something" does not happen, then the contract is null and void and the contract will specify what will happen. In many instances the buyers will get back their earnest money (the good faith cash they put down with the offer).

Most times, the contingency revolves around financing and the buyer's ability to get a loan. A financing contingency states that an offer is contingent on the buyer being able to procure financing for the property. It will often be specific about the type of financing (FHA, VA, Conventional Loan, etc), the terms (interest rate, down payment, etc), and the time period.

Another type of contingency sometimes found in a contract would specify that another property must sell first and by a certain date in order for this contract to move forward. If that contingency is not met, then this contract would be invalid. Prior to the financial crisis and perhaps earlier, sales contracts with contingencies for the sale of another property first while not commonplace were seen occasionally. In a buyer's market, for example, a seller would often capitulate and accept an offer contingent upon the sale of another home first. Today that is a rarity. What is seen oftentimes now is a statement that the contract is contingent upon the successful closing of a home that is under contract and scheduled to close by a certain date. This is protective measure for the buyer that is put in place by his agent. If the buyer cannot for whatever reason close on his property, then he most likely would not be able to qualify for the next home currently under contract (with the contingency). In this instance if the contingency is not met, i.e., the first home does not close, then the contract on the second home will be null and void and the earnest money will be handled according to the terms agreed upon, in most instances returned to the prospective buyer.

A **contingency** is a statement that is added to the purchase and sale contract. It allows that if a certain condition is not met then the contract may be terminated without penalty to either party.

A successful home inspection is another contingency that we see often, with the buyer able to walk away from the deal if in the opinion of the buyer, too many significant problems are found during the inspection. In many cases the seller and buyer will agree on which repairs will be made and which will not be made, with all major issues negotiated between the buyer and the seller. In some cases homes will sell "as is" with the buyer taking on the burden of any necessary repairs.

Also known as a "Due Diligence Period" or a "Due Diligence Contingency," this contingency says that buyers have a set amount of time (often ranging from 14–21 days but fully negotiable) where the buyer can do whatever he needs to do to ensure that he wants to buy the property. This generally means that he may inspect any systems or conditions related to the home and complete his loan approval process. At the end of the Due Diligence period, as we will discuss later, the buyer may for any or no reason declare that he is not going forward with the contract. We will cover inspections and due diligence in more depth in a later chapter.

This is how a typical contingency would be worded in a contract:

Buyer shall have 21 days from the date of agreement executed by all parties ("Financing Contingency Period") to determine if buyer has the ability to obtain a loan with the following terms:

* Loan Amount: 95% of the total purchase price of the property (This is an example, the percentage could vary.)
* Term: 30 years (Most loans are written for 30 years but sometimes 10 or 15 or in the case of adjustable rate mortgages may be 1,3,5 or 7.)
* Interest Rate: No Higher Than 4.5% (Again an example, any number could go here. From the 45-day seller's perspective, a number that is somewhat higher than a current market rate is desirable and will allow a margin in case rates were to go up.)
* Loan Type: FHA (This is an example which could as easily be VA or a conventional loan.)

Now that you know some of the key elements that should go into your game plan and some of the market forces that will be working for and against you in your quest to sell your home within 45 days, it is time to look at the members of your selling team, the roles that they will play, and some important questions to ask them during the interview process.

Four Things to Remember from Chapter 1

* Selling your home within 45 days requires a solid game plan for success. This game plan should be well thought out and you should readily consider the ideas offered by your advisors.
* Homes that are priced right and in excellent selling condition are selling at a higher percentage of the asking price and often getting multiple offers. It is a great idea to look at as many as possible of the homes competing with yours.
* Across most of the nation, properties have been depreciating

since 2007 but in many areas have come back some since 2012. It is important to understand the local market, the number of properties on the market, whether that number is on the rise or is falling, and most importantly, the absorption rate for your market. This will allow you to set a realistic game plan and to begin to understand the importance of updating and pricing correctly.

* The old real estate adage "location, location, location" has been replaced by "condition, condition, condition" and "price, price, price."

CHAPTER 2

Getting Your Team Together

If everyone is moving forward together, then success takes care of itself.

—HENRY FORD

THERE ARE PLENTY of accomplished professionals who navigate the real estate market on a daily basis and who are ready to help you sell your property. They range from real estate agents to home stagers to general contractors and many others.

In this chapter we will look first at some of the budgeting that you will want to do before you put your team together and then we will show you how to assemble a group to get your home sold within 45 days. The budgeting aspect is very important even if you feel that your home is already "sales ready." Your budget will vary according to the condition of your home and the amount of available cash on hand to get the repairs and/or renovations accomplished.

Be honest with yourself in terms of what truly needs to be done (as opposed to what you may like to get by with doing) and balance that with your budget.

As you learned in the last chapter, there are certain things you will want to do before you put your home on the market and some of them cost money. General contractors (for repairs), stagers (to set up the home's interior and exterior for maximum impact), and home inspectors (for pre-inspections) will all demand hourly or flat fees for their work. It is important to factor these costs in early and properly budget for them. The last thing you want to do is run out of liquid cash halfway through a bathroom renovation or have to return the stager's rented furniture before the home is sold!

It Is All About Teamwork

Once you have determined your budget for repairs and renovations, you will put a team of capable, reputable, experienced professionals together to help you sell your home. In most cases your team will consist of a Realtor, a home stager, a general contractor (for small repairs and updates), a home inspector, a landscaper, an appraiser, an attorney, and an accountant. You may or may not need the services of each of these professionals, but here is a rundown of the tasks that each will perform and a detailed list of questions to ask each one before you hire him or her.

Your Real Estate Agent

We could write an entire book on the tasks that a real estate agent will perform for you during the selling process, but we will boil it down to the basics and let you confer with your own Realtor for the added details. One of the most detailed lists of agent tasks was developed by the National Association of Realtors® and presented to the House Financial Services Committee on Housing in answer to government questions about industry pricing.

As part of NAR's testimony, the organization submitted a list 184 things that listing agents may do in a real estate transaction. The line-up includes pre-listing activities (make appointment with seller for listing presentation, send a written or e-mail confirmation of appointment and call to confirm, prepare "comparable market analysis"

National Association of Realtors (NAR)

This large trade association has over one million Realtor members and promotes the free enterprise system and the right to own, use and transfer real property. Its members, Realtors, have subscribed to the NAR code of ethics and take regular training on ethical business practices.

(CMA) to establish market value, etc.); listing appointment presentation tasks (give seller an overview of current market conditions and projections, present company's profile and position or "niche" in the marketplace, present CMA results, including comparables, solds, current listings and expired listings, and so forth); and those activities that take place after the listing agreement is signed (review current title information, confirm lot size via owner's copy of certified survey, and obtain and review house plans). Be sure to ask an agent if he is willing to show you some of the comparable homes for sale in your area.

The agent's duties do not end there. They also enter the properties into the MLS database, add the property to the company's active listings, and take photos of the property to upload into the MLS. Then comes the marketing. Agents create print and Internet ads with seller's input, coordinate showings with owners, tenants and other agents, and install electronic lockboxes on the home. They prepare mailing and contact lists, develop property fliers and feedback forms, and review comparable MLS listings regularly to ensure that the property remains competitive in price, terms, conditions and availability. Some agents will create a marketing video for your home. This walk-through video helps an out-of-town prospective buyer understand the flow of the home and how rooms relate to each other. These videos can be e-mailed or posted to YouTube.

Once a buyer has placed an offer on the home, the agent will receive and review all Offer to Purchase contracts submitted by buyers or buyers' agents, evaluate offer(s) and prepare a "net sheet" on each for owner to compare; counsel seller on offers, and confirm buyer prequalification by calling the loan officer. The agent will negotiate all offers on seller's behalf and prepare and convey any counteroffers, acceptance or amendments to buyer's agent. The list of duties that your agent will perform during this period is extensive and includes confirming the acceptance of any deposit monies, verification of buyer's employment (in some instances), following loan processing through to the underwriter, and contacting the lender weekly to ensure processing is on track.

Agents also perform a wide variety of tasks related to home inspections, the home appraisal, the closing process, and the post-closing period. Consider your agent your biggest ally during the selling process and turn to him or her to handle a broad spectrum of responsibilities for you as a seller.

In fact, Realtors more than earn their commissions (discussed later in this book) when it comes to selling homes. Before you select your real estate agent, NAR suggests asking the following important questions to ensure that you choose a top-notch professional who meets your needs:

1. How long have you been in residential real estate sales? Is it your full-time job? While experience is no guarantee of skill, real estate—like many other professions—is mostly learned from experiences that have happened in previous transactions, i.e., on the job.

2. What designations do you hold? Designations such as GRI (Graduate of the Realtor Institute), CRS (Certified Residential Specialist), ABR (Accredited Buyer Representative), CDPE (Certified Distressed Property Expert), IRES (International Real Estate Specialist) SFR (Short Sales, Foreclosures, REO "specialist")—which require that agents take additional, specialized real estate training—are held by only about one-quarter of real estate practitioners. There are many other designations and these are proliferating on an annual basis. This is because there is truly a need for special training in certain niche areas. Designations mean additional training, plain and simple, and they position a Realtor within a group that often shares not only specialized knowledge but referral clients as well. I know more than several brokers and agents that rely on the CRS designation to place their referrals to other areas and this is true of the other designations as well. It is also important to understand the benefit that might come into play by hiring a member of one of these groups. There are at least an additional thirty or so designations relating to the housing industry in areas relating to residential sales, international sales and marketing, relocation, property management, land construction, appraisal, technology and finance. The point is that a Realtor does not have to obtain any designations and there are certainly good Realtors who have chosen not to do so. The real estate agent or broker who has a designation is an individual who has an in-

terest in a certain body of information within the industry and has taken the time and effort and paid the expense associated with earning the designation. Most of the time this person has specialized knowledge that may come to bear in the process of selling your home within 45 days.

3. How many homes did you sell in the past twelve months and how many did your real estate brokerage sell in the last twelve months? By asking this question, you will get a good idea of how much experience the practitioner has. Ask this question in a specific way and then ask for a list of addresses. Most practitioners are happy to provide this information. All things considered, why would you want an agent who sold six homes last year (an average of one every two months) when you can have one who sold five or six or more homes every month? Trust me when I say that someone working full time with an extensive database and the online and relocation resources available today should be selling no fewer than three homes per month. Less than that and perhaps you should keep looking.

4. How many days did it take you to sell the average home? How did that compare to the overall market? The Realtor you interview should have these facts on hand and be able to present market statistics from the local MLS to provide a comparison. Be aware that days on the market is sometimes a misleading number. A home may have been on the market last year with a seller that was a FSBO for six months. Then the home may have been listed by a broker at a price above the market for an additional six months. Then it may have taken a one-month break and come back on the market as a well priced new listing and sold in three weeks. This often gets reported as sold in 21 days instead of the total time it was on the market! Agents are able to track the history of most homes and will give you the specific answers on a neighborhood comparable sale if you ask. Just be aware that many brokerages will "paint" the sale in its best light saying that it sold quickly when in fact it may have taken much longer than represented to actually have sold the property. Remember, too, that the premise of this book is that to sell a home in 45 days or less, it takes pricing that is at or slightly below that of the market.

5. How close to the initial asking prices of the homes you sold
    were the final sale prices? This is one indication of how skilled
    the Realtor is at pricing homes and marketing to suitable buy-
    ers. Of course, other factors also may be at play, including an
    exceptionally hot or cool real estate market. Understand that
    the key point here is the "initial" pricing of the home. An
    agent who overprices a home intentionally or unintentional-
    ly has done you a disservice. Also, an agent who takes a list-
    ing that he knows is overpriced because the seller has con-
    vinced the agent that it needs to be so is just not on top of his
    game. In many years of real estate practice, I have heard every
    reason why a seller wants or needs more for his home. I un-
    derstand them and I sometimes sympathize with them, but
    I will not let them overprice the home. Most overpricing re-
    lates to one of three things. The home was refinanced some
    time ago and the money was spent on something unrelat-
    ed to the home, such as sending a child to college or paying
    for a car. This in no way relates to the value of the home but
    now must be paid off when the home sells. The seller feels the
    "need" to compensate for this expenditure by making sure the
    home sells for enough to cover it. Secondly, the seller is mov-
    ing to a larger home or perhaps relocating to another area and
    again the pervasive sentiment is that the seller "needs" to get
    this much out of the home. Finally, the seller has been laid
    off or otherwise accepted lower-paying employment and now
    "needs" to sell the home at an inflated price to compensate
    for life's circumstances. I care about how these circumstances
    affect the seller. However, the market does not care. The buy-
    er looking at the home does not care at all about the plight or
    circumstance of the seller. And so when the initial question is
    asked, and it is an important question, "What is the percent-
    age of the initial sales price that you have been able to achieve
    as a final sales price?" recognize that when a home is priced at
    market value (with no inflation built in for superfluous items),
    the answer should be a relatively high percentage. An accept-
    able range for this answer should be in the 95% to 98% range.
    One thing to remember is that the results are based not only
    on the pricing but also on the agent's skill set and finally on

the overall condition of the market. In one local market, the average achieved price was 99% in the sellers market of 2007, dipping to a low of 94.5% in the buyers market of early 2009, and rising again to 97.5% in the more neutral recent market.

6. What types of specific marketing systems and approaches will you use to sell my home? You do not want someone who is going to put a For Sale sign in the yard and hope for the best. Look for someone who has aggressive and innovative approaches and knows how to market your property competitively on the Internet. Buyers today want information fast, so it is important that your Realtor is responsive. Internet marketing is crucial. It is estimated that over 90% of consumers get their real estate information over the Internet. Now, every agent will profess to use the Internet but how many use it proficiently? Look at the individual websites, particularly Realtor. com, Zillow, Trulia and Craigslist. This is where more information is provided than all other real estate websites combined. You can get a good feel about the agent by checking the websites before you ever arrange an interview. Check the quality of the photography and whether the maximum number of pictures is being used. The latest trend in real estate marketing is by video and it will be the primary focus over the next year or two. Does the agent utilize video and what are his or her methods of getting the video distributed to potential buyers?

7. Will you represent me exclusively, or will you represent both the buyer and the seller in the transaction? While it is usually legal to represent both parties in a transaction, it is important to understand where the practitioner's obligations lie. Your Realtor is required to explain his or her agency relationship to you and describe the rights of each party. This is not only practical and useful information for you as the seller, but it is the law in most states. Be wary if the agent does not have an agency statement or description in his listing presentation. Consumer protection laws demand that Realtors identify their employers. Now, it is not impossible for a Realtor to represent both sides in a transaction, but it must be disclosed and done only with the written consent of all parties.

8. Can you recommend service providers who can help me ob-

tain a mortgage, make home repairs, and help with other things I need done? Because Realtors are immersed in the industry, they are wonderful resources as you seek lenders, home improvement companies, and other home service providers. Practitioners should generally recommend more than one provider and let you know if they have any special relationship with or receive compensation from any of the providers. Most Realtors have a professional services disclosure that is a protection for them, their firm and for you the seller. The Realtor must be clear (and the form explains) that they are "recommending" the particular service provider, but that you as the consumer of any recommended service should first satisfy yourself as to the competency and pricing of the recommended parties and their services. This is only good practice on your part. Ask the service provider direct questions before you authorize their service and understand how much they may charge and how they expect to be paid. Once you, the seller, have signed this form, you are saying to the Realtor that you will take the responsibility of checking out the provider before you commit to hiring them.

9. What type of support and supervision does your brokerage office provide to you? Having resources such as in-house support staff, access to a real estate attorney, and assistance with technology can help an agent sell your home. A real estate office should have a number of services available. First, the office should provide meeting facilities for the Realtor and his clients and all of the ancillary technology services that you would need and expect. Secondly, the office should have a full-time broker in charge (BIC) supervising the activities of the Realtor and ready to act as an intermediary if needed. Most offices affiliate with a real estate attorney and it is a good idea to ask if this is the case. This allows for real estate legal opinions and conversations with that attorney if needed. If there is no "company" attorney, the Realtor should be doing enough business to have formed a relationship or two with local real estate attorneys and should be able to ask that they be available to answer your questions if needed. Finally, most offices do have on

staff personnel to help with technology challenges. It is important to know if your Realtor has this support capability.

10. What's your business philosophy? While there is no right answer to this question, the response will help you assess what is important to the agent and determine how closely the agent's goals and business emphasis mesh with your goals. Most agents should understand the goal of selling the home, but you want to work with someone that keeps both your goals and your life values in mind. The agent should be trustworthy, skillful, loyal and perhaps have other attributes that you consider important. Over the years, I have seen agents hired for their religious affiliations, for their political affiliations and for various other philosophies that they have developed and with which the seller/client has bonded. This is a matter of style in a sense. In the estimation of many sellers, the listing appointment is not about the skills of the applicant, it is about their character and all that that may entail. The question of whom to hire is one that should be given ample consideration.

11. How will you keep me informed about the progress of my transaction? How frequently? Again, this is not a question with a correct answer, but it reflects your desires. Do you want updates twice a week or do you not want to be bothered unless there is a hot prospect? Do you prefer telephone, e-mail, or a personal visit?

12. Could you please give me the names and telephone numbers of your three most recent clients? Ask recent clients if they would work with this Realtor again. Find out whether they were pleased with the communication style, follow-up, and work ethic of the Realtor.

Your Home Stager

Your home stager will turn your living space into an attractive abode that is both inviting and attractive for potential buyers. In some cases this may mean de-cluttering the space and moving furniture around, but in other cases it may require prop and furniture rentals and more elbow grease. Your home stager will handle these and other tasks in exchange for a fee.

Home Staging

Home staging is the best-proven way to get the best price for your home. Staging sets the scene to create immediate interest for the prospective buyer. It involves looking at all aspects of the home and property and includes landscaping, design, colors, furniture placement and more. Staging of a home has been shown to sell homes faster and at a higher price because of the appeal created. Home stagers receive training through Stagedhomes.com, an organization created by Barb Schwarz.

The most prestigious designation for a home stager is that of ASP (Accredited Staging Professional). The idea behind staging is not decorating a home. It is de-cluttering, depersonalizing and preparing a seller's home so that it looks like a model home and a potential buyer can imagine himself living there. Savvy home sellers recognize that the money they spend for home staging comes back to them many times over. In fact, staged homes have been proven to sell more quickly than those that are not staged and also have been proven to command a higher price.

Some sellers decide to interview two home stagers before choosing one to help sell their home. Others are very happy to have a stager visit and then hire them based on their ideas and credentials. Ask to see their portfolios. Look at the homes, the photos, and the videos in those portfolios, and then talk to the stager about their experiences with those properties. Ask about their average list-to-sell ratio to find out what their success rate has been. Discuss any challenge that they have run into when staging homes and recognize that in some instances, the challenge may be the seller himself. Ask how the stager overcame those issues to get the home into tip-top shape.

Be sure to ask your stager these additional questions before hiring them:

1. What's your presentation plan for my home?
2. Can you show me a similar example from your portfolio?
3. Do you have previous staging references that I may contact?
4. What type of contract do you use and may I review it in advance?
5. Do you offer any type of guarantee?

6. How long will the staging process take?
7. What other services do you provide? Can you bring any other marketing ideas to my project?
8. What are your fees? (flat fee, hourly fee, etc.)

Use the information that you gather to select the best possible stager for your home—someone who will work on your side to get your property sold in 45 days! Many sellers proclaim that they do not have or want to spend the money on staging their home. As a Realtor, I can say definitively that the money is well spent on this process. Staged homes will sell for more money and are set apart from their competition. Home staging makes a home look cleaner, brighter, bigger, warmer, and best of all, it makes a potential buyer want to purchase it. Isn't that what this is all about? I always tell sellers that the money spent on staging is far less than the first price reduction that may be needed if the home is not staged.

Top Ten Home Features on Their Way Out

These are tough times in the building industry and builders and buyers have agreed that new homes in the near future will be more practical with fewer wish-list items. This list represents the items least likely to be included in a new home as well as items that buyers are no longer willing to pay for:

1. Outdoor kitchens
2. Outdoor Fireplaces
3. Sunrooms
4. Two-story family rooms
5. Media rooms
6. Two-story foyers
7. Walking trails in the neighborhood
8. Luxury master bathrooms with multiple head showers
9. Formal living rooms
10. Whirlpool tubs

While you are probably not going to add any of these features to your home, be aware that buyers really do not care as much about these and are probably unwilling to pay an extra price for these amenities.

Your General Contractor

A general contractor performs a variety of tasks, depending on the types of projects you need help with and the condition of your home. Under the "GC" umbrella you will find specialists such as roofing, electrical, or heating/air conditioning contractors. For now, we will just call them home improvement "contractors," understanding that they can take on various construction projects around your home if needed.

Here are some of the key questions that the National Association of the Remodeling Industry (NARI) says consumers should ask before hiring a home improvement contractor:

1. How long have you been in business?
2. Who will be assigned as project supervisor for the job?
3. Who will be working on the project? Are they employees or subcontractors?
4. Does your company carry workers compensation and liability insurance? (Always verify this information by calling the agency.)
5. What is your approach to a project such as this?
6. How many projects like mine have you completed in the past year?
7. May I have a list of references from those projects?
8. May I have a list of business referrals or suppliers?
9. What percentage of your business is repeat or referral business?
10. Are you a member of a national trade association?

You will also want to ask the contractor if any of his or her employees have been certified in remodeling or had any special training or education, such as earning a Certified Remodeler (CR), Certified Remodeler Specialist (CRS), Certified Kitchen & Bath Remodeler (CKBR), Certified Lead Carpenter (CLC), Green Certified Professional (GCP), Certified Remodeler Project Manager (CRPM) or Universal Design Certified Professional (UDCP) designation.

Choose your general contractor carefully. I am sure you have heard the horror stories about unfinished projects and endless "add-ons" that cropped up during remodeling projects. Go over the questions above carefully and if any red flags go up during the interview process, move onto the next name on your list.

A general contractor is not an absolute must and it depends on the condition of your home as to whether or not you need one. Sometimes a handyman or a repair expert will be fine to do the job. Just make sure that you understand the scope of the work and that you seek advice about which would be best for you.

Your Home Inspector

Hiring a home inspector to do a pre-inspection on your home before it goes under contract can ward off potential problems, allow you to make basic fixes, and help cut down on the time between contract signing and closing.

A home inspector will do a thorough inspection of your home, take dozens (if not hundreds) of photos, pinpoint problem areas, determine the remaining useful life of components like the roof and the HVAC system, and hand over a report detailing those findings. With that report in hand you will have a good idea of what needs to be addressed—and what would have come up as a "problem area" on the buyer's home inspection report (which is generated after the purchase contract has been signed).

As a seller, you will have a myriad of home inspectors from which to select. The U.S. Department of Housing and Urban Development (HUD) offers a detailed list of questions that consumers should ask their home inspectors. For starters, an inspector should ensure that their inspection and inspection report will meet all applicable requirements in your state and will comply with a well-recognized standard of practice and code of ethics. You should be able to request and see a copy of these items ahead of time and ask any questions you may have. If there is any area you want to make sure is inspected, be sure to identify that information upfront.

Also find out how long the inspector has been practicing in the home inspection profession and how many inspections they have completed. The inspector should be able to provide his or her history in the profession and perhaps even offer a few names as referrals. Newer inspectors can be very qualified, and many inspectors work with a partner or have access to more experienced inspectors to assist them in the inspection.

You want an inspector who is specifically experienced in residential inspection. Related experience in construction or engineering is helpful, says HUD, but is no substitute for training and experience in the unique discipline of home inspection. If the inspection is for a commercial property, then this question of experience should be asked about as well.

Home Inspection

A home inspection is a process by which a licensed professional home inspector visually examines all of the systems and components found in the home and reports on them according to how they measure up to certain established standards. A home inspector will not necessarily look in depth into things not readily visible, for instance, a furnace. The inspector may recommend a further examination by someone more qualified if he suspects a problem in a certain area. The home inspector will email a report detailing what he has found complete with photos showing areas that may need work or replacement. The cost of a home inspection varies according to the square footage and complexity of the home but will usually range from $300 to $500.

The average on-site inspection time for a single inspector is one to three hours for a typical single-family house; anything significantly less may not be enough time to perform a thorough inspection. Additional inspectors may be brought in for very large properties and buildings. Costs vary dramatically, depending on the region, size and age of the house, scope of services and other factors. A typical range is based upon the square footage of the home but should be in the range of $300–$500. Consider the value of the home inspection in terms of the investment being made. Cost does not necessarily reflect quality.

The report is also important. Ask to see samples and determine whether or not you can understand the inspector's reporting style and if the time parameters fulfill your needs. Most inspectors provide their full report within 24 hours of the inspection. As a seller, you should attend the inspection if at all possible. This is a valuable educational opportunity, and an inspector's refusal to allow your presence should raise a red flag. Never pass up this opportunity to see your home through the eyes of an expert. Inspection reports should be filled with photos of any areas needing attention.

Your home Inspector will look at the:

Roof

Heating System (One note is that home inspectors will not inspect the inside of your heater, heat pump or furnace. There may be an interior problem, such as a cracked heat exchanger, that may not show up on a pre-inspection. If you have doubts and the unit is old, call an HVAC contractor to check it out more thoroughly.)

Cooling System

Electrical

Plumbing

Appliances

Interior of Home

Exterior

Garage/Carport

Attic

Basement

Crawl space

Finally, ask about the inspector's certifications, licenses, and organizational affiliations. There are many state and national associations for home inspectors. Request to see their membership ID, and perform whatever due diligence you deem appropriate. A commitment to continuing education is another good measure of an inspector's professionalism and service to the consumer. This is especially important in cases where the home is older or includes unique elements requiring additional or updated training.

Your Landscaper

If you do not already have a regular landscaper mowing your lawn, trimming the trees and hedges, and making suggestions about pest control and other issues, now is the time to get one. There is nothing quite like a beautifully landscaped yard to catch a buyer's eye right from the curb. A good landscaper can help you create curb appeal, while also making suggestions about new plants, tree and stump removal, and other areas that can beautify your home. If your home's curb appeal makes a great first impression, everyone will want to see inside your home!

If you are hiring a new landscaper to help with the selling process, be sure to ask him or her the following questions:

1. Does your landscape company have Workman's Compensation Insurance? Without it, you could be exposed to liability claims should a worker get hurt on your property.
2. Do you have a list of referrals that I can contact? Call them and find out what their experiences were with the landscaper.
3. Do you go beyond just mowing the grass to provide comprehensive plant maintenance, yard lighting, and sprinkler repair? Ideally, your landscaper should be able to provide a menu of ongoing services.
4. Do you do landscape designs and/or drawings that I can see before you get to work?
5. Where do you buy your trees and shrubs? Locally grown trees and shrubs are optimal since the plants will be accustomed to the climate and will live longer.
6. What are your rates for regular lawn mowing and maintenance? How much do you charge for additional services, such as tree planting and landscape lighting?
7. How long have you been in business and how many people do you employ?
8. Will you hire subcontractors for this job? If so, for what will they be responsible?
9. What type of service-after-the-sale do you offer?
10. What is a realistic budget for my new landscape?
11. Do you provide a written warranty with your work? How long is the warranty and what does it cover?

Your Property Appraiser

Property appraisers provide a professional opinion on the value of your home. They develop estimated market value and include it in a report that owners, lenders, buyers, and others use to make decisions related to your home.

An appraiser has credentials upon which a lender can rely. Loans are made on values set by an appraiser. Let me say that in most instances where I have listed a home as a Realtor, an appraisal has not been needed. If a home has plenty of comparable sales to analyze and come up with a market value, then there is probably not the need for an appraisal. The majority of homes have something to which they can be compared. That said, there are always exceptions to the rule. If a home is unique in some way, if there are simply no comparables or if it is in a remote location, for example, I have seen sellers rely on an appraisal. The appraiser will have to compare the property to another that is perhaps out of the area or even an older sale and then make adjustments accordingly. I have also seen appraisers use a replacement value analysis when they truly have a one-of-a kind property.

Before arriving onsite the appraiser typically already knows the basics about the structure and the exterior areas (square footage, room sizes, etc.). He or she will snap a few photos of your home, conduct a brief onsite inspection (to get a feel for "overall" condition) and then compare it to several others homes or "comps" in the area or make the adjustments previously mentioned.

The International Society of Appraisers provides a thorough list of points that consumers should go over with their appraisers before hiring one. First, ask the professional why they are qualified to appraise your property. A qualified appraiser has formal education in appraisal theory, principles, procedures, ethics, and law. The appraiser should be up to date on the latest appraisal standards. Continuing education and testing are the only ways to ensure this competence. The appraiser you hire should be familiar with the type of property you want appraised and know how to value it correctly. Expertise on a particular type of property is not enough if the "expert" does not know how to evaluate an item for its appropriate worth.

Find out about the inspector's formal appraisal education. Obtaining a copy of the appraiser's professional profile or resume can help you evaluate the appraiser's credentials; the burden is on the consumer to evaluate an appraiser's qualifications. Also ask about membership in appraisal societies.

There are many appraisal organizations, but only a few require members to take courses and pass tests before being admitted as full members. (ISA is such an organization, International Society of Appraisers.) An MAI appraiser is one that is a Member of the Appraisal Institute. You will often hear the term an MAI appraisal. Technically there is no such thing; it is actually an appraisal that has been prepared by someone who holds the designation. You do hear the MAI appraisal routinely and it is one on which a lender, buyer or seller can rely.

MAI Appraisal

An MAI appraisal is one done by a member of the Appraisal Institute who has had specialized training in the valuation of homes. This is the appraisal on which a lender may rely and is the basis for how much may be loaned on a home. Although there are several methods of valuing a home, the appraiser will most often use the direct sales comparison approach. This will set your value looking at other similar homes sold recently in close proximity with similar features.

Membership in a professional association is important because it shows that the appraiser is involved with the profession, has peer recognition, has access to updated information, and is subject to a code of ethics and conduct. If the appraiser claims membership in a group that trains and tests its members, be sure to ask if this appraiser has personally gone through the training and testing.

Appraisers should also be able to discuss how they will handle items that fall outside of their specialty areas. No appraiser should claim expertise in everything. ISA recognizes over 230 areas of specialty knowledge. A good appraiser knows his or her limits and is expected to consult with other experts when necessary.

It is also important to discuss fees. Do not hire an appraiser who charges a percentage of the appraised value or charges a "contingency" fee. These practices are clearly conflicts of interests and may result in biased values. The IRS will not accept an appraisal done with such fee arrangements.

Finally, once the appraisal is completed, you should receive a formal, typewritten report that gives you the information you need in a complete and organized way. With this report in hand, you and your Realtor will be able to go through the motions of finalizing the sales process.

Please recognize that if you decide to engage an appraiser, the report and value generated will only be useful to you, the seller, in determining the market value of the property. A lender engages its own appraiser to verify that the property is within the value of the loan. A lender cannot use an appraisal that has been ordered by a party to the transaction (seller or buyer).

While some sellers will rely on an appraisal, many sellers would rather trust the opinion of a Realtor who is more closely tied to the actual market value—in other words, the amount that a buyer is willing to pay and a seller is willing to accept under normal circumstances. The Realtor will provide a CMA (Comparative Market Analysis) or sometimes a BPO (Brokers Price Opinion). In many cases these tools are as valuable as a full appraisal and they are free. Just make sure that you feel the Realtor is being absolutely honest with you in his assessment of value. Using several Realtors to prepare this report will give you an idea of the range of value. It has been my experience that sometimes a Realtor will tell you what you want to hear rather than the absolute truth for the purpose of obtaining a listing. So beware if you decide to rely upon the Realtor's CMA or BPO and make sure at least that the range of value is in agreement with several others.

Your Attorney

A good real estate attorney who has experience working with properties similar to yours can help you address all legal issues associated with the sale of your home and avoid legal challenges that might arise during the process. Not all states require an attorney to be at the closing table during a real estate transaction. An attorney can review paperwork like the purchase agreement, particularly when it comes to explaining the form and making changes and additions to reflect the desires of the buyer and the seller. In most states, real estate practitioners are strongly cautioned that all forms relating to real estate transactions are simply designed to "fill in the blanks." Any verbiage other than simply filling in the blanks must be reviewed by a real estate attorney.

Do understand that the real estate attorney works for and is paid by the buyer; and, in most simple transactions, there is little or no interaction between the seller of a home and the closing attorney other than to provide information relating to the payoff of any and all liens and to provide the sellers social security number and forwarding address. The only time I would recommend "interviewing" attorneys would be in the case of a complicated transaction or perhaps a 1031 tax deferred exchange. In these instances additional fees may be warranted and these need to be understood at the offset.

Here are a few questions that you may want to ask if you interview an attorney:

1. What percent of the practice involves real estate?
2. How many years have you been practicing real estate law?
3. What exactly do your fees cover, and what do they not cover?
4. Do you have a letter of engagement that I can review? (This will outline what the attorney will do for you and the associated fee.)
5. Do you foresee any issues with taking on my transaction (such as a conflict of interest)?

Asking these and other questions will help you ascertain whether a specific attorney will be able to handle your closing effectively. Do not take chances, assuming that any lawyer can handle your real estate closing and/or your more complicated legal needs. Ask friends and family members for referrals, do your homework, and take the necessary steps to hire the best professional for your situation.

In most states, and in most instances, the closing attorney is paid for by the buyer and is almost always available to answer questions relating to the transaction. The buyer is the client of the attorney. That attorney should often be available to answer questions as well for the seller of the property and/or seller's agent, but it is important to remember that the attorney has a fiduciary relationship and an allegiance to the buyer who is his client. If the attorney refuses to an-

Closing Agent

Some states allow a closing agent to close the real estate transaction. This person is merely allowed to oversee the correct signing of all forms by the buyer and seller in a real estate transaction. A real estate attorney will already have overseen the researching of the title and will have reviewed the HUD-1 settlement statement before the closing agent has all parties to the transaction sign the closing documents. He will be familiar with the lender and closing regulations as well as the process and documentation involved in facilitating a closing.

swer any questions for the seller or the seller's agent, they should consult their own attorney. However, this is rarely the case.

Recognize too that the Realtor you hire should have a good relationship with several attorneys with whom he works regularly (hopefully, closing many transactions!). This attorney should have a good working relationship with the Realtor and should view the Realtor as a source of clients and, as such, be willing to answer questions and provide useful information to you when needed.

Although in many instances, the seller does not have much interaction with the attorney, this changes when the seller opts to offer seller financing, offers a lease with an option to purchase, or attempts a short sale or a sale by offering a contract for deed (land sales contract). In these instances a good real estate attorney is a valuable part of your team and without that attorney's guidance, the chances of a quick and successful closing are lessened.

Your Accountant

Because the sale or purchase of a home is the largest transaction that most people will get involved in during their lifetimes, it is crucial that all financial, tax, and related points are covered when the home is sold and not when the IRS comes calling with a penalty notice 12 months later.

An accountant can help you address any tax or capital gains issues associated with the home's sale and also help you most efficiently parlay your profits into a new home (see the chapter on buying your next home later in this book).

Because you will work closely with your accountant and come to trust him or her with your most intimate financial details, you will want to take the time to thoroughly interview all of the candidates before making a decision. Look first at qualifications and experience, and always insist on hiring a Certified Public Accountant (CPA). A CPA designation is proof of expert knowledge in accounting. A CPA has passed examinations administered by the American Institute of Certified Public Accountants (AICPA) and state-administered examinations. The CPA should also hold a license to practice in the respective state and must engage in continuing education to maintain the license.

Qualifications and experience are not always enough when gauging the suitability of a potential accountant. There exist numerous qualified accountants who have poor reputations. It is always good to ask the accountant for references with whom you can verify the quality of their services. It is now possible to hire an accountant from online marketplaces such Elance.com, Guru.com, Odesk.com and others. The advantage with such websites is that you can immediately confirm the accountant's reputation from the feedback they have received from past clients.

Gains or Losses

Knowing the basis of value in your home is important in determining whether or not your sale results in a gain or a loss for tax purposes. Your basis results from how you acquired the home either by buying or building it or perhaps it was inherited or given to you as a gift. From there, any improvement that adds to the value of the home (but not repairs) and that remains with the home is generally added to the basis. When you sell you will subtract all costs and expenses associated with preparing and closing the home to get your net figure. The difference in these two numbers will give you a net gain or a loss, which will be used to calculate the tax, if any, that may be due from the sale. Always consult a professional accountant to help determine the effect of the sale and what may need to be reported.

The AICPA also advises consumers to ask their prospective CPAs for referrals and to discuss the professional's areas of specialization. Some accountants only specialize in certain accounting aspects, for example, taxes or credit control. Be sure to verify that the accountant has practical experience with real estate transactions.

Fees are another important topic to discuss during the interview. Accountants base their fees on a number of factors such as the type of services required, the time required to perform the services, the level of expertise and experience required, and the complexity of the work. Some accountants charge an hourly-based fee for some services, task-based pricing for others or a fixed-fee basis.

Please know that in the laws of most states, a real estate practitioner is prohibited from giving advice regarding tax and accounting matters.

Now that you know how to put your team together it is time to turn the page and find out more about the pre-inspection process and how it can help you sell your home within 45 days.

Four Things to Remember from Chapter 2

* Develop a budget before you start getting into home improvement projects.
* Understand that most of the team members you select will need to be paid upon completion of the work; sometimes they will be paid at closing.
* Take the time to interview all professionals before signing any contracts or agreements.
* Real estate agents, home stagers, general contractors, and other professionals can help you get your home in shape for your home showings.

CHAPTER 3

Why a Pre-Inspection is a Must

⌒ Truth is confirmed by inspection and delay;
falsehood by haste and uncertainty.

—TACITUS

T HERE WAS A TIME when home inspections were saved until the very last minute, with both buyers and sellers standing by with their fingers crossed, hoping that no big issues surfaced. These days, sellers are taking matters into their own hands and getting pre-inspections before they even put their properties on the market. For just a few hundred dollars and a few hours of your time (if you choose to attend the inspection), you can get peace of mind, knowing exactly what—if anything—may be wrong with your home.

This is an excellent idea because it allows the seller to deal with any deficiencies or problems on their time schedules and to have sufficient time to gather the best quotes to remedy any problem.

The buyer will still have his or her own home inspection done, of course, but in most cases the pre-inspection will hit on any problems that the final inspection would reveal. It is an insurance policy, in effect, for sellers who want to avoid the hassle and cost of having to handle repairs and surprises at the last minute. As you can see, this is

Septic System Inspections

There are many things that may affect a septic system. First, the design of the system must be evaluated. Many systems use a solid-liquid separation tank that is 1000 to 1500 gallons. It is important to know how often it has been pumped and when it was last pumped. The septic field and absorption area and the piping are checked to see if they are functioning properly. An early sign of system failure is "lush growth." The saying, "the grass is always greener over the septic tank," is not true when it comes to a properly operating septic system.

---

also another great way to get your home sold within 45 days, because you *know* from your pre-inspection that the buyer's inspection will not unveil unusual or expensive surprises.

A pre-inspection is also an excellent tool in today's competitive marketplace, where buyers will be impressed by the fact that you are a conscientious and serious seller who is not afraid to have a third party inspect the property. It will set you apart and send potential buyers a positive message about your property and about you as its owner. This report is strictly optional as to whether or not the seller wishes to disclose it to the buyer. However, there are certain conditions that are considered material facts and must be disclosed to the buyer if they are uncovered by this report. Please consult your real estate practitioner or your attorney as to what must be or may not be disclosed. Regardless of the disclosures that are made, a pre-inspection or inspection report is the property of the party who has ordered the inspection and who has paid for the report. The inspecting company will not release the report to anyone else except that party, and will need that party's permission to release the report.

Many sellers have asked the question, "Can I do this pre-inspection myself?" Even if the seller has some experience in construction, he is probably not familiar with all of the home's components. Most inspectors have done hundreds of inspections and will look at the home with an unbiased eye. Most sellers cannot do this.

Most home inspections are based on the square footage of the home and range in price from $300 to $500. Prices can vary based on the location, how far the inspector may have to travel and on the age of the home. I would never recommend that you choose an inspector on price alone. It is much more important to choose someone with a lot of experience inspecting homes that are similar to yours. A bargain price may not be such a bargain if you are dealing with an inexperienced inspector.

Finally, if you were planning to do any remodeling or address any cosmetic issues with the property before listing it, the inspection can give you a more accurate picture of exactly which areas need the most attention. This is particularly helpful for owners who are working on a budget and who can only afford to take on one or two key projects.

When you are getting ready for the inspection it's important to make all areas of your property available. If the crawlspace is locked, do not forget to unlock it. Also if there are excessive boxes and other items in the attic or garage, these may need to be moved. Make sure that the furnace, air-conditioning equipment and electrical boxes are uncovered and in plain view. It is always helpful if you are present to answer questions.

It is important to note that doing a pre-inspection does not guarantee that the second inspection (should the buyer ask for one, and they probably will) will not turn up items that the first professional missed. What is *does* guarantee is that you have spent both time and money to identify any basic problems the home may have and that you have had the opportunity to make your home defect-free.

Let's look at crawlspaces and structural elements beneath your home. The presence of water in the crawl space usually represents a problem. If the moisture content in the wooden members beneath the home exceeds 19%, then the member has been compromised and

The 19% Rule of Thumb

The durability of wood is a function of water. Moisture content is measured by how much water is in a piece of wood relative to the wood itself. Dry lumber is defined as wood with moisture content no greater than 19%. A number higher than that could indicate problems. Where this often occurs is in the crawlspace beneath a home where water has become trapped and moisture has been absorbed into the wood. This can occur by vaporization even when the wood is not in direct contact with the water. This situation if not remedied may cause the wood to rot. A home inspection will note if this condition exists and what would be necessary to repair. In many instances the fix for this is the installation of a vapor barrier (plastic sheeting) installed on the ground beneath the home.

should be replaced. Many times the remedy is a French drain to correct the water problem and perhaps polyethylene sheeting to prevent the water from absorbing into the wood.

The crawl space beneath the home represents the area where a large number of problems are found. This is often because the owner may have never been in the area or at least not for a long time. The presence of water additionally may indicate mold or mildew.

Radon

Radon gas is a naturally occurring byproduct of decaying uranium and has been linked to over twenty thousand lung cancer deaths per year. Nearly 1 in 15 homes in the U. S. is estimated to have elevated radon levels. For this reason, radon testing has become much more common. The testing will determine if the radon gas levels in the home have reached dangerous levels. If levels exceed 4 picocuries per liter of indoor air, then a mitigation system is needed in the home.

Your inspection report will cover at least the following elements (if not more, depending on the inspector and the type of report used):

Roof
Plumbing
Electrical system
Heating and Air Conditioning (HVAC)
Doors and Windows
Walls, Floors, Ceilings and Stairs
Basements and Foundations
Land and Property
Bathrooms and Kitchens
Garages, Porches, Driveways
Patios and Decks
Exterior, Wood, Brick Veneer, Siding
Insulation
Gutters and Downspouts
Structural Elements of the home

Inspectors may also check for (which may mean a separate and optional inspection report on the inspector's part):

* Termites and other pests
* Mold
* Asbestos
* Carbon Monoxide (CO)
* Underground Fuel Tanks
* Radon
* Septic Systems
* Wells
* Security Systems

Asbestos Inspection

In older homes, asbestos can exist and can sometimes present a problem. This product was banned in 1978 from building materials. The problem comes when the asbestos is friable or easily crumbled or pulverized into powder by hand. The most common uses were acoustic ceilings, plasters, wallboards and thermal insulation for pipes and water heaters although it was common in many other building materials. It can cause serious health problems. Non-friable asbestos contains a binder such as cement and though less risky can be a problem if it is moved, chipped or broken as might happen in the case of remodeling. If asbestos is detected, it is advisable to contact an asbestos removal expert. The presence of asbestos is a problem for almost any potential buyer and should be handled upfront.

Deciphering the Pre-Inspection Report

An objective inspection report can save you a lot of time, money, and hassle, but it also requires a bit of reviewing and studying on your part. Bring up any immediate questions with the home inspector, who should be able to pinpoint and justify his or her comments and feedback. The reports typically span 30 to 50 pages and also include photos, so get your reading glasses on, pour yourself a glass of 2004 Cabernet, and get ready for some serious reading!

Talk to your real estate agent about the report (see the next section of this chapter) and go over it thoroughly to make sure you understand both the high points and the low points that are detailed in the report. The report itself should not have any information regarding costs since this is sometimes seen as a conflict of interest if the inspector is both recommending a price and then offering to make the

Underground Storage Tanks

Underground Storage Tanks (USTs) that were used for residential heating purposes and under 1100 gallons are not regulated and not required to be removed in many states, including North Carolina. Additionally, soil samples are not required in many states, including NC, unless it is obvious that a release has occurred. If a release has occurred or been detected, cleanup will be required. Potential buyers are sometimes reluctant to buy homes with underground storage tanks. Therefore, although tank owners are not required to remove non-regulated tanks, it may be a good idea in the interest of selling the property. If there is a UST on the property, owners are advised to consult their real estate advisor or to contact the Division of Waste Management in their state.

repairs. Usually you will need the help of your general contractor or perhaps just your handyman to price out any of the work and then do the repairs necessary.

Your general contractor can also help you decipher the report and determine exactly what is wrong, what needs to be fixed, and how much it is going to cost. The contractor can then create a "punch" or to-do list that addresses—in order of importance—the items that need repair or replacement based on safety, resale value, and profitability.

What Do I Need to Fix?

Once you have your report in hand and an idea of the key issues that need to be addressed, sit down with your real estate agent and discuss how you should proceed. Let's say the home inspector noticed rotting wood in the attic and identified the culprit as a roof leak. This

Termite Inspections

Termites are insects that mostly feed on dead plant material, generally in the form of wood. Many homeowners have a "termite bond" or contract with an inspection company that will make annual inspections to insure that there are no active termites beneath, in or around the home. A lender will require that a termite inspection take place on a home on which they make a loan and that the letter show a clean bill of health or that any active termites have been treated by a licensed pest control company and that any repairs done to damaged wood have been made. The termite letter will be required to be dated within thirty days of closing.

is something that should be addressed right away not only to protect your investment, but also to ensure that the buyer's inspector does not turn up this type of negative report.

You may also run across information that you feel is extraneous but that a buyer would consider "negative." Let us say the useful life remaining in your current roof is six years. Well, that may not seem like a lot to someone who expects to live there for the next 10 years, but the fact that the roof is performing its intended function basically means that the burden is not on you to replace it right now. Now, I have seen instances where buyers demanded new roofs when the remaining useful life was six years or even less; but, with some pushback, the sellers were able to say "no" and end that negotiation quickly. The useful life of a roof is an opinion of time left and is highly debatable. Your Realtor will be your best ally in helping you decide what should and should not be done.

Expect to see a lot of minor adjustments (such as GFCI receptacles on power outlets, which were not required for homes built prior to a certain year) on the report. What is important to know is the year that certain items became mandatory in local building code requirements. If your home was built prior to that date, you should be okay unless you have made some type of major remodel to your home. Then, you may be required to update the item to conform to current code.

Although you may argue against the GFCI replacements, these have saved many lives. This device senses very small differences in current between the hot and neutral wire in the outlet. If you drop an appliance into a sink or tub, it will trip the circuit immediately and you are safe. Without these, you and the future buyer are at risk. The cost for changing outlets is minimal and can be life-saving.

Again, you will want to talk to your Realtor about the issues and figure out how important it may be to get them fixed before selling. Anything that you leave as-is and that comes up on the buyer's inspection will be open for negotiation when it comes time to nail down the final sales price for your home.

It is time to switch gears and look at the concept of home staging or getting your home visually appealing for buyer traffic.

Four Things to Remember from Chapter 3

* A pre-inspection is a fairly inexpensive and simple way to ferret out property flaws before putting your home on the market.
* A seller who takes the time to have a pre-inspection report positions himself as a conscientious homeowner.
* A pre-inspection report can address any issue that may exist in a home in today's competitive market and it allows you to deal with these items on your schedule with time to obtain competitive quotes from contractors.
* Talk to your real estate agent about the points on the inspection report that should be addressed and those that can be set aside.

CHAPTER 4

Staging Your Home for Sale

> Before anything else, preparation is the key
> to success.
>
> —ALEXANDER GRAHAM BELL

I CANNOT OVEREMPHASIZE the power of home staging. I have seen it work wonders across all types of properties—even those that the owner *thought* were ready to sell as-is. With the help of an experienced home stager who has a proven knack for turning rooms into attractive, inviting spaces, you cannot only *sell* your home, but you can sell it at a top price within 45 days.

From the Realtor's perspective, I can tell you that stagers make excellent recommendations. They come in and tell the sellers things that real estate professionals sometimes have difficulty saying or per-

---

Barb Schwarz

Barb Schwarz coined the term "staging" in 1972 to describe the idea of a home seller proactively preparing their home to help maximize its appeal to potential home- buyers. She has since shared her methods and ideas and perfected the process of preparing homes for sale. "National staged homes sell 50 percent faster and spend 80 percent less time on the market than non-staged competition."

---

haps do not have the experience in identifying. They bring something to the table that no other professional can bring by speaking in a brutally honest manner with homeowners about their properties.

Like your real estate agent, stagers fill the "trusted advisor" role and also come at the property from a third-party perspective. Yellowing curtains, dated wallpaper, rooms crowded with furniture, and dirty sliding glass doors do not stand a chance against an experienced stager! These professionals really know their trade and their expertise goes a long way in helping you get your home sold quickly and for the best possible price.

In a previous chapter I walked you through the interview process that you could use with a home stager. It is important to recognize that your Realtor should have a good relationship with one or more home stagers. Ask your Realtor's opinion of the work they have done for them in the past and if the home has sold quickly or not. Now it is time to look at what that stager will do for you and the role that he or she will play in getting your property sold within 45 days. If that means that they have to point out the dirty corners, the unwashed windows, and the clutter that abounds…then so be it! Get your second glass of 2004 Cabernet!

The Staging Concept

Home staging is a concept that Barb Schwarz officially tagged in the 1970s. She has since been credited with creating the staged-home concept and the home staging industry as a whole. The strategy has evolved over the years and today it has become a necessity for just about every property that goes on the market. It is particularly germane in today's market where inventory levels are high and qualified buyers can be difficult to ferret out and where the condition of a property has become so important.

At its core, staging is about sprucing up a home to make it attrac-

Staging

This process strategically sets up or merchandises a property in a way that not only makes the property desirable to tour but creates a way for a buyer's eyes and heart to connect to it with a powerfully effective first impression that stays with them.

tive to potential buyers. It goes beyond just planting some flowers and throwing a new welcome mat on the front porch. Staging also involves de-cluttering (removing items that are cluttering up the home), bringing in new furniture pieces and props (stagers typically rent them for the duration of the listing), and doing light touch-up work (painting, scrubbing, cleaning, and so forth).

As you look around at your property you may be wondering just how much staging it will need. If you are working on a budget, for example, you probably will not be able to outfit your home with designer furniture and rugs for 45 days—nor will you have to do this. Here are the top 12 areas that HomeGain singles out as the best possible staging options, how much they cost, and what you will get out of the investment:

HomeGain Top 12 Home Improvements for Sellers (National)

Home Improvement Project	Average Cost	Home Price Increase	% Return on Investment	% of Agents Recommending
Clean and De-clutter	$100–$200	$1500–$2000	872%	98%
Home Staging	300–400	1500–2000	586	82
Lighten and Brighten	200–300	1000–1500	572	95
Landscape Front/Back	300–400	1500–2000	473	94
Repair Plumbing	300–400	1000–1500	327	88
Update Electrical	300–400	1000–1500	309	89
Replace or Shampoo Carpets	400–500	1000–1500	295	97
Paint Interior Walls	500–750	1500–2000	250	94
Repair Damaged Floors	500–750	1500–2000	250	91
Update Kitchen	1000–1500	2000–3000	237	69
Paint Outside of Home	750–1000	1500–2000	201	81
Update Bathroom	750–1000	1000–1500	172	70

© HomeGain.com, Inc.

This should give you a good idea of exactly which staging strategies will pay off and which ones will not. You can work with your Realtor and your stager to hit on the areas of most concern and then prioritize the rest of the list. As you obtain buyer feedback you will be able to adjust accordingly. Let's say you tossed the carpet shampooing idea early on but then the feedback showed that those two coffee stains were getting a lot of negative attention. Time to thoroughly clean those carpets! Go ahead and relax with the rest of that 2004 Cabernet!

Creating Mass Appeal

As a homeowner who will sell your home within 45 days, your goal is to appeal to the highest number of buyers possible. To achieve that goal you must put yourself in their shoes and see your home through the eyes of that buyer. A home stager will serve as your partner during this process. As I mentioned earlier, he or she is there to be honest with you and to share expertise and knowledge that you might not otherwise have. Plus, you are so close to your home that you may not be able to approach this process objectively. That is perfectly natural, and it is why you are relying on a team of qualified individuals to help you list and sell your home as quickly as possible and for top dollar.

Knowing how well that home staging works, the number of sellers who *do not* stage their homes consistently amazes me. It could be that they do not want to spend the money for the professional help or maybe they think they can handle it themselves. Many of them just wind up "decorating" their homes and cleaning up never realizing the value that a home stager can bring to the table (such as a higher sales price, multiple bidders, etc.).

If you do decide to hire a home stager the first step will be to conduct the interview, as discussed in the last chapter of this book. Once you have selected a stager you will set up a consultation. This will allow the stager to go over your property thoroughly, take pictures, ask questions, and make some initial suggestions. The stager will take an objective look at all of the rooms of the home and evaluate them with the eye of a highly critical buyer.

After the initial walk-through, you can expect the stager to go back to each room and provide a detailed vision and plan for turning your house into a "show home." Remember that none of the suggestions are personal nor do they reflect directly on your tastes or living habits. The stager is simply doing his or her job: prepping your home in a way that makes buyers fall in love with it. Try to understand that the stager is trying to make the home appeal to the highest number of buyers. He or she is trying to do all that it takes to raise the home to a level that makes it appealing to the highest number of potential buyers.

Once you have reviewed the suggestions with your stager and decided which of them will be implemented and which of them may not fit with your budget, it will be time to implement the plan of action. It is important to note at this stage of the game that investing a few dollars to make your home more desirable will result in a higher sales price and probably a reduced selling time. Keep this in mind as you review, approve, or turn down your stager's suggestions.

Here are some of the key areas that you can expect your stager to address during the consultation and implementation phases:

* **Lighting:** To show most effectively, the home must be well lit. Many rooms do not have overhead lights; do use lamps in these rooms to make sure that they are lit. Up the wattage of your bulbs throughout the home and if possible use incandescent rather than fluorescent bulbs. These use more power but cast everything in a warmer and more pleasing light.
* **Adding color:** Stagers will brighten dull rooms by adding color to them. Although the prevailing wisdom is to neutralize paint color, the idea of adding selective color in just the right places can and does add to the salability of the home.
* **De-cluttering:** Extra furniture and personal mementos will be toted off to mini storage for the time being. Looking at the number of items in any room is a key component of staging. Generally speaking, you want the buyer to feel undistracted by your things. Always pack up any personal items. I have had sellers say that this makes the house less livable to them. What you have to decide is this, "Do you want to continue to live in your home?" If the answer is no, then pack up all of those items and get them out of the home.
* **Cleaning:** Your home must be clean as a whistle at all times. What is hard is for an owner to "see" that the home is not really

clean. A professional cleaning service is the answer. Have them come into the home initially and give it a professional cleaning. Then consider having them come back every other week until the home is sold.

* **Kitchens:** That circa-1980s avocado green refrigerator should be upgraded. The small cost involved could completely transform your kitchen. Most buyers want stainless steel appliances today, including refrigerator, dishwasher, microwave oven and range oven. However, the refrigerator is considered personal property so you may be able to exclude that from the contract and take it with you. The countertop material of choice is granite. There are certainly other acceptable surfaces, but most buyers want and expect granite. If you are replacing the surfaces do not use anything else to save money. This is what buyers want and it will help sell your home. A tile backsplash is also a highly attractive feature in a kitchen. Ask your stager their opinion of tile, granite and appliance choices. They will be able to help you with what buyers find most desirable. Staging a kitchen may also involve less expensive ideas. Replacing stove burners, having appliances repainted and resurfacing sinks are a few ideas that work; making sure that the counters are clean and that there is a minimal look is important as well. Never leave groceries out in plain view. Sometimes having a message board with notes out is a nice touch as is leaving out a few of your kids (or grandkids) drawings for decoration. Most kitchens have a coffee maker on the counter so place a bag of coffee beans and a mug beside it for accent. I often see a bottle of wine and a couple of glasses. Sometimes tables are set with plates, napkins and silverware. Recognize that the kitchen is the heart and soul of the home. It is the focal point and maximum effort should be taken to make it as attractive and updated as possible.

* **Repairing:** Wall cracks and mars in the flooring are just two of the issues that should be addressed properly before the showings begin. All walls and ceilings should be repaired and freshly painted in neutral colors. Consider using the palette of colors from Restoration Hardware (restorationhardware.com). I see these in many well-decorated homes and have actually had buy-

ers ask sellers to use these paints in repair requests. Their paints have universal appeal. Always paint all ceilings in ceiling white. Refinishing floors has become a highly competitive and reasonably priced option. Ask for your stager's opinion on floor finish color and tone if it is time for the floors to be refinished.

* **Replacing:** Sometimes just a minor replacement (such as replacing the vinyl tile in a second bathroom) can make a significant difference in how buyers perceive a home.

* **Neutralizing color:** If you painted the ceiling of your living room sky blue and adorned it with clouds, it is probably time to change that look to a neutral color. Most buyers want the neutral earth tone colors. Any vivid and flashy colors should be rethought and neutralized.

* **Exterior:** Curb appeal is important so listen carefully to the advice that your stager gives you about the area outside of your four walls. The landscaping of your lot is crucial to your success in selling your home in 45 days or less. The first step is to walk around the property and make notes. Make sure there are no trashcans, recycle bins or garden hoses that are in plain sight. You can begin to create curb appeal by using hanging baskets, freshly planted flowers or small shrubs. Consider a wreath for the front door and above all make sure the front entranceway is clean and desirable. Trim the bushes and trees in your yard, especially if they block views from the windows or shield your home from the street. Consider investing in the landscaping by planting small shrubbery in key areas. One of the first things I would do is to hire a landscape planner for a minimal consultation. I have seen many homes sell for thousands of dollars more due to a well-planned, attractive outside area.

  · Keep the lawn mowed at all times. Make sure all leaves, grass clippings and other yard debris are removed from view. If you have a compost pile, neaten it up. Any pools, fountains, ponds or other water features should be cleaned and have as little visible equipment as possible.

  · Plant inexpensive flowers along the sidewalk, in window boxes, near the front door. Adding color will always add to the appeal of the home.

- Invest in a new welcome mat at every door.
- Make sure all gutters and downspouts are clean and free of debris.
- Install new door hardware (especially on the front door). Make sure that your door does not stick when opened or closed and that the key works easily.
- Get rid of dirt and cobwebs outside with a pressure washer. Make sure that the front door and surrounding area is thoroughly cleaned and freshly painted. This is one of the most important things that you can do to sell your home. Have someone you know and trust critique each entryway to your home but especially the front.
- Paint or replace the mailbox. Consider planting something at the mailbox area if it is a stand-alone area at the street. Putting color and a fresh look to this area will pay off. If the mailbox is attached to the home replace it. It is $50 well spent.
- Make sure that all sidewalks and driveways are blown free of leaves, dirt and debris prior to a showing of the home. Although it is unrealistic to expect this to be done for every showing, make sure that it is done at least weekly while the home is being marketed.
- Garages and carports are areas to which buyers pay special attention. Gather, clean, sort and hang as many tools and implements as possible. Lawn care equipment, mowers, gasoline cans and the like should be minimal and as clean as possible. (Just a small tip: If you have a yard tractor and if you plan to keep it, store it off the property, maybe at a neighbor's home. It will probably be included in the contract if the buyer sees it.) Make sure the floors are clean. If they have been previously painted, now would be the time to add a fresh coat of paint here. Make sure all lights, shop lights and floodlights are in good working order.

* **Wallpaper:** Make sure the tones are neutral and that surface is clean and unmarred. Or, this would be a great time to remove wallpaper from the walls and opt for a fresh coat of paint instead. If the wallpaper is well hung and there are no problems

with the seams, it can be painted over. Peel and sand out any rough spots before you prime it.

* **Popcorn and plaster ceilings:** Changing out ceilings is not as difficult as it sounds. If the drop ceilings in your home are taking away from its overall beauty, consider removing them completely for an up-to-date look. Consider removing the popcorn ceilings and replacing with a flat freshly painted one. It makes rooms feel bigger, brighter and cleaner. Trust me when I say that popcorn ceilings have been the reason that many, many buyers have given for not buying the home. Another solution to removing the popcorn ceiling is to hang and finish and paint a new sheetrock ceiling over the existing one.

* **Flooring:** Floors need to be clean and devoid of marks, mars, and other damage. Carpeting should be cleaned or replaced or stretched, depending on its condition. In homes with no carpeting, use throw rugs for decoration and accent. Have Realtors, family and/or friends offer a true opinion of getting the carpeting replaced. Use a neutral color carpet. Ask your stager or flooring retailer for samples of the most popular neutral colors. Stay away from anything that "makes a statement." Consider changing the padding as well.

* **Storage spaces:** Do not fill them up with the boxes of items that you took out of the living room! Keep these spaces cleared so that buyers can imagine how their own possessions will fit in the spaces. Do have a storage space off of the premises and do carry things from the home and store them there. Make sure that the pull-down stairs to the attic are in working condition. Many buyers want to see the attic area before purchasing a home.

* **Windows:** They should be cleaned and all hardware should be operational (or replaced). Check all insulated windows for seals that have failed. These will come up on an inspection report so you may as well deal with them now. Remove dated or heavy curtains. The more natural light you can allow into a room the better.

Stagers also go beyond the basics and look at issues like room shape. While the actual shapes cannot be changed, simple furniture arrangement, carpet placement, and the accentuation of an attractive focal point (like a fireplace) can make any room look better through the buyer's eye. If a room does not have a natural focal point, the stager will create one. A folding screen, floral arrangement, or other addition can help catch a buyer's eye quickly and help them gain perspective on how perfect the room will be for their own lifestyles. If the room is not balanced (let's say all of the furniture is on one side of the room and the rest of the space is empty), your stager may balance it out by moving things around, rearranging artwork, and so forth.

Furniture will also play a key role in the staging process. Any furniture that will stay in the home must be clean, and any pieces that are beyond repair or cleaning should be removed and put into mini-storage. Most stagers offer furniture rental options. Talk to your stager about this option and figure out the best, most affordable strategy for your home.

Speaking of affordability, it does not have to cost a fortune to stage your home. While you can do it yourself at a moderate cost, enlisting the help of a professional stager will ensure that all critical areas are addressed and that the job gets done right for that first home showing. Stagers either charge by the hour or by a flat fee, with the latter ranging from $500 and up, depending on what you need. If, for example, you need furniture rental for the duration of the listing period, then you may have to pay $1,000 to $3,000 for that service. Talk to your stager, compare prices, do your homework, and come up with a plan that meets your budget and gets your home in tip-top shape for the most discerning buyer.

Hitting the High Points

Your home stager is not there to rearrange furniture and point out areas that need paint. He or she will provide detailed suggestions for every physical aspect of your home, such as:

* **Accessorizing:** Would a new floral arrangement or a new light fixture make the difference between a "blah" home showing and a buyer who is wowed by the house?
* **Art and Mirrors:** Used conservatively and in the right places, both art work and mirrors can help dress up a home and get it into good showing shape.

* **Pets:** Not everyone is an animal lover so keep yours—and their accessories, food dishes, and litter boxes—clean and out of sight during showings.
* **Exterior:** Your stager will make suggestions on the following areas and more—
    - **Night lighting:** If you do not have it, do not get it. If you have a system in place make sure all bulbs are functioning and that the timer and controls are readily available to be shown.
    - **Sidewalks:** Make sure these are freshly pressure washed and that there are no tripping hazards.
    - **Driveways:** Any cracks from settling should be filled and the driveway should be pressure washed as well.
    - **Roof**—Many roofs have become stained in certain areas and are a negative to buyers. There are ways to fix the stained area without compromising the integrity of the roof. Be sure to ask about this.
    - **Pools:** In order for a pool to be seen as a positive to a home, it must be running and crystal clear at all times. Consider a Polaris self-cleaning system. If you purchase or have one, let it run constantly and make sure to clean the bag every day or two. I have seen pools sell homes. Everyone can picture themselves resting around an attractive pool area and enjoying this amenity, but it's up to you to set that stage. A pool can be just as detrimental if it is dirty. It will make the prospect think that they have to constantly work on it to keep it clean. That is why the automatic pool cleaning system is so valuable. While truthfully it will not do the job on its own, it will give the buyer the idea that this is not so hard or "I can do this."
    - **Playhouses:** The key elements here are the structure's age, how it has been kept up and the perceived safety (or lack thereof) of the equipment. There is so much information relating to tripping hazards, swing hazards, spacing of individual components. Consult your Realtor and your stager about this. I have seen a lot of equipment that is unsafe and has been required to be removed prior to the sale. But

I have seen very nice equipment that has added (marginally) to the home's value. The important things here are how it looks and how it functions.

- **Porches and Decks:** All areas should be cleaned, pressure washed and re-stained or repainted. Any metal or canvas awnings should be evaluated for cleaning or replacement.
- **Storage Buildings:** An asset to a property can be a storage building or a shed. Make sure the door functions properly and that the exterior is presentable. The shed should not be crammed with boxes. Move boxes off premise and let the building or shed remain as empty as possible. It will look a lot larger and more attractive when examined by the prospective buyer.

* **The Foyer, Stairs and Hallways:** They may just be travel areas to you, but these parts of the home are always inspected carefully by buyers who want to make sure the home's common areas will meet their needs. Your stager will help you clear the clutter and clean up these areas to make them as attractive as possible.

Feng Shui

Your stager may also help you arrange your home to incorporate the principles of Feng Shui, which focuses on how changes in selection, color, and arrangement of furnishings can improve the energy of "chi" (pronounced "chee") within a home. This ancient body of knowledge reveals the connection between humans and the dwellings they inhabit. The focus is on the human's well being, which can only be achieved when we are in harmony with nature and the universal flow of energy. This, in turn, creates supportive environments for fulfillment and success in all aspects of the buyer's life. This step is not going to be applicable for all buyers, but for some it may be extremely important. Do not miss the opportunity to cater to prospects that believe in the benefits of Feng Shui.

Over many years, I have encountered individuals who believe that orientation of the home matters and that it relates to the Feng Shui of the home as well as how their lives will play out. The very simple explanation involves the flow of Universal Energy and how that energy flows in the space. There is a difference in the good and bad energies. The chi is the term for this universal energy that permeates everything around us and it manifests itself in different colors, shapes and other elements.

The main goal in Feng Shui is to attract, direct and nourish the chi flow inside your home in a way that supports a good flow of chi through your body. Much, much more could be said and described about this but here is the takeaway point: Simply be aware that this could come into play with the right buyer and either plan in advance to have a basic knowledge of the principles involved or else rely on a stager who is well versed and understands at least the basic concepts. No one is asking or expecting you to put your home in a perfect state of chi but just to recognize that there are many adherents to this belief and you may need to be prepared to understand and deal with it on some level especially if it may lead to a quick sale of your home.

Staging Mistakes to Avoid

It is a proven fact that the main living areas sell a home. At minimum, you and your stager should focus on living rooms, kitchens, dining rooms, and family rooms. Bedrooms, bathrooms, dens, and home offices should be next in line for staging. Additionally, you should address any room that the future homeowner may find difficult to furnish, include porches, patios, entryways, and any rooms that have been added to the house.

As you review your stager's recommendations and decide which of them to implement, consider the following staging mistakes and try to avoid them at all costs:

1. Thinking you know what is best for your home, when in reality you are probably too close to it to know exactly what needs to happen to get it into top showing shape.
2. Trying to do it all yourself. A good stager can reduce your stress and give you market-ready insights that you can implement quickly.
3. Not asking the stager for recommendations. Talk to some of their clients, review their portfolios, and make sure they have a track record of success.
4. Tying the stager's hands. Let them do their job, which is to get your home ready to show to the most discerning buyer in your market.

5. Not removing your personal mementos. Do you want buyers to be so preoccupied with your family photos on the wall that they do not look at the rest of the home? The goal is showcasing the home itself.
6. Refusing to put furniture in mini storage. We know that old recliner is your favorite piece of furniture, but it is time to put it away for a little while and let your home shine.

The list of issues that owners run into during the staging process goes on, but you get the picture: let the stagers do their job, confer with them on important points, and then allow your home to get the royal treatment that it deserves. Even a minor staging investment can go a long way in helping you get the price you want within 45 days.

In selling or observing the sale of many homes, I have observed the concept of reducing the price of a home time and again to compensate for issues relating to a lack of conditioning, a lack of updating and most importantly, a lack of staging, which to some degree deals with the other two aspects. If a stager is going to charge you several thousands of dollars for the service of making your home stand out from the competition, it is money well spent. I truly believe that the money spent here is always less than the first price reduction and ultimately allows that you will maximize the profit in the sale of your home.

In the next chapter we will walk you through the very important process of finding the right Realtor to list your property for sale.

Four Things to Remember from Chapter 4

*   Home staging is a critical step that nearly all homeowners should address.
*   Do not take your stager's comment personally. They are there to give your entire property a constructive criticism as seen from the eyes of the buyer.
*   Home stagers do more than just arrange things and remove clutter; they bring value to the home selling process.
*   If staging your entire home stretches your budget too far, concentrate on the home's common areas (living room, kitchen, family room, dining room, etc.).

CHAPTER 5

Finding the Right Realtor®

> ༺ A true hero is not someone who thinks about
> doing what is right but one that simply does
> what is right without thinking.

> —KEVIN HEATH

YOUR REALTOR WILL BE your most important ally when selling your home, so be sure to put time and effort into picking the best one. In this chapter you will learn how to discern the best of the best from the not-so-great professionals, understand what their industry designations mean, discern between discount and full-commission agents, and understand exactly for what you are paying.

In Chapter Two we reviewed some of the most important questions to ask your Realtor before signing a listing contract, so please refer to that section for those details. Ideally, you want someone who knows how to successfully market homes for sale, who holds professional designations and takes part in continuing education, who understands the regional and national markets well, and who is not moonlighting as an agent on the weekends.

The latter point is particularly important because agents who spend 10–15 hours a week in the business cannot touch those that spend 40, 50, or 60 hours marketing homes, working with buyers, negotiating deals, and handling all of the paperwork involved with the sale of a home. You would not go to a dentist who only worked weekends as his "second job," so do not select a Realtor for whom real estate is a secondary occupation.

There is an old rule in real estate that says the top 20% of the agents sell 80% of the real estate sold. I actually believe that the top 10% now sell 90% of the real estate sold. The other interesting fact is that there is very high turnover in the industry. Over one third of all real estate licensees will not be in the business in the next four years but will be replaced by a new group.

Deciphering Designations

The top Realtors in any market usually have a number of 3- or 4-letter acronyms after their names, including ABR, CRS, GRI, and so forth. Few would argue the fact that the real estate market has become increasingly competitive over the last few years. To stand out, many professionals take continuing education courses and earn designations that identify them as specialists in certain areas of the industry.

The most common designation that you will see after an agent's name is Realtor®, which identifies the professional as a member of the National Association of Realtors®. Realtors® are committed to treat all parties to a transaction honestly and subscribe to a strict code of ethics. They are expected to maintain a higher level of knowledge of the process of buying and selling real estate.

Here are a few other designations and what they mean:

Certified Distressed Property Expert/CDPE®

A Certified Distressed Property Expert (CDPE®) understands the complexities of the distressed property market. This agent has received specialized training in foreclosures, short sales, REOs and pre-foreclosures. Since in many markets distressed properties represent up to 50 percent of all sales within that market, an agent with this designation is particularly helpful to many sellers.

Accredited Buyer's Representative/ABR®

An Accredited Buyer's Representative (ABR®) understands the homebuyer's needs and how to best serve them and also possesses specialized information to stay on top of home buying issues and trends and exclusive resources to share with clients and give them a competitive edge. Agents with ABR after their names have taken a 2-day core course in a classroom or online.

Certified Residential Specialist®/CRS®

The Council of Residential Specialists delivers the education, resources and connections agents need to achieve their goals. Beyond the referral network, the high-caliber online and classroom courses and the benefits of membership, earning the CRS Designation centers on learning proven methods for making more money. This designation requires extensive course work and the recipient must have completed a substantial number of real estate transactions.

Certified International Property Specialist/CIPS®

The Certified International Property Specialist Network (CIPS Network) comprises 2,000 real estate professionals from 50 countries and is the specialty membership group for global business practitioners of the National Association of Realtors®. The CIPS® designation prepares Realtors® to service the growing international market in their local community by focusing on culture, exchange rates, investment trends and legal issues.

International Real Estate Specialist/ RES®

This is an international designation for a group of about 5,000 agents. It allows properties throughout the world to be readily available to be shown by these agents to their clients. An agent holding this designation has a singular advantage in that he or she is able to draw from a wider range of properties found in the local MLS.

Certified Property Manager/CPM®

Managing nearly $2 trillion in real property assets, CPM® Members have the competitive edge in every area of real estate management, from residential to commercial to industrial. Property owners and investors value the designation more than any other in the industry according to independent research findings. This is particularly useful to agents that participate in the rental and management markets.

Counselor of Real Estate/CRE®

The Counselors of Real Estate is an international group of recognized professionals who provide seasoned, objective advice on real property and land-related matters. Only 1,100 practitioners throughout the world carry the CRE® designation. Membership is by invitation only.

NAR's Green Designation/GREEN

The National Association of Realtors® created NAR›s Green Designation to provide ongoing education, resources and tools so that real estate practitioners can successfully seek out, understand, and market properties with green features. The program offers specific themes, ranging from sustainability, green building science and business application.

Seniors Real Estate Specialist/SRES®

The SRES® Designation program educates Realtors® on how to profitably and ethically serve the real estate needs of the fastest growing market in real estate, clients aged 50+. By earning the SRES® designation, members gain access to valuable member benefits, useful resources and networking opportunities across the U.S. and Canada.

Short Sales & Foreclosure Resource/SFR®

Knowing how to help sellers maneuver the complexities of short sales as well as help buyers pursue short sale and foreclosure opportunities are not merely good skills to have in today's market—they are critical. Realtors® with the SFR certification can be a trusted resource for short sales and foreclosures.

This is not an exhaustive list of every designation that your prospective Realtor will hold, but it does give you an idea of what types of educational opportunities the top agents are adding to their repertoires. You do not need an agent who has every single acronym after his or her name, but you do want someone on your side that is committed to the industry and to lifelong learning.

Planning and Recommendations

One of the most valuable assets your real estate agent will bring to the table will be his or her ability to deftly handle both the preplanning phase of your home sale, and the during- and post-phases. As a homeowner you likely know the mechanics behind the sales process (having purchased your own property at some point), but you may not know how all of the pieces of the puzzle fit together in today's real estate market.

A good agent will help you through these issues and should be able to give you a brief "overview" during the interview process to prove their prowess in this area. A good agent will also serve as a sounding board by making recommendations, listening carefully to your feedback, and then helping you make the best possible decisions regarding the sale of your home.

One of the first tasks your Realtor will handle is the creation of a Comparative Market Analysis or a CMA. By looking carefully at the comparable properties that have sold recently and the active listings that are currently on the market, your agent will be able to come up with a good sales price range for your property. The Realtor will use a 4-step process to develop a solid CMA. First, they will set the criteria by looking only at the most relevant set of comparables. The criteria may include:

* **Type:** Homes are compared to homes, condos to condos, etc.
* **Date of sale:** In a fast-changing market, the most recent comparables are best. Most Realtors will use data no older than six months. Occasionally, if there is a lack of comparable sales, an older "comp" may be used but if so it will need to be adjusted for the time since the sale was made. The time adjustment would need to follow the general trend of the overall market.
* **Size:** For comparison, the comps should preferably be within 15 percent of your home's square footage. Sometimes those homes may vary by somewhat more than this percentage. If there is a larger variance, just make sure that the comparable sale is of a similar type of home. In other words, if your home is a ranch style home, it should not be compared to a larger two-story home.

* **Last sale price:** Homes at the very high or low end of the estimated price range may be removed. Just understand why these may have been removed. Obviously on the very low end of the price scale a home may have been a "distressed" sale. On the highest end of price, look at what features this home may have had to cause it to sell above the norm.
* **Neighborhood & school district:** If possible look for those in the same neighborhood and school district as your home. School districts are constantly changing. There are always desirable, even strongly preferable schools. Look at the school district boundary lines and ask how these may have changed over time. If a particular school district is vitally important to you, then try to use every available resource to understand if any change is in the works.
* **Views & waterfront access:** Only look for those comparables that have similar exposure as your home. Waterfront properties should not be compared to water view properties.
* **Number of bedrooms & baths:** Properties with great variations from your home should be excluded.
* **Age, style and condition:** These issues are only relevant if your home varies significantly from the proposed comps. In other words, do not compare your recently renovated home to a fixer-upper or if this has been done, be sure to make adjustments for the updates. Unfortunately, most updates do not bring a dollar for dollar return. And those updates done several years ago may bring substantially less than what they cost.
* **Lot size:** Again, this is only an issue if the lot sizes are very different from yours. I usually see buyers willing to pay more on a lot that is about twice the size with all other factors being equal. So if two homes are in the same area and have very similar features except for the size of the lot, the price will need to be adjusted if the lot size of home A is roughly twice the size of home B. Otherwise a buyer will generally pay no more for it.

Your agent will use the criteria above to review various market sources (sales records, current listings on the MLS, etc.) and build a solid list of 4–6 comparable properties. Before creating a report that identifies a price and/or price range for your home, sometimes you or your agent may want to drive by the properties in person to make sure they are indeed comparable (at least from the outside).

Another variable you will want to discuss with your agent is the average historic appreciation or depreciation in your neighborhood, community, or city. This will play a key role in figuring out a viable sales price. For the last four years, for example, some markets have seen annual depreciation rates of 4–5 percent on average. That means a home that was listed at $300,000 two years ago is now worth more like $284,000. The converse of this is true as well. In some markets there has been recent appreciation Talk to your agent about exactly what is going on in your market and how the depreciation or appreciation trends will impact your pricing strategy.

Comparative Market Analysis (CMA)

This report is prepared by a Realtor to help a home seller figure out the value of the home. Homes that have sold within the last six months are the comparable sales and should have similarities to your home. Since many homes have different features the report will assess the value of a particular feature and add or subtract it when comparing.

The distressed market—namely, the high number of short-sale and foreclosure sales that are currently on the market in many regions of the nation—will also impact how you price, market, and sell your home. While you certainly do not want to fire sale a home just because there are "foreclosure" signs posted around your neighborhood. You do want to discuss the issue with your Realtor and come up with a good way to differentiate your non-distressed property from those that are held by banks and lenders. One way to do this is by promising a quick, clean closing—something that many distressed sales cannot do. This is because banks are overloaded with distressed sale property offers and not always able to address them quickly—or even within the allotted time frames on the purchase and sale contracts.

There are ways to find out the approximate number of distressed properties within a certain radius of your home. It is always good to know not only the number but also the trend. If there are fourteen distressed properties within a one-mile radius, that may be of concern to a seller. However, if the number has fallen from thirty homes within the same radius in the past three months, that might be regarded as very good news indeed.

Some lenders are setting a preapproved price on short sales and the overall distressed market situation is improving. Your Realtor should have a thorough understanding of this market. First, your home may be a candidate for a short sale and you need all the knowledge and experience such an agent can provide. But even if you are in the category a traditional sale and want it to happen quickly, if the Realtor you choose has a good working knowledge of distressed properties, he can position yours with buyers to make it more attractive to them.

Knowing that your home will breeze through the inspection process (because you followed the pre-inspection suggestion outlined in Chapter Four of this book) and the lender approval process can help you gain an edge over those bank-owned properties that could languish on the market due to indecision on the part of the lien holders.

Avoiding the Three Ps

There is a standing joke in the real estate industry and it goes like this: some real estate agents follow the three Ps of marketing—they PLACE a sign in the yard, they PUT the property in the MLS, and then they PRAY that it is going to sell (or that another agent will sell the home).

You want to avoid agents who follow the three Ps at all costs. A well-respected local broker estimates that perhaps half of the 7,000 total agents in his market are good agents and do not follow this principal. Many of the rest are part-time or some-time agents who do only the bare minimum when it comes to marketing. The guy who sells cars through the week and then sells real estate on the weekends falls into this category.

Active Listings

These are the homes currently for sale and the competition for your home if located in the same neighborhood or general geographic area. Looking at several of these active listings at open houses or with your agent helps you understand if they are priced at market value and how they may affect you in competing for buyers.

As we mentioned earlier in this chapter and in the Q&A portion of Chapter Two, you want to find an agent who is truly committed to the business. Look for someone who has one or more assistants and partners and who is not just sitting in the corner of his bedroom on Saturday afternoon pulling homes from the MLS system for an unqualified buyer.

You should also be wary of flat-fee or discount brokers who, for a fee, will put your home in the MLS and handle a very limited number of marketing activities for your home. You may be tempted to take this route, based on the low price associated with such agents, but they simply cannot do everything that needs to be done to sell your home within 45 days. They will not put the same concerted effort into making sure your home has maximum exposure to the largest possible buyer audience—something that is critical for your short selling period. Discount brokers have their place I am sure but it is often not for a quick sale.

Now is a great time to explain exactly how the agent commission works and how it ultimately breaks down. For starters, commissions are negotiable and cannot be set. Commissions cannot be agreed to be set at a certain percentage by brokerages. This violates federal anti-trust laws.

Expired Listings

These homes were actively on the market but the listing ended or "expired" before they were sold. Ask your agent for a list of these homes. Usually, these did not sell because they were priced above market value given their condition.

Withdrawn Listings

These properties were taken off the market for a variety of reasons. Some sellers change their minds and no longer want to sell. Others take the home off the market because it was priced too high and had little or no activity. Agents sometimes withdraw listings so they can put them back on as a new listing and make it appear to buyers that the home has just come on the market since buyers gravitate to "new" listings.

However, you will find that in many instances the full-service, commission-based agents will command rates that hover in the 5–7 percent range. In most cases, the commission is split with a buyer's agent. From there, the remaining amount is shared with the agent's broker and, of course, Uncle Sam. All marketing and transaction expenses that were not covered separately by the seller are also subtracted from the agent's check, which typically breaks down as follows:

Home sales price:	$200,000
Commission rate:	6%
Total commission:	$12,000
50% to the cooperating broker:	$6,000
50% (depending on the agent-broker arrangement) to the broker of record:	$3,000
Total expenses to sell the home:	$900
25% (depending on the agent's tax bracket) of what is left goes to Uncle Sam:	$525
Your selling agent's net pay:	$1,575 (for 45 days or 6 weeks of work = $263 per week)

As you can see from this example, agents are not exactly the tycoons that they are made out to be in the media and on TV. Sure, the "Millionaire Agents" that work in Hollywood and that are featured on Bravo TV take home big dollars but the typical Realtor working your city probably does not.

Keep this in mind as you shop for agents and understand what they bring to the table. Also remember that you get what you pay for and in most cases the part-time or discount broker is not going to deliver the results you need within your 45-day selling time frame.

Covering Their Assets

Another important area that you will want to discuss with your Realtor before making a hiring decision is Errors & Omissions (E&O) insurance. Namely, you want to make sure your agent is covered by this insurance. According to a large, national E&O provider, an average of 27 claims a day (across the nation) are filed at that company alone. The average claim was for $32,000. The claim typically involved a Realtor who tried to handle something on his or her own without expert assistance, for example, a realtor who donned a tool belt and fixed a leaky pipe that later caused major damage to the home. I see examples of this time and time again in my market, and they serve as warning signs for sellers who work with agents who are not covered by E&O insurance.

Also known as professional liability insurance, E&O covers damages resulting from the conduct of an agent's professional services, which is typically excluded from the standard, general liability policies that most also carry. E&O covers brokerages and individual agents in the event that a party to the transaction holds you, the seller, and your agent responsible for a service you provided, or failed to provide, that did not have the expected or promised results.

E & O Insurance

Errors and Omissions (E&O) insurance also known as professional liability insurance helps protect agents, their companies and their clients (you) against the cost of defending against a claim of negligence and damages that could be awarded. Make sure your agent is covered by E&O insurance.

E&O covers the agent for errors (or omissions) that they have made or that the client "perceives" that they have made. Most E&O policies cover judgments, settlements and defense costs. They provide protection for the agent and peace of mind for you as the seller/client in the event that an error or omission on the Realtor's part has created financial loss for you.

Deadly Mistakes to Avoid

With so many Realtors to choose from and an abbreviated amount of time in which to sell your home, it is easy to make some common errors during the selection process. Here are 10 deadly mistakes that you will want to avoid at all costs:

10 deadly mistakes when selecting a Realtor:

1. Selecting the agent who promises to list your home at the top price. (Some agents will tell you want you want to hear to get the listing.) Listing your home at an unrealistically high price

will cause fewer showings and probably no offers. Your home needs to be listed at a realistically achievable price.

2. Finding someone who offers you the lowest commission rate. In most instances, cheapest does not mean the best in terms of the marketing and/or the negotiating skills.

3. Working with a part-time agent. An agent who is not in touch with the market each and every day will not be able to keep up with all of the nuances and changes in the market and will not be fully informed about the many changes occurring daily on numerous properties.

4. Assuming that "any agent" is a good agent and that he or she will market your home to the fullest extent. Marketing a home is an art. Many agents do not understand the process of correctly marketing a home.

5. Not asking enough questions (particularly about pricing the home correctly and about the marketing that will be done to promote the home) during the interview process. Be sure to understand exactly how the pricing of your home has been determined and what you are getting in the way of marketing.

6. Letting a family member or co-worker list your home, even if they are not necessarily the right person to take on the job. This has been the number one mistake that many sellers have made. If your family member needs money, just write them a check. Do not list your home with them.

7. Hiring someone based on a flashy, high-tech listing presentation. (Look at multiple presentations before making your choice.)

8. Not asking for references and/or talking to past clients about the agent's success record. If an agent has sold a number of homes, he or she should have a number of happy clients. Beware of an agent who either does not offer references or has a wake of unsatisfied clients. Chances are you will end up that way, too.

9. Not looking at the brokerage/company behind the agent and its track record and reputation in the area. Relocation and referral business is critical to getting your home sold. Without the right connections to relocation, your home may sell but it may take much longer.

10. Assuming Realtors are a homogenous group because they have all passed the same test and follow the same ethics and therefore must be similar in abilities. Nothing can be further from the truth. All agents are different and possess varied qualities so interview them carefully before making your selection.

Once you have found a Realtor that will best suit your needs, and one with whom you can work closely over the next 45 days, your next task will be to set a selling price. In the next chapter we will cover this critical step in the listing process.

Four Things to Remember from Chapter 5

* All agents are *not* alike.
* Some agents will promise you the world to get your listing but not deliver on those promises.
* Avoid part-time, discount, and flat-fee brokers who will not offer the marketing plan needed to get your home sold within 45 days.
* There are 10 deadly mistakes that you can easily avoid when selecting the agent who will expose your home to the highest number of buyers.

CHAPTER 6

Setting Your Sales Price

> ⌒ *Price is what you pay. Value is what you get.*
>
> —WARREN BUFFETT

IT IS TIME TO LOOK CAREFULLY at a crucial step in the 45-day selling process: setting your sales price. Despite what some may say and what you may have heard, throwing a high price out there and hoping that it sticks simply does not work. In fact, it will tend to work against you in any market. Another approach that does not work is setting the price based on what *you* paid for the home, as many sellers found out during the most recent housing recession. Finally, assuming that you will get at least what your neighbor got for his home (or higher) also does not work. Prices fluctuate and homes sell for "what the market will bear" and not what the seller thinks he or she deserves or needs.

In this chapter we will look at how to price your home correctly, how to check out the competition, the value of determining regular price reductions in advance, and learning how to measure your home accurately.

The Price is Right

There is more to pricing your home for sale than just going by the price you paid for it, adding a decent markup, and having your agent upload the listing to the MLS. To get a true reflection of your home's current market value, here are a few starting steps that you will want to take:

Examining Comparable Sales

Comparable sales are those most closely resembling your home. Make sure the CMA report compares your home to homes that are similar in age, square footage, location, condition and have similar amenities.

* Consider how much money a ready, willing, and able buyer will pay for your home based on recent comparable sales.
* Forget about the wonderful memories you have had in the home and the hours spent out in the garden. These are not "selling points" and they do not impact price. Be completely objective and look at your home through the eyes of a prospective buyer.
* Have your agent complete a CMA showing the prices of comparable recently sold homes, current listings, and expired listings. (See Chapter 5 for more details on CMAs.)
* Look at the current listings in the MLS as your "competition" on the market. Will you be competing against a high volume of newly built homes, or is the housing stock in the area older? Where does your home fit into the picture, age-wise? If you have any doubts about what a particular competing home has to offer, ask your Realtor to show you that property.
* Conduct your own market research. Visit open houses in the vicinity and compare them to your home (size, condition, amenities, etc.). Look at them from an impartial viewpoint: all things being equal, whose home would *you* buy?
* Calculate price per square foot (see the section on measuring your home later in this chapter) for your home and for other current listings on the market.
* Look at current market conditions. Are home prices moving upwards or downwards? Are listings moving quickly or are they staying on the market for months on end? How is the national economy faring? What does the local job market look like? How is the local relocation business looking in your area?

Consider the current market absorption rate. In the current conditions with the current housing inventory, how long would it take the market to sell every house that is for sale in your market? In a healthy real estate market, this should be between five and six months worth of inventory. In many current markets, the absorption rate is as long as twelve to twenty-four months. This is the classic definition of a "buyer's market." Know the trend as well. If inventory is falling, the market is at least moving in the right direction for a seller to sell quickly.

One way to get an accurate price assessment for your home is by having an appraisal done *before* you put the home on the market. This is not a typical step, but it is one that will give you a very good idea not only of what your home is worth but also of what a bank will be willing to lend on your home once a buyer is in place. Under the right circumstances, it can pay to have an appraiser go through the motions of developing a presale analysis to pinpoint a current market value for your home.

An appraisal picks up where the CMA leaves off and is generally very accurate. It is not necessarily more accurate than a CMA but is done by a professional appraiser who has the credentials upon which a lender may rely. The appraiser can be especially useful when working within the 45-day time frame for which you are aiming since their pricing opinion can ward off any questions on the buyer's or buyers agent's part regarding the home's asking price. It is a common ploy for the buyer's agent to remark, "We just do not feel comfortable with the ability of this home to appraise." Whether or not they really believe this, I think most times it is just a game to get you to accept a lower price.

There have been problems with appraisals in many markets where distressed properties have been in abundance. These properties sim-

---

Appeal to the "herd mentality"

A buyer does not want to be the only one interested in a house. When you set the price at the lower end of the price range, you could stimulate interest from more than one buyer and create a herd mentality. Having more than one competing offer to purchase is a good thing.

---

ply have a downward influence on the value of all other properties. If you think about it, it only makes sense. The sale of each distressed property, whether it is a short sale or a foreclosure, takes a buyer out of the market. This is a buyer who may otherwise have been a candidate for your home. The higher the number of these distressed properties, the higher the number of buyers purchasing them. This results in fewer buyers and downward pricing pressure.

Do not get too exact with your asking price

I had a seller once whose home was in the range of $350K and insisted on pricing his home at $363,772. Really. The oddity of this pricing calls attention to the home for no good reason. Over time, I came to realize that the buyers felt that this seller had calculated his costs to the penny and would not be flexible in entertaining an offer. The goal is to keep the seller in the background and showcase the home, not draw attention to the seller.

Careful Measuring

If you want to sell your property within 45 days, you will want to make sure you have all of your ducks in a row before you start showing your home to potential buyers. If you do not have a floor plan sketch of your home, for example, now is the time to have a builder, an appraiser or other professional draw one up for you. The sketch will come in handy for marketing purposes—people love to see how rooms are arranged, how big they are, what type of extra "nooks" and spaces they will be getting, and so forth. You can show all of this on a floor plan.

You will also want to obtain an accurate measurement of the square footage of your home. When you bought your home, for example, there may have been one measure (say, 2,500 square foot) on the home listing flier, another in the property appraiser's database (2,467 square foot), and another given by the owner herself (3,000 square feet under roof!). To avoid confusion and possible problems, it is in your best interest to have your home accurately measured to determine the square footage.

There are generally two types of measurement, GLA and HLA. The first is a simple gross area measurement (to determine the square footage of the home plus any accessory structures) that arrives at an accurate Gross Living Area (GLA). The more important measurement is what is known as Heating Living Area (HLA). This is the measurement of the conditioned space of the home. Most dollar-per-square-foot calculations are made on the heated living area. In many areas of the country, this is a measurement to which buyer's are quite attuned.

Over the last few years and in many states, heated living area (HLA) is represented within a range of square footage in MLS. This is to avoid any inaccuracies or misunderstandings of the actual HLA. Furthermore, representing HLA in a range is a protection to the seller and to the agent. In years past, sellers and their real estate agents have been sued for inaccuracies. Gross Living Area (GLA) includes sizes of unheated (but under roof) porches, garages, attached carports, staircases, fireplaces and other unheated storage spaces to the house.

Individual room measurements are often inserted into the floor plan and can be used for a variety of functions. In some cases, these individual room measurements may be used for furniture placement. Square footage is an important consideration to most homebuyers. They use it as a tool to compare one home to another, often equating the size of the house to its value.

Every state handles home size differently, but in North Carolina we have gone from exact square footages to "ranges," namely due to liability issues. The North Carolina Association of Realtors (NCAR) requires an accuracy range of 5 to 10 percent when it comes to home measurements. This leaves some leeway for owners who do not have precise measurements listed in MLS.

If your state's real estate commission has not established square footage guidelines, the following recommendations from NCAR might be of help because they are based on widely accepted standards.

Measure the House

* Starting at an exterior corner, measure the length of all walls. Round measurements to the nearest inch.
* Make a sketch of the home's perimeter, recording all dimensions.
* If you must measure some areas from inside, add six inches for an exterior wall and four inches for an interior wall.

Determine Finished Living Areas

* Must be space intended for human occupancy.
* Must be heated by a conventional, permanent heating system.
* Must have walls, floors and ceilings of materials generally accepted for interior construction.
* Must be directly accessible from another finished area. That means a finished room accessed through any unfinished space cannot be counted as finished square feet.

According to NCAR, living area (sometimes referred to as "heated living area" or "heated square footage") is space that is intended for human occupancy and is:

* Heated by a conventional heating system or systems (forced air, radiant, solar, etc.) that are permanently installed in the dwelling—not a portable heater—which generates heat sufficient to make the space suitable for year-round occupancy;
* Finished, with walls, floors and ceilings of materials generally accepted for interior construction (e.g., painted drywall/sheet rock or paneled walls, carpeted or hardwood flooring, etc.) and with

a ceiling height of at least seven feet, except under beams, ducts, etc., where the height must be at least six feet four inches. [Note: In rooms with sloped ceilings (e.g., finished attics, bonus rooms, etc.) you may also include as living area the portion of the room with a ceiling height of at least five feet if at least one-half of the finished area of the room has a ceiling height of at least seven feet and it is directly accessible from another living area.]

In order to properly determine the square footage of a home, you must first determine the "heated living area" of the home. The "heated living area" of the home consists of only those portions of the home in which the occupants actually live and which are heated by the home's primary heating system (for example, the living room, den, kitchen, dining room, study, bedrooms, bathrooms, closets, pantry, foyer, utility room, and hallways). It includes the areas occupied by any stairwells but excludes any floor space that is topped by a ceiling that is less than five feet high. "Heated living area" does not include a garage, carport, attic, unfinished basement, outside storage room, porch, balcony, or deck, whether or not any of these features are attached.

The amount of living area and "other area" in dwellings is based upon exterior measurements. A 100-foot-long tape measure is recommended for use in measuring the exterior of dwellings, and a 30-foot retractable tape for measuring interior and hard-to-reach spaces. A tape measure that indicates linear footage in "tenths of a foot" will greatly simplify your calculations.

Begin at one corner of the dwelling and proceed with measuring each exterior wall. Round off your measurements to the nearest inch (or tenth-of-a-foot if your tape indicates footage in that manner). Make a sketch of the structure. Write down each measurement as you go and record it on your sketch. A clipboard and graph paper are helpful in sketching the dwelling and recording the measurements. Measure living area and "other unheated area under roof," but identify them separately on your sketch.

When you cannot measure an exterior surface (such as in the case of attics and below-grade areas), measure the perimeter walls of the area from the inside of the dwelling. Remember to add six inches for each exterior wall and add four inches for each interior wall that you encounter in order to arrive at the exterior dimensions.

Measuring your home is not mandatory, but it is a good idea for anyone who wants to most accurately present their home to a group of buyers who are ready, willing, and able to purchase a house within the next 45 days. It also gives you peace of mind, as an owner, knowing that this important figure is accurate within a specific, required range.

Automated Home Valuations

These may be valuable but are many times far rougher than many sellers can believe. Valuations that are 20% to 40% lower or higher than a property's eventual selling price are not uncommon as the sites will acknowledge. Use them as a guide to get you in the ballpark but recognize that there are flaws. Your agent should be able to point out inconsistencies and let you know if the automated home value reflects its "true market value."

Regular Price Reductions

The last thing you probably want to think about right now is *dropping* the asking price on a home that you likely felt was worth more in the first place, but this is an important point that you should address with your real estate agent early in the game.

The goal is to get the home out in front of the market and then to react to the feedback given by buyers in a timely and appropriate manner. This ensures that your listing never looks like it is "languishing" on the market and shows both buyers and other agents that you are a serious seller. Remember, our pricing decisions are based on the current market value of the home, and in many instances, this current market value has fallen since the home was purchased. The current market value is a function of what is going on in the real estate market around you, the current sales, the number of ready, willing and able buyers and the competition from other properties for sale.

Current market conditions will be the first consideration when

Price is not a "set and forget" procedure

Pricing is an ongoing discussion between the seller and the agent. A lot of factors may come into play during the course of the listing and not all of them may be anticipated. Be open to adjusting the price as the market demands.

coming up with a schedule of regular price reductions. If you are dealing with a slightly depreciating market, for example, then these reductions will help you follow the market down at close range, rather then letting it get too far out in front of you. When writing up listing agreements, for example, it is wise to factor in the market's current depreciation rate. Let's say it is 2 percent and that the home's initial price is set at $300,000. That means that this home's value is depreciating at a rate of $6,000 per year or $500 per month. In the listing agreement, it is best to include a listing addendum (an additional document that is added to the original listing agreement) that reflects a $500 per month price reduction to offset the ongoing depreciation.

Other considerations that come into play include buyer and broker feedback on the price, whether there have been any solid offers since the last price reduction, and other variables that may appear. For example, if there are fewer than a normal number of showings, and no offers, then the property is probably overpriced.

Be sure to talk to your agent about these issues and figure out how you are going to address them on a predetermined, deliberate schedule. Price reductions often should fall in the 3 to 5 percent range to make a difference and to wake the market up and let it know that you are a serious seller. Here is an example of a listing addendum for regular price reductions:

This addendum will serve to modify the listing agreement entered into by the parties above for the property above.

Scheduled Price Reductions—the sale price of the property will be lowered as follows:

$1,000 on January 31
$1,000 on February 28
$2,000 on March 31

Each price reduction whether noted here or otherwise shall extend the term of this listing agreement by 30 days for each adjustment. The listing period shall also be extended for the time with which the property is under contract should the transaction not close.

By signing this disclosure, you acknowledge that you have read and understand this addendum.

Estimates of Value

As a homeowner, you have a lot of resources at your fingertips. The Internet is a veritable hotbed of real estate-related sites that cater to buyers and sellers. Sites that automatically estimate home values are especially prevalent and have names like Zillow, Trulia, and Yahoo Real Estate, to name just a few.

These sites offer a valuable service to homeowners during the "homework" stage and help sellers do basic estimates, size up the competition and see what is going on in the market. What the sites *do not* provide are official estimates of value nor do they offer the "local" expertise that Realtors, appraisers, and other professionals in your area can give you during the selling process.

Because each site uses its own algorithm for determining property values, you will want to check out a few while you are doing your research. Do not just pick the highest value and assume that you will be able to get that price for your home. A better approach is to review the data provided by various sites and then combine that information with your own knowledge—and the knowledge and expertise provided by your Realtor—to develop a reasonable idea of the value of your property.

Can the Buyer Afford This Home?

Knowing the answer to this question puts you far ahead of the game when you are negotiating with a buyer (or when your agent is negotiating with the buyer's agent).

Lenders will take into consideration:

1. The buyer's income
2. The buyer's length of time with their current employer
3. The debt to income ratio (how much debt they have compared to how much pre-income tax money they bring in to cover that debt
4. The cash the buyer has to put down

Find out as much as you can about the buyer or have your agent find out. Do not be afraid to ask these financial questions of the buyer. Time wasted with unqualified buyers is time lost.

Property Tax Assessments

One measure of value that both you and your potential buyers will have at your disposal is the property tax assessment for your home. Much like the online valuation services opinions, this is just one more opinion of what your home is worth, based on what the tax assessor says it is worth. This is probably going to be the least accurate assessment because the numbers are typically old (particularly by today's fast-paced market standards) and do not factor in key trends that your Realtor's CMA will address.

Tax Assessments

Many tax assessments are automated and riddled with errors. If yours is high it may be challenged and possibly reduced. Bear in mind that many buyers erroneously believe that the selling price of a home relates to the assessed value. Nothing could be more fictitious. Assessments that in many cases are not even close can form the basis in the buyers mind for their offer or at least they may justify a low offer based on a low tax value. Your agent should be ready for this and should be able to explain (and prove) any discrepancies in an errant tax assessment.

Although this measurement often misses the mark, it is generally in the range of what your property is worth and, more importantly, it is often what buyers from other areas perceive as an accurate value. The value set by the county assessor is a double-edge sword. If it is too low, it will of course save you money in property taxes but at the same time, it will cause buyers to be wary since it is lower than the asking price of the property. On the other hand, if the assessment is high, then it makes the buyers feel good about what they might offer for the property. However, you will be paying higher property taxes each year because of this overvaluation of the property.

In one North Carolina County alone, approximately 50,000 homeowners contested their property tax values in 2011 and this is happening all over the country. Because many counties only reevaluate a property every eight years—and because the market changed dramatically between 2003 and 2011—those homeowners were left holding high tax bills and looking at property values that were no longer accurate. Under pressure to keep property tax revenues as high as possible, municipalities in North Carolina and across the U.S. are reluctant to simply reduce tax assessment levels, but under the law and by due process property tax values can be challenged.

Tax districts use software programs with sophisticated algorithms to assess property values for specific regions. Although these values are supposed to assess property at actual market value, they are not always accurate. Data available in public and governmental databases, which is typically used to arrive at the valuations, may or may not be accurate. Even the slightest error (4 bedrooms versus 3 bedrooms) can have significant impact on a property's assessed value.

The software also lacks information about the actual condition of each property, is unaware of the market boundaries that define where values change, and does not factor in intangibles like "desirable school districts." These are all important points to keep in mind when you review your assessment and decide if it warrants protesting and/or how your potential buyers will react to it.

Now that you are fully educated on the fine points of coming up with a sales price, let's take a close look at the exclusive listing agreement and the role that it will play in the sale of your home.

Five Things to Remember from Chapter 6

* Overpricing your home right out of the gate can hamper your chances of selling it within 45 days.
* It is not enough to tack a few bucks onto the price that you paid for your home and hope it sells.
* It pays to check out the competition by observing other homes for sale in the immediate area and by visiting open houses in your neighborhood to see what the competition is like in the market right now.
* You must have a real estate professional prepare a comparative market analysis (CMA) to show homes similar to your home that have sold in a recent time period.
* In certain cases, you may want to use a presale appraisal to pinpoint the actual market value of your home.

CHAPTER 7

Deciphering the Exclusive Listing Agreement

Dreams become reality when we put our minds to it.

—QUEEN LATIFAH

A N EXCLUSIVE LISTING AGREEMENT is a written contract between you—the seller—and your real estate agency that is marketing your home. In this chapter we will look closely at the agreement, what is in it, what it means to you, and what it means to your agent.

At its simplest, a listing agreement sets forth the rules governing your relationship with your agent and with the agency for which he or she works. The agreement has many different facets and is not standardized across the U.S. In other words, the verbiage in the North Carolina listing agreement at which we are looking is different from that of say Colorado. Many of the elements are the same from state to state but there are differences according to the established real estate laws in each state. Be sure to check with your agent for the specific contract and what it contains.

Speaking of agents, it is also important to note that there are different types of agents and working arrangements that you may encounter during the sale of your home. Here is a quick rundown of each and the role that they will play in your home's sale:

* **Seller's agent:** They represent sellers and work in the seller's best interests to negotiate and close a deal by working with a buyer's agent representing the buyer. It is important to note that these agents represent clients under a single agency and therefore must provide fiduciary responsibility and loyalty to the client. That means that they cannot share unauthorized information with the buying party or the buyer's agent unless the seller agrees. They can and must share all pertinent data and factual material relating to the home and its condition. They must perform duties, be honest, and follow professional ethics. In short, they are working to get the highest price in the shortest time with the least inconvenience to the seller.

* **Buyer's agent:** This professional represents buyers and works in their best interests to negotiate and close a deal by working with the seller's agent. This person also represents a single agency and must follow the fiduciary obligations and trust issues relating to the buyer. They may not disclose any buyer information to the seller's agent except with the permission of the buyer. They may and should share information regarding the buyer's ability to perform and this would include a prequalification or qualification letter or an approval letter from the lender. In most cases, the buyer and the buyer's agent will sign a buyer's agency agreement, which outlines both parties' obligations and duties.

* **Dual agency with two agents:** Because agents work for brokers, it is possible that your home is listed by one agent of Firm XYZ and then sold by another agent of Firm XYZ. This is what is known as "dual agency." Both the seller and the buyer must agree upon dual agency in writing prior to offer acceptance. The laws governing these arrangements vary from state to state.

* **Dual agency with the same agent:** There are also times when an agent represents both the seller and the buyer in the same transaction. This agent must treat both parties equally, fairly and honestly. They cannot share confidential information with either party. Dual Agency must be disclosed to all parties in the transaction and be approved by those parties prior to offer acceptance.

* **Designated agency:** Recently, some states have developed rules that recognize a newer dual agency practice known as "designated agency." This type of agency is used when a real estate firm has an in-house dual agency, where an individual agent represents only the interests of the seller and another agent is appointed by the firm to represent only the interests of the buyer. One agent at a brokerage may help a buyer buy property that is listed by another of the brokerage's agents, for example. The real estate firm then acts as the dual agent, thus eradicating any conflict of interest among the agents and their clients.

Reviewing the Contract

As you read over the exclusive listing agreement, you will notice that it specifically states that the agreement is "exclusive" between the parties. That means the agency with which you contract is the only one who represents your property on the market. Put simply, this exclusivity means that you will not deal with any other agents directly and that any marketing will be conducted by the listing firm and that any and all offers will be presented to you by that firm.

The listing agreement will also state that your home will be assigned a listing number for the Multiple Listing Service (MLS). Other agents will use this number to identify your property and to arrange showings for their respective buyers. Consider this your home's "inventory number."

On the contract, you will also find a date of contract (the date that it is signed) and expiration date (when it expires and is no longer valid). In many cases you will sign a 6-month agreement, although the date range is negotiable. The next portion of the listing agreement concerns everything that will go with the property. Your agent will ask you a series of questions as he or she fills out the agreement. Be as specific as you would like with this section to avoid confusion when it comes time to move and take those window treatments or blinds or other personal property with you!

Here is an example of this section of the exclusive listing form:

INCLUDING (if any) all property that integrally belongs to or is part of the real estate (except rental items), whether attached or detached, such as wall to wall carpeting and vinyl, light fixtures and bulbs, ceiling fan(s), shades, rods, blinds, awnings, storm windows, storm doors, screens, plumbing fixtures, sump pump, water heater, water softener, automatic heating equipment, fuel tank, air conditioning equipment (window or central), door chimes, built-in items, electrical service cable, door opener and control(s), other attached fixtures, radio and/or attached TV receiving equipment, fence, trees, bushes, and plants (yes, you must leave any flowers, bushes or other ornamental landscaping unless otherwise noted in the contract).

OTHER ITEMS EITHER INCLUDED OR EXCLUDED (SPECIFY): Here is where you can list anything that is currently in the home that you would like to, or that you do not want to, include in the sales price of your home. Remember—buyers can ask for everything but if the item in question is not "attached" to your home, then it is considered personal property. Please note that in most instances, dishwashers, built-in range ovens, built-in microwaves, garbage disposals and trash compactors are fixtures and are expected to remain with the property. Refrigerators, freezers, washers and dryers are not attached, are not fixtures, and are the personal property of the sellers.

The next item that you will discuss with your agent is his or her commission. This is a negotiable number that in most states ranges from 5–7 percent, although agents are not—by law—allowed to conspire to fix that number. The commission is paid by the seller, who is responsible to pay it if during the listing period an acceptable Offer to Purchase and Contract is agreed to by all parties and if the property then actually goes to closing and is sold. Sometimes there is a negotiable time period at the end of the listing agreement that allows the listing agent additional time to negotiate a contract with someone who has seen the property during the listing period. Should a contract be written and accepted during this time period, the commission is still due and payable by the seller.

In other words, if your agent introduced you to a buyer who came back—after the listing agreement expired—and bought your home, then you are responsible for the commission if the sale occurred in the protected additional listing period. In the commission section of the contract you will also notice the amount of the commission that will be allocated to the "cooperating broker," which in most cases will be the buyer's agent. In most markets this will be 50%, although that rate can also vary according to the listing firm with agreement by the seller.

Theoretically, when an agent brings a ready, willing, able buyer with no contingencies at a full price cash contract, your agent has earned his or her fee.

Should something happen and you decide not to sell your home, then you are still liable for this commission, which is typically paid out at the closing table. In some cases, sellers will offer bonuses to agents who sell their properties. If this is something that you want to do with your home, the details will be listed in the exclusive agency agreement and—if earned by the buyer's agent—will have to be approved by the buyer before distribution of the funds.

The Pitfalls of Dual Agency

Dual Agency comes with pitfalls and potential risks. Real estate agents have a duty to protect the fiduciary interests of their clients and to deal fairly with all parties in a transaction. Agents must have prior written consent for dual agency, that is, representing both parties, before entering into a transaction. From a buyer's perspective, buyers feel that since they have negotiated with the broker and talked to him about the deal, the buyer believes that the broker is representing them. Most brokers, however, are representing the seller. From a seller's perspective, the seller feels that the broker owes him a greater degree of loyalty since it is the seller paying the commission. Consumer groups (and courts) tend to take the position that dual agents provide less not more to both the seller and the buyer.

While a honest and thoughtful broker may act as a good facilitator of a transaction, many would argue that it is impossible for one person to act simultaneously to get the "highest price and best terms for the seller" while trying to get the "lowest price and best terms for the buyer." While this condition happens everyday in the real estate world, agents are routinely challenged by buyers and sellers regarding circumstances involving dual agency and should give serious thought to the potential consequences of entering into a dual agency situation.

Other key points that you will go over with your agent before signing the exclusive listing agreement are covered in the next section, which includes an example of a full agreement and covers the specifics that you will find on the document.

Doing the Legwork

It is important to remember that an exclusive listing contract is an agreement and that both parties should "agree" to its terms before signing. The contract is not difficult to understand, but if any red flags arise during the review process be sure to discuss them with your agent.

Pay particular attention to the way the form is filled out and if it meets your needs; do not wait until you are sitting across from the buyer at the closing table to mention that certain items on the agreement are *not* included in the sale, for example.

Designated Agency

When faced with the dilemma of Dual Agency and the challenges it presents, a real estate firm may appoint a different agent to represent either the seller or the buyer.

For example: Agent Adam lists a property for Seller Sam on Maple Street and immediately gets a call from Buyer Ben about the property. Agent Adam discloses that he is working for Seller Sam and explains agency and provides and explains a state mandated brochure, which describes Agency to Buyer Ben and shows the property to him. Buyer Ben thinks about making an offer and enters into a buyer agency agreement with Agent Adam. Adam, who has disclosed that he is acting as agent for both parties, has a written agreement with both parties and has disclosed this to both parties, thinks about the consequences of representing both parties in a dual agency situation and decides against it. Adam consults the broker in charge of his firm who "designates" another agent Dan to represent Buyer Ben. Now Adam is representing the seller and Dan is representing the buyer. The firm for which they both work still represents both parties and is a dual agency in the transaction. However an agent has been designated to represent one of the parties in this case, the buyer. This special form of dual agency is called Designated Dual Agency. It is not a perfect situation since Adam may have learned certain facts about Buyer Ben that may now give him an advantage. Or maybe he learned nothing. It is a better situation to have the two agents representing their respective parties than to have the one agent trying to accomplish goals that are at opposite ends of the spectrum.

A reputable, experienced real estate agent will explain every detail of the contract. If you still have concerns, it will be wise to consult with a real estate attorney before signing on the dotted line. Understanding the listing agreement is one of the most important and fundamental steps on the way to selling your home within 45 days.

Here is an example of an exclusive listing agreement. The agreement you sign may vary from this one but these are the major elements. Just make sure you review it and ask for explanations of anything you do not understand.

EXCLUSIVE LISTING AGREEMENT

1. THIS AGREEMENT IS ENTERED INTO BY AND BETWEEN PROSPECTIVE SELLER(S) (print name per title) hereinafter called "Owner" and (Brokerage/Firm) OWNER'S BROKER, hereinafter called "Broker" or "Agent". The term "Broker" shall also include Broker's affiliated licenses (brokers and salespersons). The terms "Owner" and/or "Seller" shall include seller, landlord or optionor. The term "Buyer" shall include buyer, tenant or optionee. The terms "sell" and "sale: shall include sell, lease, rent, exchange or option. Owner or Owner's duly authorized agent whose signature appears below, hereby grants to the undersigned BROKER, the exclusive right to (sell) (rent) (lease) for an irrevocable period beginning the day of _____, and ending at 11:59 P.M. the day of _____, (the "Exclusive Period") the following property.

2. THE REAL PROPERTY located in County, North Carolina, legally described as Address:_____
with legal description _____ deed book _____
page _____.
Other (Parking, Storage Areas, etc.): _____
_____

3. INCLUDING (if any) all property that integrally belongs to or is part of the real estate (except rental items), whether attached or detached, such as wall to wall carpeting and vinyl, light fixtures and bulbs, ceiling fan(s), shades, rods, blinds, awnings, storm windows, storm doors, screens, plumbing fixtures, sump pump, water heater, water softener, automatic heating equipment, fuel tank, air

conditioning equipment (window or central), door chimes, built-in items and electrical service cable, door opener and control(s), other attached fixtures, radio and/or attached TV receiving equipment, fence, trees, bushes, and plants.

OTHER ITEMS EITHER INCLUDED OR EXCLUDED (SPECIFY):

4. GROSS SALES PRICE to be $ on the following terms:

POSSESSION will be given and Owner will pay to Broker a PROFESSIONAL SERVICE FEE of $ or (%) percent of the gross sale price, whichever is greater if:

- a. Broker procures a Buyer during the Exclusive Period ready, willing and able to purchase at the above price and terms, or on any other price and terms agreeable to Owner; or:
- b. Owner or anyone else sells, exchanges, leases, rents or otherwise transfers the property during the Exclusive Period at any price or on any terms (or as provided in paragraph 9); or:
- c. The property is sold, transferred, leased, rented, or exchanged, by any person, within days after the end of the Exclusive Period (the Protection Period), to any person, firm or corporation, to whom Broker or any person representing Broker has presented for sale this property during the Exclusive Period, if Broker supplies Owner with a list of names and addresses of persons at or before the end of the Exclusive Period. Provided, however, that Owner shall not be obligated to pay the Professional Service Fee if: (1) a valid listing agreement for the Property is entered into during the Protection Period with another licensed real estate broker and the sale of the Property is made during the Protection Period; and (2) Owner does not reserve the parties on the protected list from the new listing; or:
- d. Owner prevents the sale of this property by any adverse action, such as prohibiting the buyer from making improvements to the property required of the buyer prior to settlement by a lender, or attempting to cancel this agreement without cause. The professional service fee shall be pay-

able in cash in the county in this state where Broker has his principal office, at the time of the transaction settlement. Owner authorizes Broker or other escrow agent to pay Broker from Owner's proceeds of the sale.

5. COOPERATIVE BROKERAGE ARRANGEMENTS. Owner agrees that Broker may cooperate with other brokers and offer a commission of ($) or (%) percent of the gross sale price to cooperating brokers, including brokers solely representing a buyer. Broker shall disclose to Owner, in writing, any policy that would limit the participation of any other brokerage. Fees to referring brokers may be as negotiated with Broker.

6. BROKER is given permission to: (1) Submit this property to the Multiple Listing Service along with all marketing information including utility and tax information both before and after closing; (2) advertise this property; (3) (may) (may not) place a for sale sign thereon; (4) remove all other for sale signs; (5) (may) (may not) place a lock box thereon; (6) show the property at all reasonable times; (7) show other property and provide comparative data to prospective buyers; (8) recommend property inspections at buyer's expense. Broker may also make the following selling statement to prospective buyers:

Broker (may) (may not) disclose this reason for selling:

_____

7. INQUIRIES. Owner agrees to refer to Broker all inquiries from any person received during the Exclusive Period.

8. RENTAL LIMITATIONS. If the subject property is being offered for sale, owner agrees that this property will not be rented during the term of this agreement, unless the lease specifically provides that the property may be shown upon an hours notice to the tenant during reasonable hours and that possession shall be given to a buyer within days of accepted offer. Is this property being sold subject to tenant's rights? (yes) (no). If yes, attach lease(s) and/or rental agreement(s).

9. EARNEST MONEY. Broker may: (1) accept earnest money deposits; (2) hold earnest money checks until both buyer and sell-

er have executed a sales agreement; (3) deposit earnest money in Broker's trust account; (4) hold earnest money until the transaction has been consummated or otherwise terminated; (5) require written releases from all parties before releasing trust funds. If a buyer deposits earnest money and thereafter defaults, the balance of the earnest money shall be paid to Owner; and Owner (agrees) (does not agree) to pay a sum equal to one-half of the earnest money (but not exceeding the amount of the Professional Service Fee) to Broker for Broker's Services.

10. HAZARDOUS MATERIALS AND DEFECTS. Owner represents that there are no known hazardous materials or contaminations of any kind, nor any known defects, structural or otherwise, in, or on or about the property, except (if none, so state) _____.

11. EQUIPMENT, FIXTURES AND MECHANICAL SYSTEMS. Owner agrees that all equipment and fixtures, including appliances (if any), electrical, plumbing, heating, and cooling, as part of this sale, will be in operating condition and performing the function for which they were intended, on either the date of possession or settlement, whichever takes place first, except (if none, so state) _____.

12. INDEMNIFICATION. Owner warrants that all information given herein, and set forth on any property data sheet provided to Broker, is correct to the best of the Owner's knowledge and belief and indemnifies Broker from all damages that may arise out of undisclosed, or incorrect facts or statements of Owner. Owner (has) (has not) reviewed the property data sheet and if reviewed accepts data thereon by signing below. If reviewed, initialed by Owner, and attached, it is made a part of this Agreement.

13. REMEDIES OF THE PARTIES. If Broker successfully defends any court action brought against Broker by Owner, or any other person involved in the sale of this property, or if it is necessary to employ an attorney to collect any fees, Owner agrees to pay all usual and reasonable court costs and attorney fees expended by Broker. This listing agreement and any contract arising therefrom, shall be deemed to have been made in the State of North Carolina

and any and all performance thereunder or breach thereof shall be interpreted, governed and construed pursuant to the laws of the State of North Carolina and the parties consent that the North Carolina District Court in and for County shall be the forum in which to bring any cause of action arising out of or under this agreement, or any subsequent agreement entered into by Owner as a result of Broker's efforts concerning the above described property. The parties agree that such court shall have jurisdiction of the parties for such action.

14. AGENCY DISCLOSURE. Owner acknowledges receipt of the disclosure "Agency/Policy Disclosure and Acknowledgement" from Broker. Owner agrees, as a part of Broker's real estate business, Broker and Broker's affiliated licensees may represent buyers as clients and enter into written Buyer Agency Agreement to serve as buyer's Agent. Owner (desires) (does not desire) that Broker to show to buyer(s) such Seller client property which meets buyer's price range and needs. A Dual Agency Potential/Consent Agreement (is) (is not) attached. If attached, it shall be made a part hereof. An Appointed Agency Agreement (is) (is not) attached. If attached, it shall be made a part hereof.

15. PROPERTY STATUS. The property (is) (is not) residential. If residential property (has) (has not) been owned and used as Owner's principal residence for two (2) out of the past five (5) years. Owner is advised to consult tax advisor.

16. BROKERAGE SERVICES ONLY. Owner acknowledges that Broker is acting as a Real Estate Broker only and not as an attorney, tax advisor, lender, appraiser, surveyor, structural engineer, property inspector, consultant or other professional service advisor. Owner is hereby advised to seek such other professional advice as may be important to Owner.

17. RELEASE OF INFORMATION. Owner authorized lender(s), contract holder(s), and utility companies to provide Broker with any and all information regarding the above-described property.

18. FAX TRANSMISSION. The facsimile transmission of a signed copy hereof, as well as any addendums to this agreement shall

constitute a binding agreement. The parties agree to confirm this agreement by mail or personal delivery of the original signed agreement between the parties.

19. ENTIRE AGREEMENT. This Exclusive Listing Agreement constitutes the entire agreement between the parties relating to Broker's representation of Owner, and supersedes any prior listing agreement, whether oral or written.

20. AGREEMENT shall be binding upon the heirs, assigns, executors, and administrators of the parties and only agreements noted herein, shall be binding upon the parties. This property is offered without respect to race, color, creed, sex, national origin, religion, physical/mental disability/handicap or familial status/presence of children.

Your Home Warranty

Your exclusive listing agreement will include language about home warranties. A home warranty is a service contract that covers replacements and repair costs of various home systems and appliances. It generally covers appliances and equipment such as electrical systems, plumbing systems, dishwashers, stoves and other key components that may become inoperable or defective during a certain time period specified in the contract.

Many home warranties will cover the seller of the property during the time that it is listed and up until the moment of closing. Then

Home Warranties

Although home warranty policies would appear to offer peace of mind, some people have misguided expectations about what the home warranty policy will cover. Be sure to read the Home Warranty pamphlet in its entirety to understand exactly what is covered and for what period of time. Many times additional coverage can be placed on items not covered under the basic plan, read that as *standard* plan. Coverage on items such as pool pumps, hot tubs, saunas, solar heating systems and many other things can be purchased but at an additional cost. Do not assume something is covered. Ask your agent or ask the warranty company. All of the home warranty companies have toll-free numbers and are happy to answer specific questions.

they will cover the buyer of the property in most instances for one year after the purchase. The buyers may then continue the warranty on a year-to-year basis. These contracts do not cover all home repairs and vary across warranty providers. Most of the time there is a service or trade call fee. This may cost from $50 to $75 per occurrence. In other words, if the compressor on your air conditioner fails and is covered under the warranty, then the replacement—which in actuality may be several thousand dollars—would only cost you the trade call fee. On the other hand, if you make a call for a leaky sink faucet, you would still pay the trade call fee.

Referral Fees on Home Warranties

Prior to 2010, agents and brokers were routinely paid $40 to $75 for each referral they made that resulted in a home warranty. In June of that year, the U. S. Department of Housing and Urban Development issued a ruling that neither agents nor brokers were allowed to accept fees from home warranty companies for promoting their products.

For the fairly inexpensive price of about $350 to $500, depending on the specific coverage and size of the home, a home warranty can help you compete with both existing and new homes in your market. The peace of mind that a buyer gets from knowing that the coming year may not find him paying money out of pocket to replace damaged or worn out appliances or systems is quite valuable, particularly in today's economy and job market. So the first function of a home warranty is to provide a sense of well being about the property. There is an additional benefit to the seller of the property; he or she is covered during the listing period on the same items. Sometimes once a property goes under contract and inspections are made and repairs warranted, the home warranty is instrumental in causing those repairs to be made.

The home warranty also takes the pressure off of you as a seller since small issues can be handled and covered by the warranty. Small issues that the home inspector turns up will remain just small issues as long as the buyer knows that the item will be covered in case it fails at a later date (within the terms of the warranty). It is important to note that nearly anything in the home can be added to the policy (for an additional fee, of course) in order to present the most complete package possible to your buyer. Additional coverage could include swimming pool equipment, wet bar refrigerator, garage door opener, central vacuum or the well pump.

The Number of Home Warranties

American Home Shield, a leading warranty company, has over 1.4 million customers with warranties. A recent survey of the one million Angie's List members indicates that 24% of the members have a home warranty. Nearly two-thirds of those taking the poll that had a warranty said it came with the purchase of their home.

It is now time to take a look at a host of factors and issues that affect the sale of your home. In the next chapter we will go through some general issues and drill down into factors like current liens, synthetic stucco construction, and unpaid real property taxes.

Four Things to Remember from Chapter 7

* Understanding the exclusive listing agreement is an important step on your way to selling your home within 45 days.
* Explaining agency as it relates to both the buyer and seller in a transaction is a good business practice and in most states, it is the law to explain working with real estate agents.
* Different types of real estate agents fulfill different roles for the home-selling and home-buying public.
* Adding a home warranty to your agreement can provide great peace of mind for the buyer and take some of the pressure off of the seller.

CHAPTER 8

Issues Affecting the Sale of Your Home

> ∼ *Always turn a negative situation into a positive situation.*
>
> —MICHAEL JORDAN

IN THE REAL ESTATE WORLD, Murphy's Law may appear from time to time, "If something can go wrong, it will go wrong." It is just the nature of the business based on the sheer number of people and entities involved, the price of the typical home, and the complexities involved in the whole selling/buying experience. The more prepared you can be to deal with challenges and contingencies, the better off you will be.

In this chapter we will take a brief look at a number of issues that could impact the sale of your home beginning with fair housing laws.

Fair Housing

The federal Fair Housing Amendments Act of 1988 protects homebuyers and renters from illegal discrimination. Buyers have the right to buy any home they can afford in any neighborhood, and the Act makes it illegal to discriminate because of such factors as race, color, national origin, religion, sex, physical or mental disability or handicap, or familial status (meaning, whether they have children or are pregnant). These groups of people are known as protected classes. It is also illegal for a real estate agent to steer an individual or a family to a certain neighborhood or area based on demographics.

Real estate professionals, lenders or others involved with the home buying and selling process who unfairly deny someone the right to own (or rent) a home are said to be "discriminating," and thus violating the Fair Housing Act. Fair Housing violations are more common than most people would think in this day and age. They can range from the single mother denied the right to purchase a condo in a neighborhood perceived to be, but not legally registered as, an over-55 community to the minority homebuyer who is "steered" to neighborhoods by a real estate agent who "thinks" they belong in a certain area.

Are Only Physical Disabilities Covered as a Protected Class?

The answer to this question is no. Besides physical disabilities, discrimination may not be made on the basis of an emotional or mental disability as well.

As a seller, it is important to be aware of these types of discriminations and the buyer's legal rights should an infraction occur. Often, the problems arise during the lending process, where again no one can refuse to give out a loan based on race, color, national origin, religion, sex, familial status, disability or handicap. (A lender is allowed to offer a loan on less favorable terms, or even turn down an application, based on valid issues like insufficient income, unacceptable credit history or poor past track record with mortgage loans.)

According to the U.S. Department of Housing and Urban Development (HUD), it is also illegal to threaten, coerce, intimidate or interfere with anyone exercising a fair housing right or assisting others

Sexual Harassment

Courts have held that the law's ban on housing discrimination based on sex includes coverage when claims of sexual harassment are made. It must be shown that the sexual conduct was unwelcome.

who exercise that right, advertise or make any statements that indicate a limitation or preference based on race, color, national origin, religion, sex, familial status, disability or handicap. For example, it is illegal to advertise that a house is for sale to "whites only," or to "families only," says HUD.

Over many years in the real estate business, I have occasionally had a seller remark to me that he would not sell his home to a member of a minority group. In these instances, I have said that I would not be able to help that seller because what he had espoused doing violated federal law as well as being morally and ethically reprehensible.

Be aware as a seller that this type of attitude while rare is offensive and will jeopardize not only the quick sale of your home which is the intent of this book but will also jeopardize you the seller in a number of ways.

Familial Status

Familial status is a protected category or class and generally means that a seller or a landlord may not discriminate against families with children under the age of 18 with regard to housing. This protection is broad and also covers women who are pregnant and people in the process of adopting a child.

Permission to Market Your Home

As you read in the last chapter, the exclusive listing agreement includes verbiage concerning the marketing of your home, yard signs, and lockboxes that will allow agents entry even if you are not home.

We will delve further into the marketing tactics for today's homeowners later in this book, but for now it is important that you know the value of such activities and how your agent will be focused on getting your home the maximum exposure possible across the widest swaths of potential buyers. To do this, your agent needs the flexibility to use a combination of traditional (yard signs, open houses, property brochures, etc.) and new age (dedicated websites, social networking mentions, etc.) marketing methods.

The Due Diligence Period

Your agent may refer to this period as the "contingent inspection period" or the "due diligence period." The two names are often used interchangeably and refer to the period of time that the buyer has to inspect the home in exchange for paying a negotiable due diligence fee (sometimes that fee may be zero dollars). After that period expires, their earnest money (which they put down when they signed the contract) goes "hard"—in other words, it may be nonrefundable should the buyer change his or her mind about purchasing the home.

In January 2011, the North Carolina Bar Association and the North Carolina Association of Realtors released a new version of the "Offer to Purchase and Contract" document. In that document, NCAR introduced a new way of handling the due diligence period. It allows the buyer to pay a fee directly to the seller for the opportunity to perform due diligence on the property during a specified time period and depending on what is discovered, having the right to walk away from the deal without losing the earnest money. During this period, the seller cannot sell the house to anyone else; however, they can take back up offers. Generally speaking, by 5 p.m. on the last day of the due diligence period, the buyer or buyer's agent must notify the seller or seller's agent if they intend to declare their intent to walk away from the contract.

The Due Diligence Period

Due Diligence period is defined as a period of time during which the buyer can thoroughly investigate a property to determine whether they are satisfied with the aspects of the property and want to move forward with the contract or if they are dissatisfied in which case they would have the right to terminate the contract and cancel the purchase.

Property Taxes and Insurance

Property taxes and insurance are two critical points that you will want to have up to date and accurate before selling your home. Expect a property tax record review and an insurance record review to take place before you can close on the sale, as both reviews will reveal important information that may impact the sale of your home.

If, for example, the seller has not paid property taxes for a year and is currently in arrears, that obligation to the taxing authority will need to be settled before the seller can sell his or her home (or at the latest at the closing table). On the other hand, many sellers pay taxes before they are due. In this case, a proration will be performed by the closing attorney refunding some of the taxes to the seller for the balance of the year in which he will not be occupying the home but for which he has already paid. This portion of the taxes will be refunded to the seller and collected from the buyer at closing.

Buyers and sellers may also encounter what is known as a C.L.U.E. report, or a Comprehensive Loss Underwriting Exchange, which is generated on the home by the insurance industry. This report will show the history of the insurance coverage on the property, five year's worth of claims on the home (if there are any), and areas that could be of potential concern for the buyer, who can use the information when making his or her offer. In other words, it is important for a buyer to do due diligence on the insurability of a property during the due diligence period. There are instances where claims have been made long ago that may affect one's ability to purchase insurance (required by any lender) on the property.

Understanding the Risks of Marketing a Home

Much of this is common sense, but just to reiterate what we have been saying throughout this book: selling your home within 45 days requires honesty, diligence, and a sincere desire to sell your property. Part of that means coming to terms with any issues that need to be revealed (on your seller disclosure form) and discussing them with your agent before deciding how to address them.

Simple disclosures—such as whether this is your primary residence and how long you have owned it and lived in it—can play a key role in the sale of your home. Be sure to take an upfront, honest approach to the sale of your home and you will not go wrong. We will cover this topic in more depth later.

Earnest Money and Trust Accounts

Nearly every real estate transaction involves earnest money deposits. Although not essential to the creation of a valid and binding offer to purchase and contract agreement, it is rare for such transactions to not require the buyer to make an earnest money deposit.

The offer to purchase and contract agreement will govern where the earnest money will be held. The earnest money is most often turned over to the real estate broker who in turn holds the money in a trust account for the parties to the transaction. Many times, the earnest money will be held by the brokerage representing the buyer. Sometimes, it will be held by the brokerage representing the seller. A real estate attorney or a title company may also hold the earnest money.

In most cases, real estate brokers hold the earnest money in non-interest bearing trust accounts. Real estate licensing laws place some definite obligations on the broker with respect to the earnest money deposit. In North Carolina and South Carolina, the holder of the earnest money must deposit the check into a broker's trust account within three (3) business days from the signing and dating of the contract by all parties.

The earnest money amount can be negotiated. Usually, it will be a small percentage of the purchase price, and it will vary depending on market conditions, the price and type of property (vacant land, resale of a home, new construction), as well as other factors.

Flood Zones

If your home is located in a flood zone, you (and soon, your buyer) will have to carry flood insurance on your home that most certainly will be required by your lender. This flood insurance in nearly all instances is underwritten by FEMA. Because you own your home and carry insurance on it, you probably already know whether or not it is in a flood zone. You can check with your county appraiser and/or zoning board to find out the specific answer to this question.

C.L.U.E. Report

Comprehensive Loss Underwriting Exchange (C.L.U.E.) is a claims history database generated by LexisNexis that allows insurance companies to access consumer claims on a property. The database contains up to 7 years of personal property claims history. Insurance companies can access the database and consumers can access information on their own properties.

In some instances homes that were not previously in a flood zone will find that the flood zone has been redefined and now they are required to carry flood insurance. It always pays to check this information. If you portray the home as not needing flood insurance and if the buyer finds out at the closing table that flood insurance is now required, then you will have a major issue on your hands.

When you list your home on the MLS it will likely include "flood" or "non-flood" as information for buyers who are concerned about this particular issue. Flood insurance can be an issue impacting the sale of your home because it requires a separate policy (and, as such, an additional insurance premium). It is incumbent upon the seller and the seller's agent to know and disclose this pertinent fact.

Synthetic Stucco

Synthetic stucco has come under fire recently for its unfortunate characteristic to cause moisture to be trapped and retained within wall areas of the home and for the resulting structural failures that have occurred because of such moisture retention. Officially known as EIFS or Exterior Insulation and Finish Systems, the product is a multi-layered exterior finish. Newer EIFS systems include a drainage setup to help keep moisture from being trapped behind the covering. Older versions of synthetic stucco did not include such accompaniments and have been known to create structural issues within the homes in which they were used.

The material can create issues such as mold or mildew on the interior or exterior of the home, swollen wood around door and window frames, blistered or peeling paint, and cracked EIFS or cracked sealant. NAR advises sellers who know that their homes include synthetic stucco to avoid potentially misleading representations about the condition of the EIFS or the underlying framing.

For instance, stating that the house is "dry" or that the EIFS application defects have been "repaired" is an invitation to the courthouse, says NAR. There is no way to verify reliably the condition of all the wood under the siding without removing that siding. Nor does any accepted EIFS repair protocol exist. In fact, many engineers contend that an EIFS house cannot be repaired, short of stripping the structure completely of its EIFS exterior and re-siding with another material.

Encourage the buyer to obtain an EIFS inspection preferably by a structural engineer rather than a home inspector (because the more invasive testing methods engineers use are more likely to find moisture problems). Finally, NAR advises sellers to transfer any potential responsibility back to the buyers. Give instructions to buyers regarding resources (such as www.buildingdefects.com) designed to inform them about the product and the surrounding controversy.

The state of North Carolina currently requires a disclosure statement by the seller if a home contains EIFS.

Homeowners Associations

Homeowners associations, or "HOAs" are legal organizations that maintain common areas and enforce deed restrictions. In most cases, a HOA will oversee a condominium, townhome, or neighborhood development. These groups use Covenants, Conditions & Restrictions (CC&Rs), which are issued to each homeowner and then enforced by the HOA in order to maintain quality and the value of the properties that are under their domain. If your home is in a development with an HOA, there are several issues that could come up during the sale.

For starters, the HOA collects monthly, quarterly, and/or annual fees in amounts that must be revealed to the buyer. The CC&Rs are also important because in many cases they define what an owner may or may not do with their property. You as the seller will be asked to share the CC&Rs with the buyer (in most cases, a copy of the book stays with the home when it is sold). In many cases, the CC&Rs are readily available online under the neighborhood or management company's website.

A bigger issue right now is the fact that many HOAs have struggled with the insolvency issue in the current market conditions. Because their own billings have gotten more and more difficult to collect (due to job losses, property depreciation, foreclosures, short sales and so forth), the solvency of HOAs has come into question numerous times over the last couple of years.

In North Carolina, for example, there have been many examples of insolvent HOAs. This not only poses a problem for the seller, but it also puts up significant challenges for the buyer since getting a loan for a property whose HOA is insolvent is virtually impossible.

If there is an HOA involved, the financial status of the HOA could be a big issue on whether you can sell your property within 45 days. Be sure to thoroughly check out your HOA early in the process to ensure solvency. If you know that there is a problem, you are required to disclose that information to a potential buyer.

Homeowner Associations (HOAs)

An HOA allows people with shared neighborhood values an opportunity to enforce regulations affecting the neighborhood or community. These often include architectural review and a degree of conformity regarding the general appearance and rights and restrictions regarding neighborhood activities. The HOA is often responsible for the upkeep of a neighborhood's amenities and will pass through the costs on a pro rata share to the homeowners of properties in its jurisdiction. Membership in an HOA by a residential buyer is typically a condition of purchase.

Termite Bonds

A termite bond is a contract between a homeowner and a termite control company. It allows the homeowner to pay a "retainer" fee to that company for the service of inspecting a home periodically to check for wood-destroying insects or organisms. The bond outlines the frequency and type of treatment to be provided and may include re-treatment and repair guarantees at no additional charge. It also should allow for repairs to structures damaged by termites or other wood-boring pests should damage occur while the home is under the protection of the bond.

Termite Bonds may be offered during the home inspection process when a home is sold or after treatment has been provided for an active infestation. In most cases, the terms of the bond dictate that a pest management professional will inspect the home on a regular basis (quarterly or annually depending on the contract) and provide additional treatment when needed.

A home with a termite bond shows potential buyers that the seller has taken the necessary precautions to ensure that the property does not become one of the approximately 600,000 U.S. homes that are damaged by termites each year—a problem that is rarely covered by traditional homeowners insurance. Prices for termite bonds vary depending on the terms of the bond, type of species covered by the bond, treatment included, the region of the country and pest control company. If you are going to purchase a termite bond, make sure that it is transferable to the new owner when the home is sold and find out if there is a charge for the transfer. The information must be disclosed to the buyer.

The Purchase Contract

It is important to you, the buyer, and your agent(s) to carefully review the purchase contract before signing it. Depending on your individual situation, you may also want your real estate attorney to review the document to ensure that everything is properly covered and that nothing is left out (or, left in that should not be there) and that all terms are clear and concise.

Other important documents that you will go over with your agent (depending upon which state your property is located) include the Working With Real Estate Agents brochure and the Home Inspection brochure. North Carolina's Working With Real Estate Agents brochure, for example, addresses the various types of agency relationships that may be available to you. It helps you decide which relationship you want to have with a real estate agent and also provides useful information about the various services real estate agents can provide buyers and sellers. It also explains how real estate agents are paid.

Another document that you may be asked to sign relates to professional services disclosures. Real estate agents usually make recommendations on home stagers, lenders, inspectors, insurance agents, surveyors, general contractors, home warranty providers, attorneys and other professionals, but it is important that you reach out to those companies and individuals recommended and screen them yourself before making a decision on any professional who will assist you with selling your home in 45 days. Be sure to understand the services they provide and the payment that they expect upon rendering these services.

Current Liens

On the exclusive listing agreement the seller will reveal whether there is a mortgage (deed of trust) on the property and whether there are any second lien-holders (HELOCs) that have to be paid off when the home is sold. It is important to be honest in this section because 1) the truth will be revealed when the title search is performed and 2) if you owe more than the home is worth, it could negatively impact your ability to sell your home within 45 days. If the latter is the case, see Chapter 17 of this book for in-depth details on how to list your home and sell it as a short sale. Please note that if you have a current and open home equity line of credit on your home, this will need to be cancelled prior to the closing and proof will need to be provided to the closing attorney.

When reviewing the current liens on your home it is important to understand the difference between a *deed of trust* and a *mortgage*. A deed of trust is a deed wherein legal title in real property is transferred to a trustee that holds it as security for a loan (debt) between a borrower (the trustor) and lender (the beneficiary). Mortgages involve two parties and generally find the mortgagee (the lender) giving legal title directly to the mortgagor (the borrower). North Carolina is a deed of trust state.

When Your Home Is Worth Less Than Owed

In some cases, you may owe more money on your mortgage than your home is currently worth. This is a reality that has befallen many homeowners over the last few years, namely due to declining property values. In Chapter 17 of this book we will go over the specific steps you will want to take if you find yourself in this situation.

Schools

School districts play a significant role in the sale or purchase of a home particularly if the buyers have young families—or if they are planning to start a family. This issue can work for or against you as a seller. A mediocre home in a top performing school district that has an excellent reputation may sell quickly, for example, while a beautiful, large home in a less desirable school district may require some incentive to sell within 45 days. Although schools are quite important, please remember that homes may not be advertised in a neighborhood that is a great "family" neighborhood since technically that is a violation of Fair Housing laws.

Most of the time buyers will look at the elementary, middle, and high schools that are located within the home's "zoned" district. They will also look at test scores and other measures upon which school ratings are based. It is important to note that school zoning changes are possible under certain circumstances, although most decisions are tied to transportation and busing and therefore difficult to alter.

Check with your school district for their rules regarding school redistricting. It may be important as a seller to add a disclaimer regarding the district in which the home is currently located if it is subject to change. It should be the buyer or the buyer's agent's responsibility to check this information thoroughly if it is important to the purchaser.

Schools

Of interest to every parent, schools often make or break the quick sale of a home. Be sure to investigate the schools surrounding your home for sale at *www.schooldigger.com*. There is information here relating to every aspect of nearly every school in the U.S. including test scores, rankings and reviews. Talk to your agent. If the public schools to which your home is assigned are less than desirable, be sure to know any and every alternative including magnet schools and private school choices.

Walk Scores

Today's homebuyers have a plethora of information at their fingertips and some of that information is specific to your property. Your home's Walk Score, for example, is available on www.walkscore.com and it creates a public access "walkability" index for your home. One home may be extremely "walkable" while another may be tagged as "car dependent."

Of course, you cannot singlehandedly improve your home's Walk Score, but it is helpful to be aware of this measure and to understand its value to some buyers. If the score is high on the walkability scale, you may want to use that positive attribute in some of the marketing materials for your home. Discuss this point with your agent.

Taxes, Fees & Liens

Any federal, state, or local income tax that has not been paid must be paid by the time your home closes. Otherwise, if unpaid, it may constitute a lien on the property, which may make selling your home in 45 days difficult. Condominium or HOA fees that are unpaid can have a similar impact, as can any mechanics, labor, or materials liens that service providers have filed at the county courthouse.

Other issues of which to be aware include any judgments that have been filed against you personally or any other legal matters that *may* result in a judgment against the property. The Uniform Commercial Code (UCC) fixture filings can also impact the ability to sell your home in 45 days. If you have filed for bankruptcy or if there are any leases signed on the property, the closing may also be postponed.

Think through the possibilities of any judgments or liens and reveal your concerns to your agent early so that you can work through any issues of this nature affecting the sale of the home. Otherwise, this may result in a delay of the closing.

VA/FHA Appraisals

If your buyer is using an VA or FHA loan, he or she will need to have a special home appraisal inspection completed. These appraisals are slightly more detailed and costlier than those used for conventional loans.

VA and FHA Appraisals

VA and FHA appraisals are somewhat different than those done for conventional loans. FHA appraisers are concerned with the health and safety of the borrowers and they look at not only the standard things but also they take it a little farther. These appraisers look at things like handrails on steps, cracked windows, lack of screens, evidence of rodent or insect infestation, slip hazards, trip hazards, peeling paint, etc. They want to see that windows are easily opened in case of a fire and they look at the remaining life of a roof and HVAC equipment. These appraisers will check for evidence of mold and mildew, any environmental contaminants and things like earth to wood contact and perhaps the evidence of termites. While it goes without saying that many of these things should already be done, especially if you are trying to accomplish a quick sale within 45 days, there are times when it seems that FHA appraisers are overly cautious and demanding especially if you are the seller looking at their report.

Be aware that any value placed on a property by a VA or FHA appraiser will remain with the property and cannot be changed for a period of six months.

VA and FHA appraisers are required to perform certain minimum inspections as well as evaluate the market value of the property. Such appraisals may turn up issues that the home inspector or that a traditional appraiser may not catch. As a seller, you will want to be aware of any possible repairs that "must" be done for the sale to close and to discuss with your agent exactly how the repairs and the costs of such repairs shall be handled.

Assessments

A property tax is sometimes confused with a special assessment tax. These are two different forms of taxation. A property tax is based upon the fair market value of the property being taxed. A special assessment is a tax that in some instances is levied upon a property for some benefit provided by the taxing authority, e.g., sidewalks, streetlights, etc. In condominiums or townhomes, there is sometimes an assessment by the owners association to make repairs to the roof or other infrastructure of the property. These can be referred to simply as assessments and as such, must be disclosed by the seller to a prospective buyer.

Surveys, Deeds & Covenants

These legal instruments can have an impact on the sale of your home. In many cases these factors will not create any negative issues for you during the sale, but it is important to be aware of them:

* **Property surveys:** A sketch or map of a property that shows its boundaries and other physical features. The survey also shows the relative location of a house, shed, other building and fences on the property, and it usually includes the position of any public or municipal easements. A property survey will also disclose any encroachments from neighboring parcels or any encroachments from the subject property onto neighboring parcels. Surveys may be done whenever a piece of property changes ownership and are always required when a loan is involved.
* **Notes:** A mortgage note is a promissory note associated with a specified mortgage loan. Simply put, it is the borrower's promise to pay back the loan.

* **General Warranty Deed:** This is a type of deed where the seller guarantees that they hold clear title to a piece of real estate and has the right to sell it to the buyer. (See the next section of this chapter on marketable title for more information on how this is done.) This is the strongest and most preferable type of deed for the buyer. It contains five specific guarantees regarding the transfer of the property.
* **Special Warranty Deed:** A special warranty deed is a deed in which the seller warrants or guarantees the title only against defects arising during the period of his or her ownership of the property. The grantor makes no warranty against defects existing before the time of his or her ownership.
* **Covenants:** A covenant is a promise in a written contract or a deed of real property. There are different types of covenants, such as a covenant of warranty, which is a promise to guarantee the title to the property is free of any claims against it, a promise agreeing to joint use of an easement for access to real property. Mutual covenants among members of a homeowners association are promises to respect the rules of conduct or restrictions on the use of the property.

Marketable Title—Owner's Title Insurance

When the ownership of your home transfers to the buyer, you will also convey "marketable title" to that new owner. A marketable title can be transferred to a new owner without the likelihood that claims will be made on it by another party.

Marketable title is critical in all real estate transactions because buyers expect to receive property to which no one else can lay claim. They do not expect that their ownership will later be challenged. Marketability of title is addressed in the purchase contract and is typically assured by the owner's title insurance policy.

Title insurance is used by homebuyers and lenders for protection against back taxes, undisclosed liens, legal judgments, forgeries, fraud and a host of other potential legal/financial problems that can arise and which may attach to the home when purchasing or refinancing property. Title insurance is important because it may correct any defects or possible "clouds" on the title that may exist.

Easements

An easement is a limited property right for a third party (such as a neighbor, a municipality, or a utility company) to do something on land that is not theirs. For example, easements are often granted to utility companies to run power lines and cable lines across land that does not technically belong to them. A homeowner may also grant an easement to a neighbor if the homeowner's property prohibits road access.

Easements can be either expressed (stated by the land owner formally) or implied. Regardless of expression, the easement generally provides only a limited amount of rights. Easements classified as "appurtenant" are said to "run with the land" and are part of the formal ownership of the land. An easement in gross is a personal easement that does not necessarily transfer when the ownership of the land transfers. It is important for you, as a seller, to know if there are any easements affecting the sale of your property and if so to consult your real estate advisor or an attorney to understand how these will affect both you and the new buyer.

Legally Binding Contracts

As a final note for this chapter, it is important to note that any agreements you sign as part of the sale of your property—including the exclusive listing agreement and the purchase and sales contract—are legally binding. If you do not understand what you are signing or the obligations attached to it, and if your agent cannot help you understand all implications of what you are signing, then you will want to consult an attorney to help with the process. As with any legal document, do not sign off on anything unless you completely understand what you are signing and are in agreement with its terms and conditions.

Any changes or addenda to signed contracts must be in writing, and email is an acceptable conveyance in most states. Please understand in your state if email is acceptably legally binding. (In North Carolina and most states, it is legally binding.)

Should you and your agent agree to cancel your contract, you will both sign a Cancellation of Agreement form that releases you and your agent from the duties and obligations outlined in the agreement.

Now that you have a good understanding of the list of obstacles that could stand in your way during the sales process, let's look closely at the various pieces of paperwork that have to be addressed during the process.

Four Things to Remember from Chapter 8

* Many different issues can arise during the sales process, but none are insurmountable.
* Being upfront with your Realtor about liens, judgments, easements and any other issues affecting the home or its title can help you both avoid surprises and issues down the road.
* Taking out a termite bond on your home and providing a home warranty are ways to show buyers that you are serious about providing the necessary protection to allow for the home to sell.
* All contracts are legally binding and any changes to them must be made in writing.

CHAPTER 9

Seller Disclosures

∿ *Honesty is the best policy.*

—BENJAMIN FRANKLIN

As you read in previous chapters, home sellers must disclose any and all material facts about their properties to prospective buyers during the sale process. A leaky roof, bad plumbing, and/or faulty electrical systems should be discussed with your agent at the beginning. He or she will counsel you on exactly how disclosures should be handled in order to avoid unnecessary delays and/or lawsuits on the part of the buyer. Any material fact relating to condition must be disclosed. In this litigious world, anything affecting the home that is known by the seller and undisclosed will be a problem later.

In this chapter we will look first at the residential property disclosure and the material facts that you will be required to reveal. Then we will give you a laundry list of the major home components of which you (or your contractor) should be aware.

Residential Property Disclosure

Owners of residential real estate (single-family homes, individual condominiums, townhouses, and the like, and buildings with up to four dwelling units) are required to furnish purchasers a Residential

Property and Owners' Association Disclosure Statement ("Disclosure Statement"). This form is the only one approved for this purpose. A disclosure statement must be furnished in connection with the sale, exchange, option and sale under a lease with option to purchase (unless the tenant is already occupying or intends to occupy the dwelling). A disclosure statement is not required for some transactions, including the first sale of a dwelling that has never been inhabited and transactions of residential property made pursuant to a lease with option to purchase where the lessee occupies or intends to occupy the dwelling.

Here are a few questions that will be on your Residential Property Disclosure Statement—all of which will need to be answered in some manner. I say in some manner because an answer may be a simple yes or no or no representation. No Representation is not as common an answer, but it may be seen or used in the following circumstances:

1. An estate sale where the owner is deceased and the questions are being answered by someone who has never lived in the home.
2. An owner who has rented the property for a long period of time and may know some of the answers but not all of them.
3. A lender who has not had any personal experience with the home.
4. Someone who has inherited the property.
5. An owner who simply does not want to answer the questions and by law does not have to answer them.

Not answering these questions about the condition of the property is often justified, but it sometimes raises a red flag to the buyer. The question posed is, "Why is the seller not answering? Does he or she have something to hide?" After seeing this situation over many years and hearing these questions, I believe that the buyers will now inspect more thoroughly and will be overly cautious in regard to any questionable component of the home. Inasmuch as our purpose here is to sell your home within the next 45 days, it is my hope and advice that you will answer the questions with a simple yes or no and disclose everything about the home that is asked.

One other thing that I have seen come into play is when a seller answers a question with a no, indicating that there is no problem or malfunction with a particular component and then later it is discovered that there is a problem and that it is obvious that the seller must have known about it. This in and of itself may be grounds for a termination of the contract. I have seen too where a buyer has demanded a return of the due diligence fee. This fee is nonrefundable in every other circumstance except where a seller makes an intentional misstatement or in some other way may be in breach of contract. So I am cautioning you, the seller, to be truthful and complete in answering the questions on the disclosure statement.

Yes/No/No Representation

When filling out your residential property disclosure form, you must respond to each of the questions on the form by filling in the requested information or by placing a check √ in the appropriate box. Here are some important points to remember:

a. If you check "Yes" for any question (meaning there is a known problem), you must explain your answer and either describe the problem or attach a report from an engineer, contractor, pest control operator or other expert or public agency describing the problem. If you disclose what you know and/or attach a report, you will not be liable for any inaccurate or incomplete information contained in the disclosure so long as you were not grossly negligent in obtaining or transmitting the information.

b. If you check "No," you are stating that you have no actual knowledge of any problem. If you check "No" and you know there is a problem, you may be liable for making an intentional misstatement.

c. If you check "No Representation," you have no duty to disclose the conditions or characteristics of the property, even if you may know of them.

If you check "Yes" or "No" and something happens to the property to make your Disclosure Statement incorrect or inaccurate (for example, the roof begins to leak), you must promptly give the purchaser a corrected Disclosure Statement or correct the problem.

Here are a representative sampling of questions found on many property disclosure statements. These may change from state to state and some states, such as North Carolina, are asking for disclosures and information on any Home Owners Association (HOA) as well.

Are there any problems with any of the following: If you answer yes, you must explain your answer and/or attach any reports regarding the item:

1. Foundation, slab, fireplaces/chimneys, floors, windows (including storm windows and screens), doors, ceilings, interior and exterior walls, attached garage, patio, deck or other structural components
    a. Siding is: ☐Masonry ☐Wood ☐Composition/ Hardboard ☐Vinyl ☐Synthetic Stucco ☐Other_____
    b. Approximate age of structure? _____
2. Roof (leakage or other problem)? _____
    a. Approximate age of roof covering? _____
3. Water seepage, leakage, dampness or standing water in the basement, crawl space or slab? _____
4. Electrical system (outlets, wiring, panel, switches, fixtures, etc.)?
   _____
5. Plumbing system (pipes, fixtures, water heater, etc.)?_____
   _____
6. Heating and/or air conditioning? _____
    a. Heat Source is: ☐Furnace ☐Heat Pump ☐Baseboard ☐Other _____
    b. Cooling Source is: ☐Central Forced Air   ☐Wall/ Window Unit(s)   ☐Other _____
    c. Fuel Source is: ☐Electricity   ☐Natural Gas   ☐Propane ☐Oil ☐Other _____
7. Water supply (including water quality, quantity and water pressure)? _____
    a. Water supply is: ☐City/County   ☐Community System ☐Private Well   ☐Other _____
    b. Water pipes are: ☐Copper   ☐Galvanized   ☐Plastic ☐Other _____   ☐Unknown

8. Sewer service and/or septic sewer system? _____

    a. Sewage disposal system is: ☐Septic Tank   ☐Septic Tank with Pump   ☐Community System   ☐Connected to City/County System   ☐City/County System available ☐Straight pipe (wastewater does not go into a septic or other sewer system [note: use of this type of system violates state law])   ☐Other _____

9. Built-in appliances (range/oven, attached microwave, hood/fan, dishwasher, disposal, etc.)? _____

10. Present infestation, or damage from past infestation of wood destroying insects or organisms, which has not been repaired?

_____

11. Drainage, grading or soil stability of lot?_____

12. Other systems and fixtures: central vacuum, pool, hot tub, spa, attic fan, exhaust fan, ceiling fan, sump pump, irrigation system, tv cable wiring or satellite dish, or other systems? _____. Also regarding the property identified above, including the lot, other improvements, and fixtures located thereon, do you have any

13. Room additions or other structural changes? _____

_____

14. Environmental hazards (substances, materials or products) including asbestos, formaldehyde, radon gas, methane gas, lead-based paint, under ground storage tank, or other hazardous or toxic material (whether buried or covered), contaminated soil or water, or other environmental contamination? _____

_____

15. Commercial, industrial, or military noise, odor, smoke, etc. Affecting the property? _____

16. Violations of zoning ordinances, restrictive covenants or other land-use restrictions, or building codes including the failure to obtain proper permits for room additions or other structural changes? _____

17. Utility or other easements, shared driveways, party walls or encroachments from or on adjacent property? _____

_____

18. Lawsuits, foreclosures, bankruptcy, tenancies, judgments, tax liens, proposed assessments, mechanics' liens, materialmens' liens, or notice from any governmental agency that could affect title to the property? _____

19. Flood hazard or that the property is in a federally-designated floodplain? _____

20. Private road(s) or street(s) adjoining the property? _____

_____

    a. If yes, do you know of an existing owners' association or maintenance agreement to maintain the road or street?

_____

21. Is the property subject to regulation by one or more owners' association(s) and governing documents which impose various mandatory covenants, conditions, and restrictions upon the lot, including, but not limited to obligations to pay regular assessments or dues and special assessments? _____

_____

22. The property is subject to the following owners' association(s) (specify name) _____
whose regular assessments ("dues") are $_____ per _____.
The name, address, and telephone number of the president of the owners' association or the association manager are: _____

_____.

23. As of the date this Disclosure Statement is signed, there are no other dues, fees, or special assessments, which have been duly approved as required by the applicable declaration or bylaws, payable to an association to which the lot is subject, except:

_____.

24. As of the date this Disclosure Statement is signed, there are no unsatisfied judgments against or pending lawsuits involving the property or lot to be conveyed, the planned community or the association to which the property and lot are subject, with the exception of any action filed by the association for the collection of delinquent assessments on lots other than the property and lot to be conveyed, except: _____.

25. The following services and amenities are paid for by the above owners' association(s) from the regular assessments:
- ☐ Management Fees
- ☐ Exterior Building Maintenance of Property to be Conveyed
- ☐ Exterior Yard/Landscaping Maintenance of Lot to be Conveyed
- ☐ Common Areas Maintenance
- ☐ Trash Removal
- ☐ Recreational Amenity Maintenance
- ☐ Pest Treatment/Extermination
- ☐ Street Lights
- ☐ Water
- ☐ Sewer
- ☐ Stormwater Management/Drainage/Ponds
- ☐ Internet Service
- ☐ Cable
- ☐ Private Road Maintenance
- ☐ Parking Area Maintenance
- ☐ Gate and/or Security
- ☐ Other, specify) _____.

New Home Insulation Addendum

The New Home Insulation Addendum is a disclosure form regarding fiberglass (also known as glass wool) that will be completed if fiberglass is used as insulation in the home. The U.S. Department of Health and Human Services has listed fiberglass as a substance reasonably anticipated as a carcinogen. Although generally believed that fiberglass is not a risk to persons in their daily lives, this disclosure form is becoming more prevalent since that substance is used in insulation in as many as 97% of all homes in the country.

Material Facts

Material Facts include anything that would impact the buyer's decision to purchase your home or the price and terms the buyer offers. If, for example, you know that your home has a specific defect, you must disclose it. In some states, for example, sellers must notify buyers if a death has occurred on the property within the last three years. This ensures that anyone has the correct information on which to make an informed decision. In many jurisdictions, failure to reveal material facts can be grounds for declaring the sale of a property null and void.

Further, in North Carolina, if both parties do not sign the property disclosure form at the time of acceptance of the Offer to Purchase and Contract by those parties, then the buyer may nullify the contract within three days.

Here are more material facts that *may* need to be disclosed:

* The average amount of property taxes that are paid on the property each year. (This is actually a matter of public record, so why not disclose the amount?)
* The existence of debt that is secured using the property as collateral. (This information may be useful if it is determined that a seller must bring money to closing and/or if this may be a potential short sale situation.)

Some type of damage to the property (such as damage from a flood or fire).

* The need to replace plumbing fixtures or window(s) whose internal seal has failed.
* Settling that has occurred and that has affected the structural integrity of the dwelling.
* The heated square footage contained in the home.
* The amount of land that is included in the sale.
* The existence of any toxic or hazardous substances.
* The amount of finished basement space and attic space (if any).
* The possible presence of a sexual predator living within a certain distance of the home.
* Any finished or unfinished square footage that is not attached to the main structure of the home.
* The presence or past presence of a mold-related problem.
* Past or present termite damage to the home.
* In a home serviced by septic field sanitation, the permit showing the allowable number of bedrooms.

* Any reports relating to the current or past condition of a well servicing the home.
* Any reports relating to asbestos found in the home.
* Lead based paint reports, if any exist.
* The presence of radon gas or any reports related to it if radon gas has been detected.

Disclosure of Structural Changes to a Home Since Purchased

All changes or additions made to a home since you purchased it should be disclosed to a potential buyer. Any changes involving structural, mechanical, electrical or plumbing should have had the appropriate permits obtained when the work was done. It is an easy process for the buyer to check on permitting through the Building Standards Department of the local government. If you have had any major unlicensed changes performed, it is wise to disclose these changes and to go ahead and have the permits pulled. This will save time in the selling process and will need to be disclosed and addressed.

As a property owner, you will probably know many of the material facts. Others—such as the average property tax amount—you may have to look up before disclosing. Remember that the buyers will confirm anything you tell them, so be honest and upfront when filling out your residential property disclosure and when revealing any material facts about your property.

Misrepresentation

Being honest about the condition of your home and its components is important so that you do not find yourself in a legal situation for not being truthful. Legally, this would be known as "misrepresentation." It is an issue that you will want to avoid in your quest to get your home sold within 45 days. In many cases, misrepresentation involves a claim by a buyer either during the due diligence period or from the contract to closing period or sometimes even after closing that the seller misrepresented a material fact about the property. The same misrepresentation claim could be made against the agent since the agent should have made diligent efforts to find out all relevant facts about the property.

Lead-Based Paint Disclosure

If your home was built prior to 1978 you will be required to furnish a Lead-Based Paint Disclosure. This is the law and the sale of a home built prior to this date may be invalidated if the disclosure is not furnished and signed by the buyer. If a seller has any reports related to lead-based paint testing, these must be furnished as well.

There are two types of misrepresentation, negligent and willful. In negligent misrepresentation, an owner or agent overlooks something that should have been disclosed. This may present an issue but can be thought of as an "honest" mistake. Willful misrepresentation is when one has been caught "red-handed" trying to be deceptive and this will nearly always derail a transaction. If there is a problem relating to the condition of the home and the seller does not disclose it, the agent must caution the owner against such a course of action. If the agent were to withhold the now known information, both would be guilty of willful misrepresentation and both would face some type of negative consequences. The agent might lose his license to practice real estate. The seller might at the very least be sued for damages relating to the money spent on inspecting the home and the consequences could be even more severe.

Omission

Omission is another area that will endanger a seller if they are not completely honest about the condition of their properties and any known conditions that could impact the value of their homes. The seller could create a serious problem when any known issue is omitted. The withholding of any pertinent information affects the buyer and usually in a negative way. The seller and the agent can and usually will be held responsible for omissions.

Omissions fall into the negligent and willful categories as well. It is possible that a seller just did not know of a condition and it is possible that an agent did not know as well. In many instances though, an agent is held to a higher standard and should have been expected to know. Anyway, negligent omission is certainly not as serious as willful omission where a known fact relating to the home has been left out by the seller or the agent or both. It will probably be discovered at some point and the buyer may have sustained losses. Guess who will be asked to pay? When answering questions concerning the property for sale, keep in mind that both misrepresentation and omission could cause problems later.

Understanding Your Home's Components

You do not have to be a general contractor to understand how the key components work, what the current condition of the home's components may be, how old or new they are, and how well they perform their function. Most of what you will find in this section will be common sense, although the point to remember is that we do not always check the physical components of our homes on a regular basis. Now that you are selling your home, it is important to make sure that all systems are functioning properly and that you have addressed any areas of concern.

Here are a few of the components with which you will wish to familiarize yourself—or have an inspector or contractor review—before putting your home on the market:

Fireplaces and Chimneys—A fireplace and chimney inspection is important since each year over 250 deaths and over $200 million in property damage from fires result from unsafe fireplaces and chimneys. This represents about one fifth of all fires in the country. Many of the fires are contained in the chimney and cause no damage to the house. Your fireplace and chimney system (FCS) is sometimes an important part of your home heating system and needs regular examination. Just some of the problems that are sometimes encountered with FCSs include:

Spillage from factory-built fireplaces
Odor problems from fireplaces
Upstairs fireplace works but downstairs fireplace does not
Cold drafts around factory built fireplaces
Soot and smoke on ceilings
Fireplace does not draft
Cracks and crevices that allow fire and heat to escape

In older homes, the cracking of mortar and the crevices created from this cracking means that the fire, heat and smoke may escape from the FCS and pose a house fire hazard. The structural damage that occurs is associated with deterioration from age or sometimes from improper installation. The tile inner liner of the chimney and the surrounding brick and block may crack and separate perhaps as a result of the creosote that has built up in the chimney. Many times this can only be recognized by the use of specialized cameras that your inspector will use to view the inside of the chimney. In some cases these can be repaired easily and in others a poured flue system may be needed. The cost of such a system may be very expensive but necessary to maintain safety. It is important, especially in older homes, to have this inspection performed. One other problem that is seen routinely is the build up of creosote on the inside walls of a chimney. While this can cause a chimney fire, it is a relatively easy problem to cure with an inspection and cleaning.

Although there are a number of FCS inspectors, in many areas, the local fire departments will conduct an inspection free of charge as a public service.

Many sellers will exclude the condition of fireplace and chimney system from the contract. They will attempt to sell the FCS in "as is" condition and will note this information in the listing agreement and in the property disclosures. This may be your best option if you suspect a problem and your best option for selling your home within 45 days.

Basements—A basement is defined as an area beneath the first floor with a minimum height of 6'-8". Basements may be finished or unfinished and may be used for storage as well as housing the main heating and mechanical systems of the home. The electrical panels and often the main plumbing controls or cleanout connections may be in the basement. It is estimated that 90 to 95 percent of all basements will experience a water penetration problem at some point in time. Usually this water will cause more damage to personal property and possibly to the heating and mechanical systems than to the structure but there may be structural concerns as well. Excessive moisture can lead to health concerns from molds and mildew. Additionally, excessive moisture may lead to problems with termites and to the development of wood destroying fungus. If water is present or it can be determined that water has entered the basement in the past, the inspector will note what he thinks is occurring and will recommend either a solution to the intrusion of water or perhaps that a waterproofing expert be contacted.

Crawl space—Many times the same situation exists for a crawl space that may exist in a basement, that is, water penetration. Some crawl spaces are above grade but most have areas that are below the finished grade of the home. Water that penetrates into the crawl space will present the same problems that water in a basement does and additionally may create a situation where the wooden structural members beneath the home may deteriorate. When the moisture content in wood is in excess of 19 percent this condition will occur. It is the inspector's job to determine if there is excessive water and how to remedy the situation if it exists. There are also other conditions that he may note. Many times there is additional wood or other organic material, which may attract termites and which will need to be removed. Sometimes the piers that support the home are improperly built or incorrectly located and occasionally there is inadequate ventilation.

Interior of the home—Here the inspector will be looking for any areas that do not comply with building standards or current building codes. Oftentimes, there are items that have excessive wear and/or sometimes may not be performing the function for which they were intended. If there are any tripping or other safety hazards, these will be noted on the report.

Exterior—The exterior of the home will be checked for any areas where water might enter the home, the crawl space or the basement. Also checked would be areas where animals, pests or insects may enter. Siding, flashing, doors and windows would be visually inspected. All windows would be checked for cracks in glazing and to make sure that they open, close and otherwise function properly. The integrity of the window and door seals would be checked. Doors are checked for operation and for energy efficiency. Many times the faulty operation of windows and doors is a clue to settlement in the structure, which may have occurred.

Garages, carports and storage sheds—Garages and carports may be attached or detached from the main home structure and in either instance will be examined. The garage components to be checked would be similar to those of the main home including doors, windows, siding, roof and overall structural condition. Additionally, if there is a garage door it would need to be checked to make sure that it is operational and functions in a safe manner. Since 1993, garage doors have been required to have an auto-reverse feature as a protection to children. Also checked would be the garage door remote opener.

Appliances—While this may seem mundane, there are some basics to consider when checking the appliances. With a refrigerator or freezer, the inspector tries to determine if it is cooling and to make sure that it is not rusted inside or otherwise broken. Another common problem is worn out or torn gaskets which need repair. The basics for the range and oven(s), whether gas or electric, should include whether or not the burners, the broiler and the oven(s) heat. A gas range is more complicated and there may be more safety checks like the working of the oven timer or the calibration of the thermostat. When the dishwasher is in operation, the inspector makes sure it operates and also that there are no water leaks on the floor or under the sink. The dishwasher requires an air gap or loop to make sure that contaminated water does not enter the potable water system. The food disposal should be checked to make sure it is not heavily rusted or leaking. Usually the laundry appliances, even when included in the contract, are beyond the scope of a home inspection.

Roofing—The interior investigation of the attic space is where the inspector begins his roof inspection. Often the interior of the attic may reveal problems relating to ventilation, damaged wood, and past or present leak sources. Rusted nails or stains may indicate that water has penetrated the roof deck. In some extreme conditions, mold may be found. If insulation has been added (particularly blown insulation) there is a chance that the intake from the lower part of the roof, the soffit, may be obstructed. There is a chance that a ventilation calculation will need to be made to insure that the attic space has the proper airflow. Without proper airflow, the life of the roofing product will be greatly shortened. In most areas, a roof can last for twenty years or more. Inadequate ventilation as well as a large amount of snow or intense hail may damage a roof and shorten its life. Many roofs will qualify under insurance policies to be replaced if a substantial hailstorm has occurred. Your inspector should be able to note if this is the case. Many inspectors will perform an infrared roof inspection where they do not even have to touch the surface of the roof to check its integrity. The infrared rays will locate areas that are hot spots and can show him exactly where heat is escaping; this will be an area that will likely wear out much faster than normal.

In addition the inspector will note the condition of the roofing shingles and will inspect all flashings and collars on pipes and power vents or air fans that may protrude from the roof. They will inspect to see if there are additional layers under the surface layer and will check the gutter and downspout system to insure adequate drainage.

Water seeping, leakage, dampness or standing water: Are there any issues with water anywhere around the exterior of the home? If so these will be noted and may need to be remedied.

Electrical System—Arguably, the most important inspection from the standpoint of safety is the electrical inspection. Most homeowners have little comprehension of how the system works and where dangers may lie. There are still FPE panels and Zinsco panels in some homes and these routinely show up in inspection reports. Both of these panels were at one time used extensively and both worked fine for years in many homes before failing and starting fires. Understanding the grounding system for a home and if it has Ufer grounding is important, at least in the sense that it functions properly. Many homes built before 1972 and wired with aluminum are 55 times more likely to have one or more wire connections at outlets reach "Fire Hazard Conditions" than those wired with copper. There are just too many items to mention and it would be impossible to look at every connection within the home but the inspector will look at the overall system beginning with the feed from the local power company and ending in many cases at an electrical wire nut.

Plumbing—This inspector should begin at the water meter (or well) and then make a determination if the shut off valve to the home water supply is in working order. He should find out if there are any lead pipes in the home and should determine the size of the feed and often the interior water pipes. The pipes should be a minimum of ½" diameter to insure adequate flow. He should inspect the hot water heater for size, location and the age of the unit. Most plumbing lines in exposed areas will need to be inspected to see if they are insulated properly to protect from freezing. He will need to check the sewage system to make sure it is adequately tied into the municipal system or to a septic tank. Also all kitchen and bathroom faucets, showers, tubs and toilets will be examined. The venting of the system to the outside will be checked to make sure that all dangerous gases and fumes are properly exhausted.

Heating and Cooling System HVAC—This inspection is important since the HVAC system is one of the most costly to the home and is often the source of problems. First the inspector will review the system making sure it is operable, that it is located in a safe area of the home and noting its condition, past service and repair notes. He will identify the system's energy source and the method used to send the heat or air throughout the home and will check the home for proper ventilation and draft. He will check to see that the distribution system is working properly and that the controls to the units are functional. With cooling systems, he will check to see that they are operating correctly and will note their location. Most air conditioning systems have separate indoor and outdoor components as well as different lines for gas and refrigerant functions. He will review whether any part of the system shows signs of difficulty in functioning, damage or excessive wear. Most units have a life expectancy and to the chagrin of many sellers, some inspectors will use the phrase "nearing the end of its useful life." Inspectors will check electric baseboard heaters and oil furnaces in older homes. Since a general home inspector may or may not be a licensed HVAC contractor and since the report he generates is limited, he will not open and examine the inner part of the heat exchange system. He will note if he suspects that due to age of the system and its overall condition if a more specialized report may be needed by a licensed HVAC contractor. Perhaps the most expensive element of a furnace is the heat exchanger. Most gas to air heat exchangers are a piece of stamped sheet metal and the combustion fuel (natural gas) is on one side of the metal wall while the air to heat is on the other side. A cracked heat exchanger will allow the exhaust or partially used gas to seep into the home. This is an extremely dangerous condition because of the chance of carbon monoxide poisoning and must be dealt with immediately. Heat exchangers cannot be repaired. They must be replaced.

Another challenge to the inspection of the HVAC unit lies when inspecting the cooling portion during the cooler months when the external (ambient) temperature is outside of the manufacturers range for the unit. That range is from 60 degrees to 115 degrees. The 115 degrees is usually not a problem since a cooler time can always be found for the inspection. The 60 degrees is a problem throughout the cooler months and it is not always possible to get an accurate report for this reason.

Septic Systems—An individual septic system for a home is often referred to as an onsite system and is found in approximately 20% of all homes sold in the country. Of these onsite systems, approximately 10 to 20 percent malfunction each year causing pollution to the environment and creating a health risk. For this reason, it is important to have a test done on your septic system. The basics of a septic system include the wastewater piping, the septic tank, the effluent piping, a distribution box, the absorption system and the bio-mat. There are far too many types of systems to discuss here but it is important to understand your system and how it has been maintained and repaired. Most sellers I have met who are the owners of a septic system routinely say that the system has been maintained and yet over half have some type of problem or malfunction. Most states have licensed inspectors who will evaluate and test the system to make sure it is functioning properly and will explain what is needed for regular maintenance. It pays to have this inspected upfront and to address any problems.

Most homes constructed within the last thirty years will have a septic permit on file with the county in which they were constructed. This permit will indicate that the layout of the system was approved and will also indicate the numbers of occupants or more importantly bedrooms (indicating occupants) that the system was intended to serve. You should know if the system size matches the current structure and number of bedrooms and the occupancy for which it was designed and intended. Do not make the mistake of listing your home as a four-bedroom home and find out after you have signed a contract that the septic system was only permitted for a three-bedroom house. Prices for an inspection range from $200 to $400 depending on factors such as location and ease of access. If the tank needs to be pumped, this should be done before the home is marketed.

Wells—Many people get their water from wells. In fact, of around 105 million homes in the U.S., over 15 million have wells. All public water systems are protected by EPA guidelines but not so with privately owned wells. Because of this, owners of these wells are responsible for ensuring that their water is safe from contaminants. All private wells are replenished to some extent by ground water. If the ground water is polluted and then consumed it can cause illness. Ground water can be polluted by seepage through landfills, underground fuel storage tanks (USTs), fertilizers, pesticides, run off from urban areas and failed septic systems. You should have the well checked every year and should have records relating to these annual inspections. Most well water is tested for total coliform bacteria, fecal coliform bacteria, nitrates, total dissolved solids and ph levels. If any other contaminants are suspected, these should be tested for as well. A State Certified Drinking Water Laboratory should check the water. The price range is from $20 to several hundred dollars depending on the laboratory and the compounds for which you have the water tested. It pays to have this done when you market the home to determine if any problem exists.

Your inspector will also inspect the well tank for rust, for any visual leaks, for the conduit to the pressure switch, and for the operating gauge and he will note if there is a service port to which to hook a hose. An inspection should also determine the flow of the well in gallons per minute. The well inspection is a minimal cost and provides protection to your family as well as giving the assurance to a buyer that there is clean water available here and it is delivered with sufficient flow.

Termites and other pests—Termites cause billions of dollars of damage each year. While they feed primarily on wood, they will also eat or otherwise damage books, insulation and any other organic items. They will even feast on swimming pool liners. Termites will also damage trees and other plants but usually when those plants are dead or dying. The two primary signs of infestation are either discovering winged termites inside the home or noticing the earthen (mud) tubes that they build. A home may experience infestation at any time and you will want to order a separate termite inspection or infestation report since all lenders will make this a condition of the sale. A "clean" letter will need to be produced prior to the closing to show that the home has been thoroughly examined by a licensed inspector and that no active termites have been found. Termite control companies are licensed by the state and as with any inspector, it pays to interview several and ask for references. When you request inspections and estimates from more than one company, it will help verify the existence of the problem and allow you to compare services. I cannot think of an instance where the control of termites and the repair from their damage has not been a seller responsibility. Any individual seller, bank-owned or estate-owned property will recognize immediately the damage to the value of the property and should act to control and repair the damage. An additional day, week or even month to begin treatment is usually insignificant since termites work very slowly.

Most termite companies will offer the opportunity to purchase a termite bond, which is a contract between you and the treatment company that inspects annually for and addresses possible future termites. There are two types of bonds: a retreatment bond and a repair bond. The retreatment bond obligates the company to retreat the home if termites are found in the future and the repair bond obligates them to fix any termite damage up to a certain dollar amount.

The termite letter is required by all lenders and it is important to remember that the letter must be dated within 30 days of the closing. If there is a delay of some type in the closing date, then an updated letter may need to be provided at closing. The termite letter is a buyer responsibility to provide. However, if you are under a termite bond, it may be wise to order an inspection before you put the home on the market.

Mold—In some instances with crawl spaces, basements or bathrooms, the presence of mold will be observed either by you or by the general inspector of the home. In these cases it would pay to have a mold inspection since this can pose a health hazard. A mold inspection is different than mold remediation. The inspection refers to the process of assessing whether or not there is an undesirable mold growth in the home. This will probably involve mold testing. Here the inspector may take samples of the air and the surface affected to find out what type of mold may exist. His samples will be sent to a laboratory for analysis. Once the results have been obtained a remediation plan will be presented and a quote will be made to perform the removal of the mold problem.

In most instances this should be an item taken care of by you, the seller, but you should remember that you have the right to inspect and understand the remediation process if it needs to occur since mold can present health issues. Please visit *www.moldreport.com* if mold is found and more information is needed. You need to assure the buyer that there is not a problem or if a report indicates that there is a problem that you will take care of it through the remediation process.

Asbestos—Asbestos has been used since ancient times and has been recognized as a health problem for over 100 years. The material was a key component in construction materials such as drywall compound, vinyl floor tiles, adhesives, pipe insulation, acoustic ceiling tiles, some popcorn sprayed ceilings, exterior stucco and hundreds of other items. This material is known to exist in many homes and its presence should be detected in some instances by your home inspector. If he recognizes a problem, there are other specialized testing companies that will go through the home and report on any suspected building materials that may contain asbestos. In most instances asbestos use was stopped in the late 1970s. Many times the asbestos, if found, is not a health issue until it is moved or broken as in the case of a remodel or demolition. There are many older homes that contain the substance in siding or floor tiles where it remains trapped unless abrasion or breakage occurs. As a seller, if your inspection reveals asbestos, it would pay to learn as much as you can about the material, its dangers and in some instances how it may pose no problem as long as it is not removed or exposed to abrasion. Visit *www.epa.gov/asbestos/* for more information.

Carbon Monoxide—There are many ways a person can be poisoned by carbon monoxide (CO) and testing a home for its presence is important if there is a suspicion it may exist. Carbon monoxide is a deadly, colorless, odorless, tasteless, poisonous gas. The gas is produced by the incomplete burning of various fuels, including wood, coal, propane, oil and natural gas. Problems in the home can result from any appliance that uses a burned fuel as its source of power.

Many times the problem with carbon monoxide results from a furnace, range water heater, room heater or fireplace incompletely burning the fuel such as natural gas. For this reason, if your home inspector suspects that there may be an internal problem with your furnace (or other appliance), this should be enough to warrant further inspection by an expert in the field. This would usually be a licensed HVAC contractor in the case of a furnace or other home heating or water-heating device. It could also be an expert appliance technician in the case of a range/oven. One commonly experienced problem is a cracked heat exchanger in a furnace. This is a safety issue of the highest order since it allows unburned fuel and CO into the breathable air of the home. Each year over 150 people die in homes from CO poisoning. For this reason, the $200 or so you may pay for an additional furnace inspection may be the best money you ever spend. For more information understanding cracked heat exchangers go to YouTube.com and search Furnace Inspection—Cracked Heat Exchanger.

Underground Fuel Storage Tanks—As the seller of a property, it is important to know if there is an underground fuel storage tank. These home heating oil tanks are non-regulated, non-commercial underground storage tanks (USTs) and are exempt from technical regulations unless there is a leak or spill from the tank. These (USTs) are exempt from "closure" which means they do not have to be removed from the ground or filled with an inert substance such as sand and have a soil analysis performed. Even though closure is not required, a tank owner is advised to empty the tank and fill with an inert substance such as sand. Water should not be used to fill the tank. Most buyers are hesitant to purchase a property with a UST so the removal is often a good idea for the seller who wants to make the property appealing to a buyer. There are good reasons why the seller should remove the underground fuel storage tank.

The reason for removal and its regulation relates to groundwater and is an effort to keep groundwater as clean as possible. Nationally over 50% of the population depends on groundwater as its source of clean water and there are tens of thousands of (USTs) that could potentially affect groundwater. If there is contamination found, it is important to understand who is responsible for the cleanup. The "statutory tank owner" is responsible for cleaning up the contamination.

Who the "statutory tank owner" is depends on when the tank was last used. If the UST was last used before November 8, 1984, then the party who last used the tank is considered its owner (even if that party no longer owns the property). If the tank had been last used after that date, anyone that owned the property would be considered the tank owner even if that person never used it. For that reason, a buyer may become the "UST tank owner" by buying the property and may share in or assume all liability if the tank then leaked at a later time. There are funds such as the North Carolina Non-commercial Leaking Petroleum Cleanup Fund that will pay up to $1M in reasonable necessary costs directly related to the cleanup of a petroleum release from your property's UST but will not pay for the actual tank removal nor for attorney's costs. If a leak is discovered while you own the property, then you are legally obligated to report it to the Division of Waste Management in most states. For the above reasons, most savvy buyers do not want to purchase a property before it is clearly understood that the owner will remove and deal with all issues regarding USTs. As a seller, you want to confront this issue in a direct and determined way. Since the cleanup fund exists, it is better to spend the money for removal of the tank and to hire a company licensed to deal with its removal. If they note a problem when it is removed, you as the seller are entitled to financial clean up help from the fund. This is certainly preferable to perhaps being notified in the future that you share in the liability and then to find that the fund has been exhausted and that no financial help is available.

Radon—Radon is a colorless, tasteless, odorless gas that is considered a health hazard due to its radioactivity. As radon decays it produces solids that can stick to dust particles and be inhaled. Because of its radioactivity, the inhaled particles can stick to the airways of the lung and increase the risk for developing lung cancer. Radon is variable from location to location and is found to accumulate in higher than normal concentrations in confined areas such as attics and basements. This gas is the second most frequent cause of lung cancer after smoking and causes approximately 21,000 deaths annually in the U. S. Any home may have a radon problem. This gas enters the home through cracks in floors, construction joints, cracks in walls, gaps around pipes and sometimes through well water.

The testing of the home for radon is not difficult and can be done by a homeowner with a self-testing kit. However, since most buyers will want to make sure that radon is not present or present in very low levels and more importantly for the safety of you and your family, it would pay for you to have a professional radon inspection company perform the test. There are two types of tests: a long-term test and a short-term test. The company you hire will perform the short-term test. Tests measure "picocuries per liter of air" or "pCi/L". The generally accepted standard set by the EPA is 4 pCi/L. That is to say, if the level is less than 4 pCi/L, then the home is acceptably safe by EPA standards. If it is higher than 4 pCi/L, a radon mitigation system should be put in place. If you perform this highly recommended test, do recognize that radon is found everywhere. The outdoor air contains around 0.4 pCi/L and it is estimated that most homes and other buildings contain around 1.3 pCi/L.

If you decide to test for radon, and you should, this can be accomplished through many home inspection companies. The testing will involve having a device left in the home for a period of 48 to 96 hours. The unit will require power to function and will continuously monitor the radon level. It will have an anti-interference feature to reveal if the unit is moved during the testing period. You should expect the cost of the test to begin at around $200 and it could be higher depending on the home. If radon mitigation is needed to lower the level, this will probably cost in the range of $1500. The buyers will look to you the seller to pay for any mitigation cost and to provide a home that is safe within the EPA standards. For more information on radon and radon testing, visit *www.epa.gov/radon*.

Stability and Foundations—We realize that you may not know everything about the underpinnings of your home, but it is important that you note any issues you may have had stabilizing or strengthening the existing foundation. The soil under your home must be able to support the home's weight and size, and movement under the earth can sometimes require owners to "underpin" their homes in order to ensure structural integrity.

Grading of the home's lot—How is the lot graded? Is it sloped? Does water run off during storms or does water collect in puddles? Have you had to deal with any other grade-related challenges? These are the same questions the buyer will ask you.

Water sealing of foundation—Was the foundation water sealed? Have you kept up with regular maintenance for water sealing of the foundation?

Here are a few other systems with which you will want to familiarize yourself (if they are included with your property), paying specific attention to 1) the age of the systems, and 2) how well they work:

Central vacuum
Pool
Hot Tub
Spa
Attic Fan
Ceiling Fans
Sump Pump (used to remove standing water in areas
    like basements)
Irrigation System (for your landscaping)
TV Cable wiring
Satellite Dish

Note that any of these may be excluded from the negotiation of the sale of your home. This is best accomplished in the Residential Property Disclosure form.

Other areas of the home with which you should be familiar include any room additions or structural changes you have made to the home. In most cases these changes will enhance your home, but in some instances the value of the structure may be impacted by the changes that you have made. Permitting, for example, can sometimes be an issue, particularly if changes were made to the structure without the necessary permits. Be sure to investigate permitting issues to avoid problems at the closing table. Permitting extends to the installation of any electrical, any new HVAC units, installation of hot water heaters and most sizeable plumbing changes.

If any zoning ordinances or restrictive covenants have been violated, the new homeowner should be made aware of the issues. If you share a driveway with your neighbor, have a utility easement (see Chapter 8 for details on easements), or have a party wall (a wall that divides the buildings of two properties that are owned by two different people), be sure to state these facts on your seller's disclosure form.

Here are other issues that may impact the sale of your home:

1. Encroachments to or from adjacent properties.
2. Lawsuits: Are there any lawsuits against you and/or your property?
3. Tenancies: Is the property under a lease?
4. Proposed assessments: Are you aware of any proposed assessments for which the new homeowner would be responsible?
5. Private roads: Are there any private roads on or around your property? Private roads must be maintained by an agreement between individuals or perhaps a HOA. The point is that this maintenance will cost something to the new homeowner and must be disclosed.
6. Homeowners Association Fees: See Chapter 8 for details on HOAs, their associated fees, and the governing documents. This is a particularly important point for any homeowner who wants to build or install outdoor structures of any kind on the property, run a home-based business, erect a fence or park a company vehicle in front of the property. The HOA's covenants and rules are also important because some organizations are charging extremely high "transfer" fees when homes in the neighborhood are sold. Be sure to go over these details early— not at the closing table!

Lead-Based Paint Disclosure

In 1992, Congress passed the Residential Lead-Based Paint Hazard Reduction Act, also known as Title X, to protect families from exposure to lead from paint, dust, and soil. Section 1018 of this law directed HUD and EPA to require the disclosure of known information on lead-based paint and lead-based paint hazards before the sale or lease of most housing built before 1978.

If your home was built after 1978 you can probably skip this section, but if it was not, then you will want to review the next few paragraphs carefully and discuss the issue with your Realtor, general contractor, and any other professional who can help you mitigate the problem.

Before ratification of a contract for housing sale or lease, sellers and landlords must:

1. Give an EPA-approved information pamphlet ("Protect Your Family From Lead In Your Home" that is currently available in English and other languages) on identifying and controlling lead-based paint hazards.

2. Disclose any known information concerning lead-based paint or lead-based paint hazards. The seller or landlord must also disclose information such as the location of the lead-based paint and/or lead-based paint hazards and the condition of the painted surfaces.

3. Provide any records and reports on lead-based paint and/or lead-based paint hazards, which are available to the seller or landlord. For multi-unit buildings, this requirement includes records and reports concerning common areas and other units and when such information was obtained as a result of a building-wide evaluation.

4. Include an attachment to the contract or lease (or language inserted in the lease itself), which includes a Lead Warning Statement and confirms that the seller or landlord has complied with all notification requirements. This attachment is to be provided in the same language used in the rest of the contract. Sellers or landlords, and agents, as well as homebuyers or tenants, must sign and date the attachment.

Sellers must provide homebuyers a minimum 10-day period to conduct a paint inspection or risk assessment for lead-based paint or lead-based paint hazards. Parties may mutually agree, in writing, to lengthen or shorten the time period for inspection. Homebuyers may waive this inspection opportunity, if they choose to do so.

The overarching point of this entire exercise is to make you aware of the complexities that may present themselves when the pre-inspection of your home is done. Not all of these conditions and challenges will exist in any one home but you may encounter several of them especially if you are attempting to sell an older home. And do not lose sight of the goal. We are aiming to sell your home in 45 days or less and the more we know and have dealt with on the front side of the listing, the better position we will find ourselves when dealing with a buyer and their inspector. Will it not be nice to say when the time comes and the buyer poses any question to you or your agent about any facet of the condition of the home, "We have had that inspected and dealt with and everything is just fine?"

Now that you know what types of issues can come up once you have the pre-inspection done and you put your home on the market, we are going to look very carefully at exactly how your Realtor will market your property for sale. In the next chapter we will examine the online and offline methods that work best and show you how your agent will leverage them to your advantage for the sale of your home within 45 days.

Four Things to Remember from Chapter 9

* Owners of residential real estate are required to furnish purchasers a Residential Property and Owners' Association Disclosure Statement ("Disclosure Statement").
* Material facts must be represented honestly and must include anything that would impact the buyer's decision to purchase your home or the price and terms the buyer offers. Do not misrepresent or omit anything that you know that may be a material fact relating to the sale of your home.
* Having a pre-inspection done on the home and knowing the condition of your home's major components can help you navigate the selling process and address any issues in advance.
* If your home was built before 1978 you will need to comply with federal laws concerning the possible presence of lead-based paint.

PART TWO

Marketing Your Home For Sale

CHAPTER 10

Marketing Your Home

   It is all about marketing; that is where the real craft comes in.

—DIRK BENEDICT

O NE OF THE MOST IMPORTANT tasks that your real estate agent will perform is the marketing of your home to potential buyers who are in your area, in other states, and even around the world (depending on the desirability and location of your property). Thanks to the Internet, you and your agent can present your property to a vast pool of potential buyers within a fairly reasonable time period.

In this section we will look at what goes into a good marketing plan, which online and offline elements should be incorporated into that plan, and how to meet your goals by using leverage of the newer technological innovations designed to expose your home to the maximum number of ready, willing, and able buyers.

Median List Price of U.S. Homes

Realtor.com, the online presence for the National Association of Realtors, reports that the median list price for a home in late-2012 was $191,500 and that inventory was at historic lows with 1.8 million units for sale.

The Basic Elements

There are few old standbys that potential buyers and the agents representing them have come to expect to see when they look at homes for sale. The first is photography—an absolute must in today's visual-intensive world. You want to make sure that your agent takes a good selection of high definition (HD) enhanced digital photos of every room, the home's exterior, and even the neighborhood and perhaps nearby amenities to show off its best features.

According to NAR, 81 percent of homebuyers say photos and detailed property descriptions are the most important features when searching online for homes. Do not be the owner who has a single photo posted on a website like Realtor.com! If the limit is 36 photos, which is the limit on Realtor.com, then max it out to that limit. The more you can "show" the prospect online, the better the chances are that he or she will want to see the home in person.

Your agent will also use the photos to develop offline materials, such as brochures, fliers, and other marketing pieces to be handed out to potential buyers, brokers, agents, and other individuals who will play a role in getting your home sold. If, for example, the agent's office is situated in an area where there is a high volume of foot traffic, then he or she will post "homes for sale" fliers on the windows or perhaps use the more high-tech version of the flier via a TV monitor that switches among various homes for sale. The fliers or the monitor should include photos and pertinent information (price, size, location, etc.).

Next, your agent will create one or more virtual tours to give potential buyers a feel for what it is like to walk through your home in person. There are vendors on the web that offer virtual tour services—from the creation of the video all the way through the hosting of the finalized tour online. Tourfactory.com provides a great source

---

Virtual Tours of Homes for Sale

A virtual tour of a home is a simulation of a home for sale usually composed of a sequence of photographs. Many times, other multimedia elements are included such as sound effects, music, narration and text.

---

for online virtual tours that links to the most websites. You will want potential buyers to feel as though they "walked" through your home and looked at everything in it—that is the magic of the online virtual tour.

Another method to send great information to potential buyers is by means of a walk-through video tour of the home, which may be placed online through YouTube or other video services or emailed out to prospects. The online video tour is a full motion product that is, in essence, a slow walk-through tour of your home. This type of tour allows buyers to understand room placement better than with mere photographs. It allows buyers to feel the "flow" of the home.

Video Tours are Effective

A video tour is used to pan and walk-through a subject property. This type of tour gives a greater actual understanding of the home since it allows a buyer to feel the flow of the home and to understand how rooms are oriented and relate to other rooms and areas of the home.

The Multiple Listing Service

There was a time in the not-too-distant past when real estate agents literally held all of the home-selling cards. Once they would list a home, a tiny black and white photo and a short description was printed up in the MLS "books," which were distributed only to registered Realtors on a weekly basis. Other agents would use those books to find homes for their buyers, check out the competition, and determine which listings were about to expire.

Fast forward to 2012 and the MLS remains an important mainstay for agents, although the control over it has loosened somewhat over the last 20 years or so. First the "online MLS" replaced those weekly book distributions with online information, and then Realtor.com contracted with NAR to serve as a massive aggregator of MLS data. Other players have come along since then and also have their share of the pie, but at its roots the MLS system—and the agents and brokers that use and support it—has not changed much. It is still "the" place to go to list homes for sale and find homes for sale. The MLS offers a distinct advantage over properties that are not included in the MLS, such as For Sale By Owner or FSBO properties. The MLS is a private, online resource, which is used frequently by nearly every single agent that belongs to the local real estate association.

Usually tied directly to a region's Realtor association or run by an outside party, the MLS is basically a database of active, expired, and sold listings that agents use to complete a myriad of tasks. Agents and brokers must be members of the MLS to use it, thus retaining that exclusivity on which the systems were built decades ago. A newer component of the MLS is known as IDX or "Internet Data Exchange." This is the system that allows Realtors to show MLS property listings on their own websites in other words to allow brokers to display each other's listings on the Internet. The IDX movement opens new doors for sellers, whose listings appear not only on the national database sites but also on the sites of brokers who tap into the IDX "data feeds" from their Multiple Listing Services.

Real Estate Sites

As you can see, there are plenty of advertising opportunities available to the homeowner online. Many of them pick up where the MLS leaves off by taking a more "proactive" approach to marketing via search engine optimization, organic search optimization, pay per click, and other methods that get certain listings to the top of that coveted Google search page.

The agent with whom you are working will have one or more of the following: a corporate website (run by the franchise under which the agency is licensed); an agency website (locally-based and focused on local agents); and/or an individual website (possibly even more than one). In some cases an agent will develop a property-specific website designed to showcase a single property (such as, "124WillowLane.com" or "256MainStreet.com"). Combined, these corporate, company, agent, and property-specific sites help to garner attention not only for the company's listings but also for those homes for sale in a specific region (via IDX, discussed earlier in this chapter).

There are also a number of national websites where homebuyers go to find listings. Here are a few of the most popular options in this category:

Realtor.com: As we noted earlier, this is a repository for all categories of property listings throughout the U.S. Homebuyers can narrow their searches to very fine details, and homeowners and agents can use features like "enhanced listings" to make their properties stand out and utilize SEO (Search Engine Optimization). Showcase listings, for example, include the following features according to Realtor.com.

- Multiple lead forms—The firms collect buyer contact information.
- Buyers fill out lead forms at the top and bottom of your listings and send their contact information directly to you. Buyers can call the agent's cell phone directly with the contact information positioned next to the listings.
- Contact information and portrait—Gives buyers an easy connection to the agent representing the home.
- Traffic Report—This lets sellers know how their listing is performing on Realtor.com. It emails regular reports to the sellers detailing how many buyers are looking at their home.

   This may help to indicate and justify that a price reduction is in order if buyer interest is waning.
- Posts up to 25 large photos—This may grab the attention of potential buyers. Homes with the most photos rise above all other listings when consumers search for homes on sites like Realtor.com.
- Open House Alerts—These may bring buyers through the door. A recent survey of agents who use Open House alerts on Realtor.com claimed a 93% success rate. Visitors were twice as likely to be "high quality potential buyers" versus visitors from newspapers or from yard signs.
- Custom headlines and property descriptions—Agents and owners are able to paint a picture with words. As evidenced by the massive exodus from newspapers to the Internet, it is evident consumers are demanding more information. Headlines that "sell" will help your listings stand out when buyers are searching.
- Full Motion Listing Videos—Although it is estimated that

only 2% of agents go to the effort to produce videos of the homes they are marketing, 73% of sellers say that they would be more willing to list with an agent who offered to shoot a video. 100 million Americans watch over a billion online videos every month so make sure they are watching your video.

- Powerful Icons on the search results page—These stand out and encourage clicks to the home for sale.

Trulia: This is a free service that allows homeowners, builders, and agents to put their listings online and get them in front of a wide audience of potential buyers. Trulia displays more than 4 million real estate and rental listings nationwide. More than 23 million unique users visit the site each month and Trulia has more than 500,000 registered real estate professionals ready to help users with their search for the perfect home. Trulia Voices, an online tool for real estate advice, is the largest real estate community on the web. To help homebuyers, renters and agents retrieve up-to-date information on the go, Trulia has also developed 10 top-rated apps for various mobile devices.

Zillow: Zillow is a home and real estate marketplace dedicated to helping homeowners, homebuyers, sellers, renters, real estate agents, mortgage professionals, landlords and property managers find and share vital information about homes, real estate and mortgages. Zillow has a database of more than 100 million U.S. homes—including homes for sale, homes for rent and homes not currently on the market. It also offers Zestimate® home values, Rent Zestimates and other useful information for homeowners and homebuyers. Like Realtor.com, Zillow also offers enhanced listings options that help agents and sellers get more attention for their individual properties.

Yahoo! Real Estate: This is another popular real estate site online that offers a myriad of services for homebuyers and sellers. Homeowners can get ballpark valuations of their homes, list them for sale, and track responses to their ads. Homebuyers can search through the site's listings, learn from its library of articles, and find real estate agents with whom to work. A few of Yahoo! Real Estate's newest offerings include expanded content coverage beyond buying and selling homes to showcase the entire spectrum of homeownership: home renovation, design and decor, moving and storage, DIY home improvement projects, smart digital homes, and home maintenance among other topics. The site also features Homes of the Week powered by Zillow. Each week it looks at seven homes for sale organized by home style (Victorian homes, Cabin homes, Cottages, Penthouses, etc.); price point (for example, what can you buy for $250,000?); and location (sometimes a city, sometimes a region—like the Gulf Coast). Finally, the "Spaces" blog features timely original content from veteran reporters and fresh voices, including bloggers familiar to real estate mavens, DIY (Do-it-yourself) enthusiasts, or design and decor fans.

MSN Real Estate: On this site you will find an array of real estate market and trend information that is geared to the homebuyer or the current homeowner. Like the other real estate sites, this one also offers listings for sale and provides visitors with articles, blogs, and other content designed to educate them on the buying and selling process.

Craigslist: This is a classified advertisements website with a section devoted to local housing for sale. It has evolved into one of the most popular channels of home marketing and it is estimated that over 5% of sales and rentals of residential properties come from this site. The challenge with Craigslist remains how to post regularly since with each minute that passes, a placed ad will sink lower into the list. The company has regulations as to how often a listing may be posted.

As a home seller, you and your agent can leverage the information found on these top, national sites to help you achieve your goal of selling your property within 45 days.

Social Media

More and more agents are using social networking sites like Facebook, Twitter, ActiveRain, FourSquare, and Google+ to get the highest level of exposure for their listings. They are using simple social networking updates (like, check out my latest listing!) to reach an audience of tech-savvy homebuyers who rely on their social networks for information, advice and support.

Agents will also post content (news, trends, community information, activities, and so forth) to their social media outlets on a regular basis and have alerts set up that let them know when someone responds to them. In many cases the results of those efforts come in the form of connections to other agents who have buyers interested in their listings. Other ways to promote listings include FourSquare "check ins" from the homes themselves (while attending an open house for the property, for example) and tweets that talk up a new listing in the site's succinct, 140-character format.

Of course, it is not enough to simply put an effort into social media marketing without measuring the results. That is where tools like Google Analytics come in. They help agents figure out what is and is not working online—either on the web or a site like Facebook—and hone their strategies accordingly. Web analytics tools track a site's statistics allowing the agent to see how many people are looking at which page, from what sites those visitors are coming and who those users are. With this information in hand, agents can measure traffic to their sites, get a grasp on their visitors' wants and needs, and measure click-through rates for new content, features and offers.

Google Analytics is free for users and takes just a couple of hours to install and configure. The program tracks how often visitors come to your site, conversions across multiple pages, visitor behavior and the percentage of people who click each link on a given page.

Key questions to consider when Google Analytics returns its results include: Which page has the highest bounce rate (the number of people who "leave" the site from that particular page)? How many visitors come to my site? How long did they stay? What pages did they view? How many took an action? From where did the visitors come? What key phrases did they use?

With the answers to these questions in hand, you and/or your agent will be able to tweak your online strategy to achieve the best possible results within the shortest timeframe.

Keywords

There are two ways to use keyword marketing in real estate. You can either buy the top keywords within a certain category (via Google Adwords, for example) or you can use a process called search engine optimization (SEO) to integrate text, content, videos, and photos in a way that gets the search engines' attention. The first option can get costly, and the second one takes time and is often a hit-or-miss proposition—namely because search engines do not always publicly reveal their algorithms and ranking methods.

One of the best ways to overcome the high cost of pay-per-click marketing is by simply using an appropriate mix of content and keywords on any website where your home is listed. Your agent should be well versed in this strategy, but it does not hurt for you to also know and recognize what does and does not work. If, for example, you notice areas in need of improvement—on a site dedicated to your listing, for example—by all means bring it to your agent's attention. By taking a proactive approach you will be in the best possible position to sell your home within 45 days or less.

Traditional Marketing Methods

Here are a few tried-and-true marketing strategies that still work well in today's market:

Your Realtor's Database

Technology may have made the real estate buying and selling process easier, but at its heart this is still a relationship-based business. People buy homes from others whom they know, like and trust. Your experienced real estate agent likely has thousands of contacts in a database, and most of those contacts know someone who is in the market for a home (if they are not also looking themselves).

As an agent I correspond in a regular manner with 6,000 to 8,000 people who are in my database. I send them information about new listings, videos of those listings, and general marketing pieces. In many cases, the buyers with whom we ultimately wind up working do come from our database (either directly or indirectly through a referral to a family member about a new listing, for example). It is important to make sure whomever you use as your agent has an extensive database of potential buyers.

Ask your real estate agent about their database and how it can be leveraged to your advantage.

Signs of All Types

Yes, folks, signs still work in today's technology-oriented real estate world. Yard signs, directional signs (Home For Sale, with an arrow pointing up the street), brokerage signs, and other customer-facing signage serves as a beacon of sort for homebuyers, particularly those that are looking for a home in a specific community or neighborhood.

One trusted source in the real estate industry says that yard signs may account for as many as 20% of all showings and as many as 10% of the sales of homes. A home without adequate signage is at a distinct disadvantage. Lead-in signs may be placed at the entrances to neighborhoods as well. Make sure to ask permission from the owner of the property or from the HOA. Generally speaking, a generic Home For Sale sign works more effectively than an agency sign here and is usually more acceptable.

Some agents use yard brochures in a box by your Home For Sale sign allowing prospective buyers the opportunity to take with them an informative printed piece about the home and its features. An additional high tech way to impart much more information is by QR coding which may be attached to the sign.

Call Capture helps identify buyers

Call Capture is a telephone-based technology that allows for the capturing of personal information from callers to a certain properly provisioned number. The system notifies the agent of the number and often the name and address of the person calling. Real estate agents have found this particularly useful to identify prospective buyers that may call about a particular home for sale. This service will register their interest and allow for a call back to the prospect. Many services allow for the call to then be forwarded to the agent or lender should a buyer so desire. Call capture service allows for a return call even if the caller is on the federal "Do Not Call" list since anyone calling falls under the 90-day business inquiry rule of the Do Not Call laws.

QR Coding

A QR Code (Quick Response Code) is a trademark for a type of matrix barcode. The code consists of black modules or square dots arranged in a square pattern on a white background. An app can be downloaded to a Smartphone that can read the QR Code. The code itself will redirect the user to a website featuring pictures and information about the home for immediate viewing. I have been at open houses where I have observed potential buyers drive up to my sign, stop and read the QR Code with their Smartphones. The advantage to the end user is the amount of material they are able to obtain quickly and easily. The advantage to the home seller is that this is paperless and efficient and imparts that same amount of information as a 12-page brochure. The advantage to the agent is that the QR Code may allow tracking so that the scanner of the code may be "tracked" and called back for follow up and hopefully to arrange a showing on your property.

Signs have come a long way over the last couple of decades. Today's more advanced signs include electronic brochures and call capture services that invite potential buyers to call in for information. When they dial the toll-free number listed on the sign, their information is captured and delivered to the agent for follow up. Voice-Pad, for example, provides agents with a complete mobile platform for capturing leads across mobile web, call capture and text. When a potential buyer calls the number, they are given a descriptive message on the home as well as the price. Anyone who may call the telephone number and/or code associated with the home leaves their electronic information including call back number and sometimes email and name. This allows an agent to call back to answer specific questions and to gauge their interest in the home. If a client registers for the service, the agent is able to regularly see the homes about which the client has inquired. This allows the agent to understand the area and price range of this buyer.

Open Houses

Open houses that target the general public still work as long as the agents behind them are willing to be creative when hosting and marketing the events. When the home is priced right, agents and sellers can (beyond road and yard signs) take a proactive approach to inviting people to the event. Many times I will walk to the ten homes on the left, the ten homes on the right and the twenty homes across the street with a descriptive flier of property where I am holding the open house. My line is always the same: "I am holding this very nice home belonging to Mr. Smith, your neighbor, open on Sunday and would like to invite you to see the home. Do you know of anyone who may be interested in moving to the neighborhood?" This is a simple but effective means of opening up a home to 40 or more neighbors who all have friends. We are just looking for one buyer here.

Buyers and buyer agents still love open houses. There is just something about browsing through property with little pressure that makes people want to participate in this age-old real estate market tactic. There are two kinds of open houses with which you may deal during the sale of your home: the broker or Realtor open house and the public open house. The first is targeted solely to local brokers and Realtors who enjoy being able to "preview" new listings and then pass the information learned along to their databases of potential buyers. Sometimes this can lead to a quick sale, but in most cases it simply puts your home into the minds of the professionals who spend their days selling homes. Sometimes food is served as a way of thanking the agents and brokers who attend the function.

The second is a public open house, which is different and caters to pretty much anyone. Expect to see your neighbors at these events as well as potential buyers. Your Realtor will handle the logistics of the open house for you, but it will be up to you to get your home into tip-top showing shape for these events. Follow the instructions outlined in Chapter Four and also those mentioned earlier in this chapter to ensure the best possible results from your open house event(s).

Other good prospects to invite include those residing in neighborhoods where the open house would be considered a "move up" and those that are in the same school district as your listing. To determine if your home is a good candidate for an open house, consider these three important points:

It must be priced right (if it is not, prospective homebuyers will know); it must be in great condition and ready to show; and it must be located in a desirable area.

Open Houses

The time-honored tradition in real estate sales is the weekend open house. This may benefit sellers but perhaps it benefits agents more. In a recent survey of Agents nationwide:

70% believed it did not help at all in the sale of the home being showcased

24% believed that an open house attracts potential buyers, 76% said it did not

75% said they were likely to "pick up" a new buyer for *another* home for sale

60% said that it helped generate new listing contracts with neighbors

The falling out of favor of open houses may be attributable to new marketing techniques including the many ways a home may be marketed over the Internet.

In twenty-plus years of selling real estate, I have never sold a home at an open house but have picked up numerous buyers for other homes and numerous listings for other properties.

High-Tech Marketing Strategies

Here are several technology-oriented marketing strategies that you should consider using:

YouTube Marketing

Video is exploding online and taking the real estate world with it on its whirlwind growth spurt. As a leading online video broadcaster, YouTube has made pretty much anyone into a videographer and provides easy ways to set up an account, create multiple channels, subscribe to specific channels and perform daily searches.

YouTube is an effective and free way to showcase your home in a video format and just one more channel that is at your use as a homeowner in the Web 2.0 technology era. YouTube is a video sharing website and is one to which other sites such as virtual tour sites may syndicate. An exclusive video for the home may be developed and assigned its own unique space here. The incredible advantage that video has over still shots is that the video captures the flow of the home. Many buyers want to understand how spaces and rooms relate to each other and this is sometimes not possible with the use of photos alone.

Mobile Texting

Texting is a convenient way to share information with mobile-savvy consumers who do not have the time or impetus to talk on the telephone or sift through email to get to the information that they want. You can use a combination of QR codes and text messages to relay information to these potential buyers, which will then allow them to dial a number and listen to a message about your listing (on their own time).

Depending on the prospect's own preferences, your agent may also use text to send out MMS messages (photos or videos), convey quick updates (such as price reductions) and handle other details. For the high percentage of mobile telephone-toting consumers who prefer this communication to any other option, texting can serve as a great "update" tool to keep potential buyers and/or their agents informed and knowledgeable.

We have walked you through many different ways to market your home in the fastest, most efficient ways possible. Now it is time to look at the next step in the home-selling process: showing your home. We will help you make all of the right decisions regarding this stage of the game and help you position your home for a fast sale.

Four Things to Remember from Chapter 10

* A dedicated URL for your home will help your agent position the property as a compelling buy for a prospect.
* Sites like Realtor.com, Trulia, and Zillow serve as national listing aggregators and disseminators of valuable real estate information.
* QR Codes have become a way to offer instant information on the home for sale.
* Social media is a way to quickly and easily market your home to a large number of potential buyers.

CHAPTER 11

Showing Your Home

> ⮑ *Even if you are on the right track, you will get*
> *run over if you just sit there.*
>
> —WILL ROGERS

I T I S T I M E to show off your home to the world. Whether you en-
joyed more of a "lived-in" look or kept your dwelling in showing
condition since buying it, now is the time to get it up to par and show
the world how beautiful, comfortable, and flexible the living space is.

The showing process is pretty straightforward:

1. Your Realtor will be contacted either by a cooperating agent
    or by a direct buyer who will ask to see the home. Sometimes
    there is a showing service like Centralized Showing Service
    (CSS) that will accept the calls on behalf of the Realtor. The
    Realtor or the CSS will call you to either leave a courtesy call
    or to speak to you directly if an appointment is required. The
    Realtor or CSS will then call back the agent who is attempt-
    ing to show the home and give them specific instructions. The
    instructions usually relate to the type of device used to secure
    the key, usually a Supralok or a combination key box of some
    type. If there is a security system on the home, this informa-

tion would be given for entry. Finally, there is almost always some type of special instruction or information that the owner may want to convey. These instructions might relate to a pet or perhaps some feature that the owner and agent want to highlight.

2. If a buyer contacts you directly (while you are standing out in the yard, for example), you will point him or her in your Realtor's direction to set up an appointment to see the home. For safety reasons it is best *never* to allow an unescorted potential buyer into your home without an appointment.

3. Now is the time to put the home into show condition if it is not already there. There are some tips following that will help you do this.

4. You then allow the buyer's agent to do his or her job by not being present during the showing. Statistics show that a buyer will stay in a home when the owner is not present for nearly twice the length of time. The whole idea is to allow the buyer to feel comfortable in the space and to envision that he or she is living there. This simply cannot be done with an owner present. Many owners feel the need to participate since they have special knowledge of the home. After showing thousands of homes to buyers I have encountered "helpful sellers" maybe a few hundred times. These encounters have never been on my real estate listings since I ask the seller to stay away during the showing. In all of these times the buyer has been polite but put off. I have never seen a buyer appreciate the seller being there and for this reason alone, I always reiterate to the seller to please leave the home for the showing.

This phase of the sale process can be somewhat disruptive, but it is essential that you stay on track and follow your agent's directions regarding the showings. This will help you sell your home as quickly as possible, and it will ensure that all potential buyers who are interested in your property get a chance to see it and put in an offer on it, if so desired. Being as flexible and available as possible during this time period will assure you the maximum number of showings.

You never know when a ready, willing, and able buyer will be in town for a few hours to see numerous homes. If your property is not ready to show, you could miss out. I have occasionally had a seller who has insisted on a 24-hour notice. While this can be done, I am sure that such a seller has missed out on showings. The average number of hours for advance notice is two hours. To sell your home in forty-five days, I would recommend one hour. This gives agents wanting to show the home maximum flexibility. I have received too many calls from buyer prospects who say they are catching a flight home in a couple of hours and want to see this one home before they fly back home.

Now, most real estate agents who are working with buyers understand that it takes an hour or two to prepare a home for a showing, and in most cases they will try to work around your schedule. If you have pets, for example, then they will need to be contained or let outside prior to the showing or preferably, by far, taken with you away from the home. Even the most docile pets are distracting. If you have family or friends staying with you from out of town (try to avoid this within your 45-day time frame if possible), then you will need some extra time to spruce up your home.

It amazes me that out-of-town guests do not pick up after themselves and leave the home in immaculate condition. We are trying to sell a home here and quickly. Explain that to them and then have them stay in a nearby hotel. Even if you pay for their stay, it will be less expensive than losing that perfect buyer who is so distracted by the mess that they simply move on to the next home on the list. Regardless of the circumstances, the key is to be as ready as possible at any minute. If you work on that philosophy, then you will not be caught off guard when Mr. and Mrs. Buyer call to see your home on a Sunday afternoon.

Sometimes agents will call from your driveway with a buyer in the car, ready to see the property. This action sometimes infuriates sellers and they will not forget that this has happened especially when they have given instructions to the contrary. Just understand in advance that this WILL happen. It is unfortunate but everyone in the world is not on your timetable. Ask for flexibility, if necessary, by requesting a one-hour window before the showing (or, at least 15 minutes). If that is not feasible, use your best judgment, knowing that your ready, willing, and able buyer could be outside, sitting in the Realtor's car.

Ultimately, you want all showings to involve a Realtor who will represent your best interests. Allow that person to do their job by being gone or if you must stay, at least make yourself scarce during the showing. Buyers tend to stay in a home longer when the seller is not around. Not wanting to speak plainly about the pros and cons of a home with their Realtor can put that buyer at unease and rush them out the door prematurely. This is certainly not in your best interest as a seller.

Making yourself scarce as the seller also helps if questions come up like, "What are the neighbors like?" or "What repairs are you willing to make?" Questions like these and others asked pointedly by the buyer are tough and sometimes you will feel like you have been put on the spot. You want to be truthful of course but you want to consider your answer carefully. I have seen answers blurted out and not thought through come back to cost sellers later. Your Realtor can answer questions such as these on your behalf either to the agent later or after they have been discussed with you. You certainly want to be truthful and not misrepresent anything but you do not want to divulge anything that is not pertinent to the home itself.

I once had a buyer and showed a home to her in which the seller was present. My buyer asked innocently why they were selling. The wife blurted out that her husband had taken a job in Arizona and that they simply had to be there in 45 days. She said they were looking at homes there and had found one that they liked in a certain school district that was important to them and she was afraid the home would be sold before they got a contract on this one. After leaving, my buyer instructed me to make a low offer with a quick closing. The buyer bought this home, I am convinced at a price thousands of dollars lower than she would have been willing to pay all because of the comments of the wife AND because "anything you say in front of a buyer can (and probably will) be used against you at a later date…" The less said, the better.

Let your disclosure form be your method of information conveyance and allow your Realtor to handle the showing process. By respecting this rule of thumb you also allow your agent to do their job and use their expertise and experience to show the home, rather than having to deflect or later explain comments you may have made. In most cases, this will help you sell your home faster and with less stress.

Using Lockboxes

When your home is put in the MLS and listed for sale, your Realtor will ask you if it is okay to put a lockbox on your front doorknob. A lockbox is a hollow metal box that attaches to the front doorknob or some secure place nearby. Inside the hollow area is another matchbox-sized space that contains the key(s) to the home. When an agent opens the lockbox with their electronic key or Smartphone, that smaller container slides out. Because the lockbox is literally a "locked box," a stranger cannot come by, open the box, get the key and gain entry to the house.

Lockboxes are an important aspect of the real estate marketing plan because they allow agents access to show your home when you are not there. These lockboxes are standalone in nature and simply serve as keeper of the keys to the home. When an agent needs to see the home without the listing agent present, they will make an appointment that, upon confirmation that a showing has been accepted, will allow the showing agent to take their client into the home.

Many of the lockboxes in use today are electronic and tied to the local MLS, which can monitor agent activity and find out exactly who has been in your home, when they arrived and when they exited. The electronic lockboxes are usually set up to work only during certain hours (say, from 9am to 8pm daily) and are coded for recognition. Other individuals who can be granted access in this fashion include property appraisers and home inspectors, if allowed by the seller and if these individuals are members of the local Association of Realtors.

One reason a lockbox is a good idea is because every Realtor Association across the country has literally thousands of professional members. These members have paid a fee to join the organization and have subscribed to NAR's *Code of Ethics and Standards of Practice*. This is a

---

Supra Lockbox

Manufactured by GE, the Supra Lockbox allows agents to use infrared technology to access the lockbox without the need for physical contact. Using an infrared key, the agent simply points the key at the box after entering their unique pin number. This system allows an owner and listing agent to know everyone who has entered the home.

---

lengthy, detailed document that is updated regularly and a document that Realtors take very seriously.

While it is not a guarantee that something does not happen in your home while you are not there, it is nice to know that the agent has at least taken an ethics course and has agreed to abide by the ethical principles set forth in the NAR Code. It is comforting to the seller to know that entry by anyone has been electronically observed and registered.

Lockboxes are also handy for Realtors who want to "preview" homes before bringing their buyers in for a look. They will make an appointment, just like they would when setting an appointment for a buyer, and they can easily access the property and get a look at the home before showing it to a client.

Ready, Set, Go!

In earlier chapters we discussed the importance of having your home clean, staged, and spruced up before showing it to the world. Refer to Chapter Four for the details on this step, if you have not already taken it. Once the showings start you will have to be able to hit the ground running. The more preparations you have done in advance, the easier this will be.

For this section we will assume that your home is clean, staged, and ready to show. The mood music is playing softly in the background, the curtains are opened wide, and the interior lighting is positioned in a way that best highlights your home. Excess furniture, knickknacks, and personal items have been stored for future use, and the home's exterior is in tip-top shape.

Here are 12 steps you will want to take to get your home in the best possible showing condition:

1. Pay attention to climate control and keep the home either cool or warm, depending on the outside temperature and elements. If a home is vacant, sometimes a showing agent will arrive early to set the temperature up in the winter or down in the summer to make it as comfortable as possible.
2. Do a 10-second tidy to make sure you did not forget any loose ends.

3. Put your pets outside or contain them in your typical manner. Be aware that if at all possible take your pets away from the home with you until the showing is complete and you return.

4. Take your children out of the house for an hour to allow the buyer the freedom to move around and spend time in the entire home.

5. Make sure your home looks open and bright. Open all curtains and turn on the lights.

6. Inform your listing agent of the high points. If you live in a neighborhood that has amenities, for example, let it be known. Make sure all this information is mentioned in your property brochures that are placed on the dining table when your home is shown.

7. Create curb appeal by making sure that the outside of your home is free of any clutter. The lawn should be mowed and any flowers or shrubs should be groomed.

8. If you really want to impress your potential buyers, place a plate of freshly baked cookies on the dining table. When they walk into your home, they will be greeted by the delicious smell. This idea has been around forever but I see buyers wowed time and time again.

9. Leave the house. The buyer will not talk about the house in front of you or open doors if you, the seller, are standing there. As mentioned earlier in this chapter, your potential buyer will spend 15–20 minutes *less* in your home if you are there.

10. Leave a bowl of wrapped candy or bottles of water near the front door along with a small note thanking the buyer for coming to see your home.

11. Turn on the gas logs in the fireplace (if it is seasonally appropriate, of course!).

12. If weather permits, open the windows—if there is too much noise outside, close them.

If you have recently had the home appraised or inspected, place copies of each report on the dining table (that is, if you and your Realtor have discussed this and it is something that will help your cause). Remember to leave out a home brochure (your agent will make one up for you) that potential buyers can take with them, and consider using a few individual note cards or post-it notes that play up the special features that are not readily obvious (the basement is finished, for example). Here are a few other items that you can leave out for potential buyers to browse:

* A short write-up on "Why we have loved this home and this neighborhood." It may not help you sell the home, but you never know to what your prospects might relate. If there is a compelling reason, e.g., incredible schools, fantastic neighbors, wonderful neighborhood traditions, that might help sway buyers into putting in an offer on your home, by all means write it down and share it. I see this occasionally, and I really think it is charming and so do buyers. Consider having a child's note as well.
* Your home's survey: Some buyers are sticklers for details and may be able to get a lot of their questions answered with this simple document.
* Homeowner Association Documents (CCRs or Conditions, Covenants, and Restrictions): These rules and regulations will impact your buyers, so let them know upfront what is in them and how they will be affected by them. Many times this will be online but it does not hurt to have a copy there at the home.
* Pre-inspection report: If it came back squeaky clean—or if you have rectified the key issues in it—by all means let buyers see that you are not afraid to show the nitty-gritty details about your property.
* Comparative Market Analysis (CMA): Want to show them how you came up with your asking price? The CMA will tell that story for you. This should support your price; you be the judge.
* A property appraisal: Put this on display only if it is current and if it supports your price. Again, you decide.

Working With Relocation Buyers

Most of the advice in this book is applicable for a wide swath of homebuyers and sellers. You can put it to work in just about any situation and expect it to work in your favor. In this section, however, we would like to address a unique segment of buyers of which you will want to be aware: relocation buyers. Depending on where you are located—and particularly if there is a good deal of business and industry in your home's vicinity—you may find yourself coming in contact with a large number of buyers who are moving into the area for the first time.

Relocation buyers are on a schedule and they work closely with their buyer's agents, who ferry them around on Saturdays and Sundays to look at properties. When that frenzy is complete for the weekend, the buyers fly back home. This compact schedule can be a positive (you may sell your home the first weekend that it is listed!) or a negative (you may have to cater to their last-minute whims in order to get your home sold).

Relocating buyers are many times given some closing costs and other benefits by their employers, may require more stringent inspections, and must "report" to the relocation companies with which they are working. Those relocation companies must also be kept informed (by the listing agent) of current CMA statuses, particularly in declining markets. They have much oversight when it comes to home pricing and the use of relocation clauses that make contracts fully assignable to them—the relocation firm—until the actual contract is signed and executed by the buyer and seller.

As you can see, there are some additional complications that can come up with working with relocation buyers, but the packages and perks that these individuals are given by their employers—and their typically short closing time frames—can offset those negatives and create a win-win situation for both buyer and seller.

Speaking of buyers, in the next chapter we are going to look at how to manage their feedback and put it to good use. We will help you discern between important feedback and frivolous feedback and show you how to act on and respond to the information.

Four Things to Remember from Chapter 11

* A lockbox helps ensure that your home can be shown without your presence.
* A Realtor should be present at all showings since safety concerns can arise when dealing directly with buyers in your home.
* Vacating your home during the showing virtually ensures that

the prospect will spend more time in it and talk more openly about it with their agent.

* In order to sell your home within 45 days you will want to keep it in tip-top showing condition at all times.

CHAPTER 12

Managing Buyer Feedback

∽ *Every human being is entitled to courtesy and consideration. Constructive criticism is not only to be expected but sought.*

—MARGARET CHASE SMITH

E VERY TIME a potential buyer sees your home in person, he or she can serve as a personal "focus group" for the product that you are selling: your property. As a seller, you should review all the feedback received and understand and factor the most important points—particularly those that are repeated by multiple buyers—into your home marketing plan.

If, for example, the first three or four people to come through your home comment on the worn carpeting, then an upgrade is in order and your agent should inform you of such. If, on the other hand, one buyer comments on the fact that the carpet looks worn, then maybe you are dealing with one particular person who does not represent the general population of buyers.

Your agent should reach out to the buyer's agents every time the home is shown and ask for a feedback summary from each one. This is typically done via email, to save time, and there are also automated, web-based systems that agents use to relay this type of information back and forth quickly and without human interaction. At certain times a telephone call from your agent to the buyer's agent is in order, especially if there have been several items that were either extremely negative or perhaps extremely positive. If the feedback is negative you will want to address it, and if it is positive then an offer may be in the works.

Find out how your agent handles the information exchange process and express your interest in being a part of it. Then, review the feedback as it comes in, determine its relevance, talk to your agent about it, and decide if any action will be necessary to ensure a faster home sale.

Always Leave When Your Home is Being Shown

When your home is being shown it is crucial that you leave and let the showing Realtor do his or her job. Some sellers feel that they have to be there to explain or try to sell the home themselves. This is the most unhelpful thing a seller can do. In a national survey of agents:

95% of agents felt the presence of the seller detracted from the chances of getting the home sold.

85% of agents said that a buyer would stay substantially longer and talk more freely about the pros and cons of a home.

Important Feedback

In this age of information overload and online social networking, pretty much everyone has something to say about everything. As a home seller, you will be sifting through a wide range of buyer feedback to get to the most important nuggets—those pieces of information that will lead you to take action and make your home more saleable.

When reviewing the feedback, consider whether the comments are common across a wide swath of homebuyers or if it is more an issue of individual preference. Remember that your home is being shown to a varied group of people who hail from different backgrounds and who have lived in many different settings. What may be old and outdated to one person may be perfectly acceptable to another; or, as Roman poet and philosopher Lucretius coined, "One man's meat is another man's poison."

Look at feedback that you can really sink your teeth into—things that can be easily and affordably fixed. Interior and exterior painting, countertop replacement, carpet removal and replacement, popcorn ceiling removal, and various other steps can be taken to make your home more appealing to buyers. Have your agent ask questions like, "What would it take for you or your buyer to make an offer on this home?" That will get buyers thinking about the most germane issues rather than spewing out a laundry list of deficiencies.

Seller Feedback

Feedback from showing agents is intended to comment on the price and condition of the home. When several comments have been made relating to a certain color, feature or area of a home, it is time to change it. When enough comments have been made relating to the price being too high, it is time to lower it.

Frivolous Feedback

Out of the dozens of people who will walk through your home during the 45-day selling period, there will be some who simply do not like it for one reason or another. They may offer what we like to call "frivolous feedback" on your home simply for the sake of it. Whether the comments are innocent or intended to ruffle your feathers (perhaps to get a "fire sale" price on the home), it is important that you keep your cool and not allow arrogant and negative comments to throw you off balance.

In many cases the buyers who are the sources of the criticism or negativity may not even be interested in buying your home. Your home simply showed up on a "list" of potential candidates that their agents found when searching for possibilities within a certain geographic region and price range. They will tell you things that you do not want to hear and nitpick at areas of your home that no one else singled out or commented on. Sometimes it is not even the buyers that are making the comments but rather the agent who has shown the home.

As an agent who has read the comments of thousands of other agents about properties I have had listed, I would sort the comments from the agents into categories. First there are the seasoned agents who are showing prequalified buyers with a measure of interest in the property. They give constructive feedback; they offer valid and well-reasoned opinions about the property. Then, there are comments from agents that are inexperienced and have not asked enough information regarding the buyer's wants or needs. These comments may include, "Client wanted a four-bedroom home," or "This buyer requires being in a neighborhood that has amenities including a pool." I want to ask them why did they take up everyone's time showing a three-bedroom home (clearly marked as such in MLS) or why in the second case, did they take up everyone's time showing a home in a neighborhood that did not have amenities (again, a searchable feature in MLS) and presumably something the agent should have already known.

What every seller wants and appreciates is feedback on any item that is changeable or fixable and has truly been a stumbling block for a buyer in regard to the sale of the home.

As a home seller, focus on the repeat feedback upon which you can take action. Use the staging and home-preparation tips covered earlier in this book to make the most logical moves in the direction of getting your home sold quickly and at the best possible price.

Responding to the Feedback

In some cases, potential buyers or their agents give certain kinds of feedback as an invitation to negotiate. For this reason, it is a good policy to respond to buyer feedback—communication that in most cases will originate with you and your agent and be conveyed to the buyer through his or her agent. As mentioned earlier in this chapter, you will want to keep your emotions out of this equation and just respond in a professional manner to the feedback, be it good, bad, or otherwise.

Let's say a buyer loved everything about your home except a single, outdated bathroom. You received a comment that said, "Loved the home and the layout, but felt that bathroom #3 was outdated and in need of a renovation." Now, let us say that this issue has been weighing on you since you first thought about selling your home, but you did not have $5,000 in your budget to update that room. Now it is standing in the way of you and at least one buyer, if not multiple buyers.

One way to handle this situation is by providing a simple response to the buyer's agent, such as: "May be willing to offer a concession and/or split the cost of upgrading the bathroom." This will get the potential buyer thinking about the possibilities and your professional attitude and willingness to make the deal happen. In some cases, it will lead to an offer and just a few dollars out of your pocket at the closing table (to cover the concession) in exchange for a sale today to a ready, willing, and able buyer. Isn't that worth a few words in response to buyer feedback?

Now that you have learned how to manage buyer feedback we will get right into the purchase offer process. In the next chapter you will find out how that process works, how to handle counteroffers and multiple offers, and how to manage the myriad of questions that buyers will ask.

Four Things to Remember from Chapter 12

* Every time a potential buyer sees your home in person, he or she can serve as a personal "focus group" for the product that you are selling: your property. Your agent should ask all buyers' agents to provide showing feedback.
* Not all of the showing feedback will be constructive or positive; some of it will be frivolous and possibly objectionable.
* When reviewing the feedback, choose your action points by looking at areas of the home that you can quickly and affordably improve.
* By responding to buyer feedback you open the door for future negotiations with a ready, willing, and able buyer.

CHAPTER 13

The Offer

> ❧ *It is the little details that are vital. Little things make big things happen.*
>
> —JOHN WOODEN

GETTING AN OFFER on your home is a major milestone in your quest to sell your home within 45 days. A buyer who shows enough interest in your home to take the time to make an offer on it is a very good sign, particularly if the offer is at or close to asking price. Of course, in many cases it will not be, but that does not take away from the fact that the milestone itself is of critical importance.

In this chapter we will look at the various steps that go into receiving, negotiating, and accepting an offer. We will also walk you through some of the most common buyer questions that you should be prepared to answer during this process.

Managing Offers

A buyer will make an offer on your home by either working through their buyer's agent (who then works directly with your agent) or—if they are working without an agent—by presenting the offer directly to your agent. (Please see Chapter Seven for in-depth information on the various agency options and how they impact you as a seller.)

The offer itself is a valid contract that is written on a Purchase and Sale Agreement, which typically contains:

* The sales price
* The approximate closing date
* The property (real and sometimes personal) that is included
* The amount of the buyer's deposit and where it will be held—usually in escrow (by a third party or occasionally by one of the real estate companies involved in the transaction)—until the closing
* In some states, the amount of the Due Diligence fee. (A non-refundable fee that goes to the seller for the purpose of taking the home off the market for a time period known as the Due Diligence Period.)
* The amount of the mortgage that the buyer needs to finance the purchase of the house and the type of loan and interest rate for which they are applying and upon which the contract is contingent
* Inspections that the buyer may want to make, such as a general home inspection and other inspections for radon, termites, etc.
* Closing costs that the buyer may be asking the seller to pay.
* Possible conditions addressed if either the buyer or seller does not go through with the sale or in any other way breaches the contract.
* Any special conditions or contingencies, which could include the seller fixing a problem with the home, the buyer obtaining financing, a satisfactory home inspection report or other items, possible appraised value upon which oftentimes the contract is contingent. (In the case of a buyer who needs a loan on the property and a lender's approval, this will be required.)

When you receive the offer your first reaction will probably be positive (if the price and terms are in the ballpark of your expectations) or negative (if the buyer thinks they are going to get your home at a fire-sale price). The important thing here is to keep emotions out of the process and look at the offer practically. Talk to your agent about the offer and figure out where you are close, where you are far apart, and what you can offer back to the buyer in a "counteroffer" that would bring you and the buyer closer together. If you have chosen an experienced agent, then he or she will be able to play a key role in this negotiation process.

The counteroffer is often going to be your next move but remember this. If the offer is accepted "as is" without a counteroffer, then it is a binding contract (assuming that all parties have executed the written document properly). There are things that each party will need to do to fulfill their respective obligations and to move the transaction along towards a successful closing but the home is said at this point to be under contract. An under contract home may be taken off the market or an owner may instruct the agent to allow additional showings and to allow for a possible backup offer.

Contract Price to List Price Ratio

You may have a price in mind that you are willing to accept only to have your offer price come in lower than that target. Be sure to ask your agent about the contract price to list price ratio. Understand what that number is for your area and MLS and also what the individual agent has been able to achieve. If, for example the local MLS has a ratio of, on average, being that the contract price is 95% of the listing price and if your home is priced correctly, you may want to look hard at any offer in that range. Part of the skill set of your agent may lie in being able to negotiate the price as high as possible but to at least fall within that range.

On the other hand, recognize that if a counteroffer is made, the first offer has, in essence, been rejected and is no longer valid. That is to say that when you as a seller make a counteroffer, this in effect kills the validity of the first offer by the potential buyer (you have rejected it) and you do run the risk of having the buyer walk away.

If you make a counteroffer, in it you will state that the you have accepted the buyer's offer but with changes to the following particular term(s), which may include:

* Total consideration (generally a higher price)
* Increasing the size of the earnest money deposit
* Increasing the size of the Due Diligence Fee
* Refusals to pay for certain reports or fees, closing costs

* Any other terms (perhaps the buyer included personal property in the contract) to which you do not agree

If the buyer rejects your counteroffer to them—and if they want to continue negotiations—then the process simply repeats itself until one of two things occurs: you both agree to the terms of the contract or one of you walks away from the negotiations.

The situation may become complex if there are multiple offers on the table at once. Your agent is required to share any and all offers with you and you are not obligated to consider any of them, meaning there is no chronological order or other rule in place here. If a $250,000 offer comes in on your home when a $200,000 and $225,000 offer are already in front of you, then you are free to sell the home to the highest bidder, provided the other terms are agreeable to you.

As a general rule your agent should notify all other agents of the existence of multiple offers and should ask them for their buyer's highest and best offer. It is always the best policy for your agent to treat all other agents exactly the same in a multiple offer situation. As a seller you can possibly leverage the multiple bids against one another to get an even better price, improve the terms, and/or gain competitive advantage. This situation generally occurs in "hot" markets, but it can also apply when the home is desirable enough to attract multiple bidders or when it is priced below its market value.

The Dollars and Cents

When you receive an offer on your home you will want to look carefully at the dollars and cents portion of the contract. Several key points will be covered in this section. Here are the four most important areas to which you will need to pay attention:

The earnest money deposit

Offers are usually accompanied by a check that is referred to as earnest money. This financial offering shows that the buyer is "earnestly" interested in buying your home. The amount of the deposit varies depending on several factors but generally does not exceed 3 percent of the purchase price and can be much less. This is a totally negotiable amount. A buyer who is trying to outbid others, for example, may offer a larger earnest money deposit. In general, earnest money checks tend to be larger in "hot" markets where buyers want to position their offers as being "stronger" and "more serious" than other offers that are on your table. When the deal closes, those earnest money funds will be applied to the buyer's side of the HUD-1 Settlement Statement as a credit to the buyers.

Additional earnest money deposit

If the buyer so chooses, he or she will include an additional money deposit when making an offer on your home. This is a move that is typically taken in hot markets where there are multiple bidders ready to purchase the property. To show that they are interested and ready to get to the closing table, buyers may make an additional money deposit to ensure their chances of winning the bidding war. It is also an amount that is sometimes triggered by an event. In other words, additional earnest money deposits are sometimes tendered by the buyer upon the successful negotiation of repairs to the home by both parties.

The price

This is the total amount of money that the buyer is willing to pay for your home. Depending on how the buyer came up with the price, it could be an arbitrary number, one that is meant to make you "come down" in price, a well-researched amount that they feel the home is worth, one that is close to your asking price, or one that exceeds your asking price (in the case of very hot markets where there is low inventory and high demand, for example). You can review the earlier chapters in this book to learn more about pricing your home and calculating its market value versus what you may think it is worth. Remember that everything is negotiable and that the price offered on the first round of negotiations with a potential buyer is usually not the price they are willing to ultimately pay. Your counteroffer will then fall somewhere between your asking price and the buyers offered price.

The due diligence fee

To prevent buyers from tying up a home and keeping it off of the market for weeks, or even months, and then deciding that it does not meet their requirements, some states (including North Carolina) have added a due diligence fee to their real estate contracts. Previously, buyers could terminate transactions up to the date of closing and get their earnest money deposits back if one of several conditions occurred or did not occur. If for example the financing fell through, a property did not appraise, or if an agreement could not be reached based on the repairs that the buyer said had to be performed, then the buyer might have had no further obligation to remain in the contract and buy the home. Conversely, the seller may have been able to exit the contract for the same reasons although generally speaking, it was the buyer who would declare the contract no longer valid due to a contingency that could not be met. At this point they would ask for the return of their earnest money.

With the new Due Diligence rule in place, the buyer pays a due diligence fee to take the home off of the market for a set period of time (the due diligence period). During that time, they will perform inspections on the home, perhaps have an appraisal done, finish the loan approval process and take any other steps necessary to ensure that the home meets their requirements. The due diligence fee, which is negotiable between the buyer and seller, comes on top of the initial earnest money deposit that a buyer must put down when making an offer. The due diligence fee is generally nonrefundable except in the event of a misrepresentation or breach of contract by the seller. In most instances, the due diligence fee is made directly to the seller and may be deposited directly by them and is intended to be simply a fee for a period of time that the seller has allowed the buyer to take the home off the market. Really, the home continues to be on the market but the thought is that other agents and buyers may perceive it is a done deal and so they may not want to take time to show the property or look at it.

The separate earnest money deposit offered by the buyer can be reclaimed by the buyer if they decide during the due diligence period that the home for any or no reason does not suit them. The seller may retain the earnest money deposit if the buyer changes their mind after the due diligence period closes, which is on the Purchase and Sale Agreement contract as 5 p.m. on the agreed upon date. If the buyer is dissatisfied before 5 p.m. on the last day of the due diligence period, they may notify the seller that they are not proceeding with the contract. Otherwise, if no notification is given, they are presumed to be "in the deal" and the earnest money is said to "go hard." That means that the earnest money may be at risk and the seller may lay claim to it if the buyer does not close on the property.

Here are some of the key steps that the buyer and their agent may take during the due diligence process:

* Conduct a property survey with licensed surveyor approved by the lender if a condition for loan approval
* Order a title search and title insurance to assure free and clear title
* Have a licensed home inspector conduct a home inspection
* Order a formal appraisal of property
* Check on availability and cost of home insurance
* Review zoning regulations to match buyer's plans for future use of the property
* Review restrictive covenants, owner's association bylaws, rules and regulations
* Explore potential flood hazards and requirement of flood insurance by lender
* Conduct a wood-destroying insect inspection
* Physically inspect the property and home
* Check for property easements and encroachments
* If property was built before 1978, conduct a lead-based paint inspection
* Have a radon inspection done by a qualified inspector

This is not an exhaustive list, but it does show the steps that buyers may take during the due diligence process. As you have already read in this book, you can take the necessary, proactive steps to mitigate any issues that might arise during this process. A pre-inspection by a licensed home inspector, for example, may help deal with any existing property defects and help you get to the closing table faster.

Multiple Offers

There may be multiple offers on your property depending on its price and desirability, and the state of the real estate market. Discuss with your agent in advance how this will be handled. Generally speaking, the agent should treat all parties fairly and in the same manner and should not disclose contract amounts to other agents except with the consent of all parties. Most agents will simply inform other offering agents of the existence of multiple offers and will ask for the buyer's "highest and best" offer to be received by a certain date and time.

Be Ready to Answer These Questions

When I am working with sellers I want them to be as prepared and knowledgeable as possible. One way I do this is by using a simple list of questions that I know buyers are going to ask and then printing up that information in a Q&A format. There are some questions for which you simply cannot be prepared, but here is a sample list that you can use to develop your own list of potential buyer questions.

1. What are the schools like and where are they located? What can you tell me about them?
2. What are the average monthly utility bills? (maybe the number one question)
3. How many gallons per minute are pumped from the well (if not on city or county water)?
4. Is there a buried oil tank on the property?
5. Have the fireplace and chimney been inspected? Does it work?
6. What are the paint and stain brands, colors, and finishes for all interior and exterior areas as well as trim?
7. How do you turn on irrigation system?
8. Is there a pest control agreement?
9. What is the moisture content under the home?
10. What are the building setbacks on the property?
11. What is the age of roof?
12. What is the age of all appliances?
13. What is the age of the HVAC system?
14. If there is a septic system, for how many bedrooms is it permitted (if home is not connected to city or county system)?

15. Where is the septic field? When was the last time the septic was pumped?
16. Who picks up trash and when? Who picks up recyclables and when?
17. How is the home heated?
18. What is the neighborhood / community like? (Remember the fair housing rules covered in Chapter 8 when answering this question.)
19. Is there a Homeowners Association (HOA)?
20. Are there judgments against the HOA? May I see the annual financial statement of the HOA? Are there any assessments from the HOA?
21. Are there architectural restrictions by HOA or community?
22. Can I park my boat/motor home/company truck in the driveway?
23. Can I have a fence / storage shed? Must it be approved?
24. Are there neighborhood amenities?
25. What are the property taxes? Has the tax value been appealed?
26. Who are the utility providers and what is their contact information?
27. What is the electrical service for the home?

The Buyer's Role

There are a few additional contract points of which you will want to be aware when receiving, accepting, and/or countering offers on your home. You will probably see the phrase "time is of the essence" multiple times during this process. Time is of the essence means that performance by one party or both parties at or within the period specified must be strictly adhered to.

Also pay attention to the property disclosure component of the contract and make sure that the proper "buyer has received" or "buyer has not received" box has been checked. In Chapter 9 you will find more details on this form and your obligations and rights as a seller with regard to this form. It is important to note that some properties—particularly those that are bank-owned—are exempt from the disclosure rule.

Two other buyer-related issues to pay attention to in the offer include buyer representation and the buyer's obligation to repair damage caused by their inspection(s). Under a Buyer Agency agreement, an agent acts solely on behalf of the buyer. A subagent of the buyer is one who has agreed to work with the buyer's agent and who, like the buyer's agent, acts solely on behalf of the buyer. Buyer's agents and their subagents will disclose to the buyer known information about the seller which may be used to benefit the buyer. From the standpoint of the seller, it makes sense not to disclose anything to the buyer's agent that you do not wish the buyer to know.

The duties a buyer's agent and subagent owe to the buyer include:

* Promoting the best interest of the buyers
* Fully disclosing to the buyer all material facts that might affect or influence the buyer's decision to tender an offer to purchase real estate
* Keeping confidential the buyer's motivations for buying
* Presenting all offers on behalf of the buyer
* Disclosing to the buyer all information about the willingness of the seller to complete the sale or to accept a lower price

These are important points for you and your agent to keep in mind as you work your way through the contract and negotiation processes. The second point deals with inspections, and the fact that buyers are obligated to pay for any repairs necessitated by the home inspection which they ordered. This is clearly spelled out in the contract.

When the offer is made on your home, an escrow agent (typically a real estate company, an attorney or title company) will be designated and an effective date (when the contract becomes fully executable) will also be included. The "effective date" of a contract is the date on which the last party signed or initialed the contract and delivered the final offer (or counteroffer) on the purchase of the home to the other party. This date is important as other dates and conditions are sometimes contingent upon it.

Lease-Options

Another contract point that may or may not be relevant in your case is known as a lease-option. A lease-option goes into effect when a buyer agrees to lease the home from the seller, sometimes for a higher-than-normal monthly fee. The excess (or any portion of the lease amount agreed to by the buyer and the seller) is used to apply toward the purchase at a later date and if the purchase is consummated. Usually there is an upfront payment to purchase the option and a set amount of time before the lease option ends. The actual purchase of the home takes place at a closing. Lease-options are usually used during a slow real estate market or in cases where a buyer has poor credit that can be repaired during the period of the lease option or when the home for some other reason has not sold.

It is important to note that only a small percentage of lease-option buyers ever wind up purchasing the home outright. As mentioned above, these buyers typically go into the lease option because they cannot qualify for a home loan and expect that they will be able to qualify after a period of time. Poor credit, lack of documentable income, or lack of savings to have a large enough down payment are the key challenges with which these potential buyers are dealing—and in many cases they will continue to be challenged by these into the future. For this reason as a seller if you are contemplating a lease option, it is important that your agent negotiate the highest amount of non-refundable earnest money deposit in case the deal does not work out. Be aware that there are legal complications to this process and an attorney must always draft and review any and all documents in a lease option.

When a lease-option contract does not become an actual sale the seller may keep any monies that were paid upfront as a deposit (assuming that the contract is prepared this way and signed by all parties). The downside to you the seller is that you will be back at square one and once again putting your home on the market again for sale and sometimes looking at repairs that must be made from the tenant. Lease-options are clearly not the top choice for someone looking to sell their home within 45 days, but they are at least something to consider in a challenged market.

Now that you have a good handle on the contract and monetary negotiation process, it is time to look at a final, important aspect of the offer and contract development process: negotiating repairs. In the next chapter we will show you how to handle this aspect of selling a home and come out on top.

Four Things to Remember from Chapter 13

* Obtaining an offer is a significant milestone in the sale of your home.
* Not all offers will be on target and some may even disappoint. Keep emotions at bay and deal with offers as they are presented.
* Your agent will work with the buyer's agent to negotiate all costs, repairs, contingencies, and other points.
* Review the list of potential buyer questions and share your answers with your real estate agent so that a prospect may have needed answers quickly.

CHAPTER 14

Negotiating Repairs

∽ Nothing astonishes men so much as common
sense and plain dealing.

—RALPH WALDO EMERSON

WHEN YOU ARE SELLING YOUR HOME, the repair request process runs the gamut from very easy to navigate to extremely difficult to negotiate. The condition of your home, the buyer's level of "pickiness," and your willingness (or, in some cases, unwillingness) to make concessions in this area will all come into play. A laid-back buyer who is handy and can fix things around the house, for example, may not be overly concerned about minute details. An elderly couple that needs a "move-in" condition home, however, may come up with a laundry list of repair requests based on a list developed by their home inspector and may well insist on every repair being done.

As you learned in earlier chapters of this book there are certain steps you can take to ward off last-minute repair issues that might arise. A pre-inspection, for example, will give you a roadmap from which to work when completing your own repairs. With this roadmap in hand you can talk to your agent and contractor about which issues need immediate attention and which do not. Then, when it comes time to field offers and repair requests, the number of surprises and requests will be greatly minimized (if not completely eliminated).

Negotiating Repairs

Negotiating repairs is often the most difficult part of the home selling process, even more so than negotiating the purchase contract. The seller often feels that he has given the home away. At the same time, the buyer may feel that he has paid the very top price the home is worth. Now some unexpected repairs are found. Most sellers need to understand that unexpected repairs are often due to a lack of maintenance by the seller and should be handled by them. Buyers should recognize the need to keep from nitpicking minor flaws in the property. All that said, it falls to the agents to represent their respective clients and to negotiate repair items. This is perhaps the most important skill an agent should have since many deals unravel because of these negotiations. Be sure to discuss this with your Agent when he or she lists the home and get a clear feeling if this is a skill you feel he or she may possess.

In this short chapter we will walk you through the process of negotiating repair requests, discuss the parties that are involved in this aspect of the property sale and help you make the best possible choices for your own situation.

The Inspection Repair Request

Once a home inspection has been conducted you will receive what is known as a "repair request form" that has been generated by items listed in the property inspection report and which the buyer feels are necessary to be completed. In most cases, this form includes those repairs important enough that the buyer wants to ensure they will be agreed to be taken care of *before* the end of the due diligence period so that the deal can proceed to the closing table.

Remember that the buyer's agent is looking out for the best interest of their client and that some buyers will literally ask for *everything and the kitchen sink* when it comes to repairs. Get the Cabernet back out! In some cases they are just hoping that you will move forward with the most critical requests, and in other cases they literally do want everything addressed prior to the final sale.

It is important not to be intimidated by the list that is put in front of you. Your agent will help you navigate the process and ensure that only those critical areas are addressed, if necessary at all. Some items and the rest of the small details may either be eliminated from the request or handled by the buyer. Many home inspectors are just being thorough and doing their job by giving an objective and constructively critical look at your home. If you took the advice in an earlier chapter and had the home pre-inspected, then this is a routine list that you may have seen before. Perhaps this list has been greatly reduced since you have presumably already dealt with many items.

Once the form is shared with you, the negotiation process begins. In many states, sellers have no contractual obligation to make any repairs whatsoever. Homes are sometimes sold "as-is," and sometimes the repairs are negotiated between buyer and seller. However, if—as a seller—you refuse to work with a buyer on repair issues you may risk termination of the deal if the buyer senses that there are major things to be done and decides to move onto other homes that are in better condition or that offer better pricing. So for that reason alone, it always pays to fix what needs to be fixed and to negotiate what you think is not as important.

A Written Repair Request Form

When repairs have been verbally agreed upon, always use a written repair request form to be signed by both buyer and seller to make sure there is a clear written agreement as to what will be repaired and who will pay for the repair.

In many cases, the requested repairs will deal with the overall condition of the property's systems (electrical, plumbing, HVAC, foundation, etc.). And while the property inspection report is broken down into separate categories for each system in the home and provides an overview of the system's condition along with any specific issues identified, it usually does not include any associated costs to remedy the problems. Your contractor will work with you to come up with those costs and your Realtor will help you decide on your most reasonable response.

Here are a few "reasonable" repair requests that buyers typically come up with after the inspection:

1. Ensuring that all lights and outlets in the home function properly.
2. Making sure all toilets, sinks and tubs function properly.

3. Ensuring that all showers operate properly.
4. Making sure that there are no plumbing leaks and that water pressure is adequate.
5. Ensuring all major systems in the home function properly, including HVAC, electrical, hot water heater, and so forth.
6. Ensuring that the roof is not leaking.
7. Ensuring that windows and doors can open and close and function as they were intended. Making sure that insulated window seals are not broken.
8. Ensuring that garage door opens and closes properly and that all remote controls (if applicable) work properly as well.
9. Making sure that wells and septic systems function as intended.
10. Inspecting all appliances that are built-in and making sure they operate properly.

Your real estate agent will serve as the intermediary during the negotiation process, and each will be "looking out" for your interests during this time. Your agent will try to pare the list down as much as possible, and the buyer's agent will be doing the opposite. In fact, the buyer's agent will want the most thorough home inspection—an attention to detail spurred on by the many liabilities and lawsuits directed at agents and inspectors who "missed" critical items during this process.

As you know, we live in an extremely litigious society where everyone wants to blame and even sue someone else when a problem arises. Historically, seller's agents have regarded home inspectors as a necessary evil in the process for their uncanny ability to point out every single shortcoming in a home, and in every way, shape, and form. Where in the past the home inspector was there to ensure that everything was in working order (i.e., performing the use for which it was intended) and within its "useful life," today's inspectors point out literally every issue, including "possible" issues (such as a roof that may not last another five years... even though it is operational right now).

Keep those pointers in mind as you and your agent handle this aspect of the sale and as you make repair concessions. Look closely at exactly what each negotiated repair will cost and compare that to the overall sales price. If you are not losing too much by making the requested repair(s) or if buyers are hard to come by and if you have only had very low offers on the home or perhaps no offer and if the repairs are significant enough that future buyers will also ask for them, then perhaps the best advice is to simply do what is necessary to make the repairs.

Once the negotiation process ends the repair request form must be signed and dated by both parties. You will then have a certain amount of time to handle the repairs. Usually it is good practice and nearly always required that a licensed general contractor complete the repairs. This insures not only a level of competency in dealing with the repair items but a party to whom to turn should something not have been done correctly. In most cases, the inspector who identified the problem will then be called back to re-inspect it and confirm that the repairs were made and the components in question are now functioning properly.

Now for the fun part: getting to the closing table. In the next chapter we will walk you through that process and show you what you can expect at the closing table and what other points needs to be addressed before you can make your way to this very important meeting.

Four Things to Remember from Chapter 14

  * Buyer's agents want the most stringent thorough home inspections possible to protect the interests of their client.
  * Buyers will use a repair request form to outline the items they want fixed before the sale can proceed.
  * You and your agent will negotiate this repair request form and come to an agreement with the prospective buyer of the property.
  * Some buyers may ask for everything to be repaired, so be prepared to negotiate carefully.

CHAPTER 15

Navigating the Closing Process

⌒ *Energy and persistence conquer all things.*

—BENJAMIN FRANKLIN

I N THE HOME-SELLING PROCESS, all roads should lead to the closing table, which is where all parties meet to transfer the deed and consummate the deal. Pretty much every step you take and every activity in which you participate will somehow be tied to this wonderful day when you sit down at a conference table at an attorney's office, title company, or other buyer-selected venue to sign all of the papers relating to the transfer of your real property to the new owner.

A few other things take place at the closing table and we will go over all of them in this chapter. We will start with a quick primer on the settlement itself and then show you what you can expect at the closing table and walk you through the various charges and items that will come up during the process.

The Closing Attorney

An attorney closes most real estate transactions, although other non-attorney closing agents may be used. Most of the time the closing attorney is chosen by and paid for by the buyer in the transaction. Sometimes when a seller pays a portion of the closing costs on behalf of a buyer, the seller may choose the closing attorney.

Settlement

Also known as "closing," settlement is the final step in executing a real estate transaction. The closing date will be determined during the negotiation phase of the bidding process and is the day when all parties consummate the purchase contract. Ownership of the property is transferred to the buyer—typically when the closing agent delivers the deed to the buyer and the closing agent records the deed with the Registrar of Deeds in the county in which the property is sold.

At the closing table, the buyer will most often deliver a cashier's check or wire transfer for the balance owed on the purchase price of the home according to the settlement statement (also sometimes known as a HUD-1 Settlement Statement).

If there is a loan involved, the lender will have sent a closing package to the attorney along with a check representing the amount for which the buyer has applied and which has been approved. The seller then signs the deed over to the buyer, the seller receives a check or bank transfer for the sale proceeds (in most instances but not in the case where a seller may owe more than what their proceeds amount to. In these instances a check will be required from them at closing. Also if the sale is a short sale, the seller will receive no proceeds since they are being "allowed" to sell while escaping some of the debt that they owed the lender). In most cases the closing agent (usually a lawyer, notary, or title company) will register the deed with the Registrar of Deeds and then the proceeds and the keys to the property may change hands.

In most cases in North Carolina, settlement takes place on the date and at the time specified in the Offer to Purchase and Contract. The meeting is usually held with a real estate attorney or his representative but can be held by a closing agent of a title company as well. This person manages the signing of any and all documents and disbursement of funds.

If you have followed the steps outlined in this book, you should have few if any issues to resolve at the closing table. In previous chapters, for example, you learned about the value of researching your home's title (to assure that there are no "unexpected" liens or clouds on the title) and the closing attorney or title company will have done this well in advance; having a pre-inspection done (to mitigate any major repair surprises); hiring a reputable agent (to ensure a smooth,

45-day-or-less process); and so forth. With this in mind, here is a look at what happens prior to and at the closing table for a well-prepared and thought-out transaction:

* Presentation of the homeowner's insurance receipt: The buyer gives the lender a receipt to prove that homeowner's insurance has been obtained for the property. This is also an item most often handled in advance by a paralegal of the closing attorney or the title agent.

* Reviewing the HUD-1 Settlement Statement (covered in more detail in the next section of this chapter): The closing agent will review the HUD-1 Settlement Statement with the buyer and seller to verify that the agreed upon dollar amounts have been entered and, if so, have both the buyer(s) and seller(s) sign the form. Ultimately, the real estate broker involved should have reviewed this statement since they are responsible under state law in many states for its accuracy as well.

* Obtaining a loan payoff amount from the current lienholder(s) and making sure that they have been paid and that any previous liens are cancelled.

* Settling the HUD-1 Statement with Cashier's Checks or Certified Funds: The buyer will give the closing agent certified checks to cover the final HUD-1 balance. The seller may, depending upon the seller balance on the HUD-1 statement, be asked to tender a cashier's check for the balance owed or may receive funds from the closing attorney, if such funds are due to the seller.

* Review all other documents: The closing agent will have the buyer and seller review and, if correct, sign all remaining documents that are part of the closing process. Here are the other basic forms that buyer and/or seller may be asked to review and/or sign at the closing table:

  · Truth-In-Lending Statement (also known as "Regulation Z"): Required by law, this standard form discloses the terms and conditions of a mortgage, including the annual percentage rate (APR), payment stream, total finance charges, amount financed, and terms of the loan. (Buyer signs.)

- Itemization of amount financed: Like the Truth-in-Lending statement, this document summarizes the finance costs, such as points, associated with the loan. (Buyer signs.)
- Promissory Note: The written undertaking, or promise, to repay a specified amount over a specified period of time. (Buyer signs.)
- Monthly payment letter: This letter breaks down the buyer's monthly payment into principal, interest, taxes, insurance, and any other monthly escrows. (Buyer signs.)
- Mortgage: The legal document evidencing the lender's interest in a property to secure repayment of debt. It puts a lien on the home as security for the loan, thus allowing the bank to foreclose if the buyer defaults on the promissory note. (Buyer signs.)
- Deed: The legal document transferring, or conveying, title to a property. (Seller signs.)
- Real Estate Settlement Procedures Act (RESPA): A statement that acknowledges that the buyers have been informed about how the closing process works and that the buyers fully understand all the closing documents and financial obligations related to their mortgage. (Buyer signs.)
- Loan Application: Confirmation that information such as employment and marital status that was given when the buyer first applied for the loan has not changed. (Buyer signs.)
- Escrow Analysis: A detailed itemization of the escrow account used in servicing the loan. (Buyer signs.)
- Tax Authorization: Grants permission to the local real estate taxing authority to send tax bills directly to the loan servicer so that payments may be made from the loan's escrow account (only applicable if the buyer is using a PITI loan, with property taxes and insurance folded into the monthly loan payment). (Buyer signs.)
- Affidavits: Sworn statements in writing by the borrower. (Buyer signs.)

- Tax and utility receipts: Various city and state receipts acknowledging various fees have been paid by the seller or that they will be paid by the buyer. (Buyer signs.)
- Acknowledgment of reports: A document that assures that the buyer has seen all reports (such as surveys and termite inspections) related to the property. (Buyer signs.)
- Abstract of Title: Provides a listing of every document that has been recorded about this particular piece of property. (Buyer signs.)
- Home Appraisal: The lender is required by law to provide a copy of the appraisal if the buyer requests a copy in writing within a reasonable time of the closing. (Buyer signs.)
- Survey: If not already distributed to the buyer, the home survey will be made available at the closing table.
- Mortgage-location survey: The boundary survey indicating whether there are any encroachments on the property. Any encroachments to or by the property and any discrepancies should have been discussed and agreed to well in advance.
- Title policy: Issued by the title company, this policy protects the buyer against ownership problems (such as existing liens on the property) and is often mailed to buyers a few weeks after closing.

* Establishing an escrow account: The lender will establish an escrow account for the buyer to cover property tax, homeowner's insurance, interim interest, and possibly private mortgage insurance. (Buyer signs.)
* Executing mortgage documents: The buyer reviews and signs all of the documents required by the lender, the most important of which are the note and security instrument (either a mortgage or a deed of trust). (Buyer signs.)
* Presentation of mortgage check: The lender gives the closing agent a check to cover the new mortgage amount.
* Receiving title to the property: A warranty deed is given to the buyer, signed by the seller.
* Receiving keys to the property: At the conclusion of the closing, and once the deed is recorded, the buyer will receive the keys to the home.

* Recordation of legal documents: The recording process is the final step in the closing process. The escrow or closing company, attorney, or the title company that handles the transaction will complete the recording. The process officially records certain documents such as the warranty deed and the security instrument, which is sometimes known as the deed of trust.

The HUD-1 Settlement Statement

Also known as the settlement statement, the HUD-1 is the final accounting of all the costs and credits associated with the successful completion of any mortgage process (refinance or purchase). This document indicates how much money the borrower will be bringing to closing. On this statement you will see all settlement charges for both the buyer and for the seller, including:

* Gross amount due from buyer: The total amount of money due for the purchase of the home.
* Gross amount due to seller: The total amount of money that the seller will gross from the sale of the home. (Occasionally, this will be a gross amount due from seller.)
* Cash at settlement to/from borrower: The net amount that the buyer has to pay (or receive) at the closing table.
* Cash at settlement to/from seller: The net amount that the seller will receive (or pay) at the closing table.
* Settlement charges: The fees, points, and charges associated with the sale of the home.
* Total real estate broker fees: The total amount of money due to the seller's agent and buyer's agent.
* Items payable in connection with the loan: These are the fees that lenders charge to process, approve and make the mortgage loan. They may include:
  · Loan Origination: This fee is usually known as a loan origination fee but sometimes is called a "point" or "points." It covers the lender's administrative costs in processing the loan. Often expressed as a percentage of the loan, the fee will vary among lenders. Generally, the buyer pays the fee unless otherwise negotiated.

- Loan Discount: Also often called "points" or "discount points," a loan discount is a one-time charge imposed by the lender or broker to lower the rate at which the lender or broker would otherwise offer the loan to you. Each "point" is equal to one percent of the mortgage amount. For example, if a lender charges two points on an $80,000 loan this amounts to a charge of $1,600.00.
- Appraisal Fee: This charge pays for an appraisal report made by an appraiser. A lender requires the appraisal and it is a requirement that the buyer pay for this item.
- Credit Report Fee: This fee covers the cost of a credit report, which shows your credit history. The lender uses the information in a credit report to help decide whether or not to approve your loan and how much money to loan to you.
- Lender's Inspection Fee: This charge covers inspections, often of newly constructed housing, made by a representative of your lender or by an outside inspector.
- Mortgage Insurance Application Fee: This fee covers the processing of an application for mortgage insurance.
- Assumption Fee: This is a fee that is charged when a buyer "assumes" or takes over the duty to pay the seller's existing mortgage loan. (This is a rare occurrence in this market.)
- Mortgage Broker Fee: Fees paid to mortgage brokers would be listed here.

* Items required by lender to be paid in advance: Your buyer may be required to prepay certain items at the time of settlement such as accrued interest, mortgage insurance premiums, hazard insurance premiums and property taxes.

* Reserves deposited with lender: These reserves will include some or all of the following—
- Hazard Insurance. Generally, this is paid for one year in advance and the lender will collect an additional three months of the premium.
- Mortgage Insurance. On an FHA loan the mortgage insurance is collected up front and financed into the purchase price. Then there is a monthly fee for the mortgage insur-

ance. On a Conventional loan there is no up front collection but there is a monthly charge added to your monthly payment for the mortgage insurance premium if it is necessary. In most cases, mortgage insurance is required if the loan to appraised value ratio is greater than 80 percent.

- City and County Property Taxes. In North Carolina property taxes are due and payable on September 1 of each year for that calendar year. The lender will require an amount at closing so that on September 1 they will have the entire calendar year amount collected and be able to pay taxes. The lender may require an additional month to be in escrow.

- Annual Assessments (HOA). Generally, these assessments are prorated to the date of closing and are simply the responsibility of the buyer/homeowner to pay in the future.

* Title Charges: Title charges may cover a variety of services performed by title companies and others.

* Recording and transfer charges: The buyer usually pays the fees for legally recording the new deed and mortgage. Transfer taxes, otherwise known as excise taxes, are collected whenever property changes hands or a mortgage loan is made. Excise taxes are paid by the seller and are set by state and/or local governments. City, county and/or state tax stamps may have to be purchased as well. In North Carolina at this time the excise tax is $2 per $1,000.00 of sales price.

* Additional settlement charges: The following charges fall under this category—

* Survey: The lender may require that a surveyor conduct a property survey. This is a protection to the buyer as well. Usually the buyer pays the surveyor's fee.

* Pest and Other Inspections: This fee is to cover inspections for termites or other pest infestation of the home.

* Lead-Based Paint Inspections: This fee is to cover inspections or evaluations for lead-based paint hazard risk assessments.

* Total Settlement Charges: The sum of all fees in the borrower's column entitled "Paid from Borrower's Funds at Settlement" is

placed here. This figure is then transferred to line 103 of Section J, "Settlement charges to borrower" in the Summary of Borrower's Transaction on page one of the HUD-1 Settlement Statement and added to the purchase price.

* Comparison of Good Faith Estimate and HUD-1 Charges: This is primarily a buyer-related issue, but it involves comparing the two documents to ensure that nothing has changed (or, that there is a viable explanation for any changes) from the time of the contract signing until the time of closing.

* Charges that can and cannot increase. There are three categories of charges on a HUD-1 Settlement Statement—those that could not increase at settlement, charges that in total could not increase more than 10% and charges that could change. The buyer should compare the charges listed in the GFE (Good Faith Estimate) column with the charges in the HUD-1 column. If the charges that cannot increase have increased or the total of the charges that cannot increase more than 10% have exceeded the 10% increase limit, the lender must reimburse the buyer at settlement or within thirty days after settlement.

Typical Home Seller Expenses

* Deed preparation (attorney fee)
* Tax stamps, an excise tax based on sales price
* Their prorated share of: property taxes, property association dues, other similar fees (prorated for date of closing)
* Real estate commission
* Fees associated with loan payoff or transferring funds into a checking account (overnight fees, electronic fund transfer)
* Any costs they have agreed to share with the buyer

Typical Home Buyer Expenses

* Home inspections
* Appraisal if required by lender
* Survey
* Their share of yearly property taxes, property association dues, and other similar fees (prorated for date of closing)

* Fees for a title search and duties performed by their attorney, title insurance policies, hazard insurance for a year, down payment and lender fees, flood zone certification fees
* Cost to record the new deed
* Funds to open lender escrow accounts for property taxes and insurance that will be paid by lender the following year

The HUD-1 Settlement Statement

The HUD-1 Settlement Statement is a standardized form in use across the country, which is used to itemize fees and credits for the buyer and the seller in a real estate transaction. At the consummation of the deal, both parties will sign acknowledging agreement to all facets of the exchange of the property from the seller to the buyer.

A Line by Line Explanation of the HUD-1 Settlement Statement

The HUD-1 is a form that the closing agent (closing attorney) uses to itemize all of the charges made to the buyer and seller in a real estate transaction. With the HUD-1 both the buyer and the seller get a complete list of all incoming funds and funds that are outgoing or disbursed. There are a few fees that are sometimes paid prior to the closing and these will be designated on the HUD-1 as POC, "(Costs) Paid Outside of Closing."

The Real Estate Settlement Procedures Act, RESPA, requires the form to be used as a standard closing or settlement form in all transactions that have federally regulated mortgage loans. Conventional lenders use and require this form as well, even if the loan does not require federally backed funds. It makes the details of the transaction easier for everyone to understand.

RESPA states that a buyer and seller should be given a copy of the HUD-1 at least one day prior to closing. This allows both parties to study it with the help of their agents or other financial advisors to make sure that everything is correct. As a seller you should never assume that the statement is correct. I have seen errors on many of these preliminary statements on both the buyer and the seller sides. Under North Carolina Real Estate law, the broker is responsible for the accuracy of the statement so most agents are used to reviewing them. As a seller you should ask questions on any items you do not understand. This is the statement that will be signed by you and the buyer at the closing table. It pays to make sure all items are correct so that the closing will be pleasant and agreeable to both parties and there will be no surprises.

Section L—Settlement Charges

Let's look first at section L on page 2. This is where the closing attorney will start. Many of the entries here are tabulated before being brought to the front page. Here is where the charges are shown for both the buyer and the seller. Keep in mind that there will not be charges on every line of the statement.

Section 700—Agency Commissions

This section deals with the commission that you the seller agreed to pay the real estate firm in the listing agreement. Lines 701 and 702 show how the commission is split between the listing firm and the firm representing the buyer. You will almost always make the payment of real estate commissions as set forth in the listing agreement. Keep in mind that the buyer may have signed a buyer's agency agreement and there are instances where the buyer may be paying an additional fee or commission to his agency as well.

Section 800—Items Payable in Connection with Loan

The buyer usually pays for the amounts in this section although occasionally if you agreed to help with the closing costs then these may be listed on the seller's side. If you for example agreed to pay $2,000 in closing costs for the buyer, these may be divided and spread over several areas such as $600 for closing attorney, $350 for survey, $400 for title insurance, etc. Each of these areas should have notation and they should add up to the amount you agreed to pay.

Line 801 shows the fee charged by the lender for originating or processing the loan. Sometimes this is a flat fee but usually it is a percentage of the loan.

Line 802 is used to show the points paid to the lender for the loan the buyer secured. The buyer is usually able to "buy down" the interest rate by paying a certain number of points. A point is one percent of the loan.

Line 803 is used to show the appraisal fee. The buyer may have paid this when he applied for the loan, and if so it will be designated as POC and will not be included in the total the buyer needs to bring to the closing.

Line 804 is used to record the cost of the credit report if it is not included in the origination fee or if it has not been previously paid (POC).

Line 805 includes the charges for the inspections done at the request of the lender. The Wood Destroying Insect Information Report is included in another area.

Line 806 is for the application fee that is charged by the Private Mortgage Insurance (PMI) Company.

Line 807 is only used when the buyer is assuming the seller's mortgage (and this is quite rare).

Lines 808 to 811 are used for miscellaneous items associated with the loan, and these may include fees paid to a mortgage broker.

Section 900—Items Required by Lender to be Paid in Advance

The buyer usually pays for these charges; these are all items that are required by the lender but they are not always paid to the lender.

Line 901 is used to show the interest that is collected at the closing for the time period between closing and the date of the first monthly payment.

Line 902 records the mortgage insurance premiums that are due at the settlement. Escrow reserves for the mortgage insurance are recorded later and in another area. If the mortgage insurance premium is a lump sum payment for the life of the loan, it should be noted here.

Line 903 is used to show the homeowners insurance premiums that must be paid at the settlement for the policy to be in effect. This is not used for the insurance premiums that will go into escrow.

Lines 904 and 905 are for miscellaneous items that may or may not be required or desired. These would include flood insurance, mortgage life insurance, creditor life insurance and disability insurance premiums.

Section 1000—Reserves Deposited with Lender

This section is used to itemize escrow funds collected by the lender from the borrower for such things as the real estate property taxes and the homeowners insurance (and occasionally for assessments that affect the property). The number of months collected will vary. The lender will usually collect enough months of property taxes upfront so that when the tax bill is due to be paid the lender will have the necessary funds on hand. The property taxes are due in early September but most lenders do not pay them until late December, just before the deadline of early January. The homeowners insurance will be due annually at or around the time of the anniversary of the closing of the property. For this reason the lender will usually escrow a few additional months at the closing just to make sure they have enough in the escrow account to pay the bill when it is issued and presented to them in about eleven months.

Line 1008 is an escrow adjustment calculated by the settlement agent by using different escrow formulas. This is to make sure that the escrow agent is not collecting and holding more funds than are necessary. The figure here is always zero or a negative number.

Section 1100—Title Charges

Title charges include fees that are directly related to the transfer of the title. These would include the title examination, title search, document preparation and the fees for the title insurance policy. These are usually charged to the buyer.

Line 1101 is used to record the title services and the lender's title insurance.

Line 1102 is used to record the settlement or closing fee charged by the closing attorney or other settlement agent.

Line 1103 is used to record the amount of the owner's title insurance policy. This protects the buyer from any claim against the property by a previous owner.

Line 1104 is used to record the amount of the lender's title insurance policy. This protects the lender from any claim against the property by a previous owner.

Line 1105 defines the limit of the Lender's title insurance policy.

Line 1106 defines the limit of the Owner's title policy.

Line 1107 defines the insurance agent's portion of the title insurance premium. This is a disclosure that was not made before December 2009.

Line 1108 discloses the underwriter's portion of the total title insurance premium.

Lines 1109–1111 are for miscellaneous title charges. These may include a fee to the county tax collector for a tax certificate.

Section 1200—Government Recording and Transfer Charges

This section is used to itemize charges for costs such as recording the deed or mortgage as well as fees for the tax stamps (also called revenue stamps).

Section 1300—Additional Settlement Charges

This section is for required services for which the buyer may shop. These might include survey fees, inspections for lead-based paint, radon inspections, structural inspections, HVAC inspections and wood destroying insect inspections. Also if a home warranty were to be provided, the charge for the warranty would be listed here.

Line 1400 is for the total settlement charges paid from borrower's and seller's funds. These are then transferred to the front page in sections J and K, lines 103 and 502.

Now let's go to page 1 and a line-by-line description.

Section J—Summary of Borrower's Transaction

Section 100—Gross Amount Due from Borrower

Line 101 states the gross sales price as per the contract.

Line 102 records the charges for any personal property such as refrigerator, washer, dryer, draperies, furniture, etc., being purchased from the seller.

Line 103 shows the total charges to the borrower brought forward from line 1400.

Lines 104 and 105 are blank but may be used for any amounts owed by the borrower or previously paid by the seller. Here is where an adjustment might be made for the borrower owing the seller a portion of the unpaid rents (if a tenant is in place).

Lines 106—112 are for the items that the seller has already paid in advance. For example, here is where the buyer would reimburse the seller for a portion of the property taxes if the seller has already paid the annual bill. Both the buyer and the seller pay for the prorated time that they own the property.

Line 120 is the gross amount due from the borrower. This is the total of Lines 101 through 112.

Section 200—Amounts Paid By or In Behalf of Borrower

These are all entries for funds the borrower will receive at closing.

Line 201 gives the buyer credit for the amount of earnest money that the buyer paid when the offer was accepted.

Line 202 is the amount of the new loan, which is being provided by the lender.

Line 203 is used when the buyer is assuming a loan that the seller has that is assumable.

Lines 204 – 209 are used to record the miscellaneous items paid by or on behalf of the buyer. This might be any allowance the seller makes in lieu of making repairs or replacing items agreed to be replaced. This area is also occasionally used when the seller accepts a note from the buyer as a part of the purchase price.

Lines 210 – 219 are for any bills that the seller has not yet paid but owes all or some portion. This area also might include rent, which the seller collected in advance and now owes some portion to the buyer. This can also include utility bills the seller owes but has not yet paid.

Line 220 is the total for all of the items in Section 200. This total is added to the borrower's proceeds.

Section 300—Cash at Settlement From/To Borrower

Line 301 is the total due from the borrower from line 120.

Line 302 is a total of all items paid by or for the borrower.

Line 303 is the difference between lines 301 and 302. This almost always gives the amount of money that the borrower (buyer) must bring to the closing. This can be a negative number and in this instance the buyer would receive money back at the closing.

Section K—Summary of Seller's Transaction

Section 400—Gross Amounts Due to the Seller—The amounts in this section are added to the seller's funds.

Line 401 states the gross sales price of the property.

Line 402 records the credits for any personal property such as refrigerator, washer, dryer, draperies, furniture, etc., being purchased from the seller by the buyer.

Lines 403—405 are for other amounts owed by the buyer or previously paid by the seller. This would include a portion of any uncollected rents. It could also include the balance in the escrow account if the buyer were assuming the seller's existing loan.

Lines 406—412 are for any items the seller has paid in advance. This is usually regarding the property taxes, which the seller may have paid in advance.

Line 420 is the gross amount due to the seller. It is the total of lines 401—412.

Section 500—Reductions in Amount Due to Seller—The amounts in this section are deducted from the seller's funds.

Line 501 is used when the seller's real estate broker or some other party is holding the earnest money deposit and will pay to the seller directly.

Line 502 contains the figure from line 1400, which amount will be the seller's total charges computed in Section L.

Line 503 is used if the borrower is assuming or taking title subject to existing liens, which are deducted from the sales price.

Lines 504—505 are for the first and second (if any) loans, which will be paid off as a part of the settlement.

Lines 506—509 are left blank for miscellaneous entries (if any).

Line 506 is used to record deposits paid by the borrower to the seller or another party who is not the settlement agent. This is slightly different than the entry in 501. These lines may be used for any other liens, which must be paid off in order to transfer clear title at the closing.

Lines 510—519 are for any bills that the seller has not yet paid, but owes all or a portion. These may include the real estate property taxes, which have not been paid and might also include any assessments that are unpaid. This also might include any rent the seller has collected for a period beyond the closing.

Line 520 is the total for all items in Section 500. This total is deducted from the seller's proceeds.

Section 600—Cash at Settlement To/From Seller

Line 601 is the gross amount due to the seller from line 420.

Line 602 contains the total amount of the seller's reductions in proceeds from line 520.

Line 603 is the difference between lines 602 and 601. Most of the time this is an amount of cash to be paid to you the seller but it is possible that the total of the first and second mortgages may exceed the proceeds. In this instance you would need to bring money to the settlement.

Page three of the HUD-1 Settlement Statement is a comparison of the Good Faith Estimate (GFE) to the actual charges on the HUD-1 form. There are some charges that cannot increase, there are some that can increase but no more than 10% and there are some charges that can change. Most of the time all of the charges are acceptable and in the range of what the lender has quoted but there are instances where buyers have been refunded money by the lender.

When the HUD-1 Settlement Statement has been reviewed and accepted, it allows the buyer to bring a cashier's check to the closing in the exact amount needed or to wire money to the closing attorney's trust account and it allows you the seller to see the exact amount that you should be receiving after the closing and the deed has been recorded. The signing of this document at the closing should be a mere formality.

Ownership, Keys and Occupancy

At the consummation of the home sale process, the new deed has to be recorded before ownership is transferred and before closing funds are disbursed and keys are handed over to the buyer(s). In many cases the closings will take place in the morning, a paralegal or other closing agent will record the deed, and then the parties will reconvene in the afternoon to receive their funds, keys, and anything else that needs to change hands. This is not a "rule" in every state, but many more states are handing down this requirement for the closing process.

Other important steps that need to take place before closing is completed include notifying utility companies of the ownership change (this can be done well in advance with just a simple telephone call or the filling out of an online form provided by the utility). One other important step in the process is the termination of your current homeowner's insurance policy. Let your insurance agent know in advance the date of the closing and then be sure to follow up and let him or her know that the closing has occurred. It is important not to cancel your policy prior to the recordation of the deed.

In most situations the owner will vacate the premise by or before the time of closing, leaving the home ready for the buyer to occupy it. Buyer occupancy prior to closing is another option but not one that we recommend due to the possible complexities involved (if the deal is derailed, for example, then evicting the renters can be complicated). Similar complications may occur when sellers retain occupancy *after* closing.

Sometimes, however, an owner will "rent" the property to the buyer in advance, and then terminate that rental agreement on the closing day when the buyer takes possession of the property in full. As long as the arrangements are well thought out and any contingencies are laid to rest before the "tenant"/buyer takes occupancy, then going forward with these unusual occupancy options is generally acceptable. Once again, an attorney should be consulted and any document regarding occupancy prior to or after closing should be prepared by the attorney.

With the closing details behind you it is time to look at one more aspect of selling a home: doing it yourself. In the next chapter we will take a brief look at the FSBO route, why you would want to use it, why you might not use it and how to navigate the process on your own.

Four Things to Remember from Chapter 15

* In the home-selling process, all roads should lead to the closing table, which ends with the home being sold.

* You can ensure a smooth closing process by taking all of the necessary steps and precautions in advance, during the 45-day selling period.
* A closing agent—typically a real estate attorney or title company representative—will orchestrate the closing.
* Keys, closing funds, and other items are generally distributed after the new deed has been recorded with the county or city government office.

CHAPTER 16

Taking the FSBO Route

⟶ A writer's job is to tell the truth.

—ANDY ROONEY

So far in this book we have worked on the assumption that you will hire (or already have hired) a competent, experienced real estate agent to sell your home. In this chapter we will turn our attention to the Do-It-Yourself or FSBO route and show you the ins and outs of attempting to sell your home on your own without an agent.

The FSBO

In today's real estate market the FSBO approach may or may not fit into the 45-day sale window. Housing inventories are high across the country, loans are harder to come by, and the Internet is literally flooded with "for sale" properties that range from very cheap to luxury. Standing out from the crowd is not easy as you already learned from earlier chapters of this book and often requires the help of a professional.

The fact is owners have sold only one to two percent of their homes on today's market. But let us say you are forgoing the agent route and are determined to do it on your own. Perhaps you have a large amount of time on your hands and are eager to get involved with a complex marketing and sales process or maybe a buyer is already in your pocket and ready to buy your one-of-a-kind, desirable home. Whatever the reason, we are sure you have thought this through carefully before proceeding.

For Sale By Owner (FSBO)

This is the process of selling a home without the services or representation of a real estate broker or real estate agent. A homeowner may represent himself or herself to sell their own property and not pay a commission. From the period 1991 to 2012 the number of FSBOs dropped from about 20% to about 10% of homes sold.

Agents Steer Clear of FSBOs

Most real estate agents do not get involved with FSBOs. Knowing that sellers are looking to save 6 percent (or so) in commissions on the sale of their homes, agents simply do not go out of their way to present FSBOs to buyers. Also driving agents away from such deals is the fact that many sellers—particularly in today's market—do not know what their home is worth. Unless they have had a professional CMA and/or appraisal done, the likelihood is that the sales price is incorrect and is very high.

This puts additional pressure on agents, who generally try to overcome an unrealistic seller's pricing expectations early in the game—not in the last few weeks leading up to closing. Agents also know that a FSBO seller may "use" the agent's services at the outset—to get an accurate CMA, for example—and then to save as much as they can they attempt to sell the home on their own. This has caused some agents not to want to show a FSBO property.

Not all agents are put off by FSBOs. The smartest ones come to showings with all of the necessary paperwork filled out and request a 3 percent commission as a co-brokerage fee. Agents know that they will probably end up doing most of the work to close the deal—so they come prepared and ready to negotiate and request a fair compensation for their work.

The Risks and Rewards

Selling a home without an experienced agent's expertise is no easy feat. Sometimes just getting through the first few steps (deciding to sell, getting a pre-inspection and staging the house for sale) leaves the homeowner exhausted and ready to concede defeat. The fact that nearly 95 percent of FSBOs *never* sell—and their owners wind up listing the home with a real estate agent—makes the 45-day mark we are striving for with this book improbable to attain. And even though sellers *think* that they are significantly saving by going FSBO, the reality is that those who work with professional real estate agents usually sell their homes for at least 6 percent higher than they would sell the home on their own.

The upside to the sale of the home is obvious. It saves the commission on the sale of the home. Some homeowners have so little equity in the property that they feel they are forced to attempt the sale themselves.

Here are a few other downsides of attempting to sell your home on your own:

* You will not be able to put it in the local MLS (only a licensed agent can do this) without paying some type of fee to some licensed professional for this service.
* You will lose significant exposure both in the local market and the national market by not having your home in the MLS (90% of homes sold in the U.S. are sold through a MLS listing).
* You will not be able to advertise your home on national websites like Realtor.com unless it is in MLS.
* A FSBO home does not receive a fraction of the exposure that a home listed by an agent receives.
* FSBOs are many times not priced correctly and some sellers end up driving off prospective buyers (most homeowners do not know how to look at comparables in their neighborhood and price their home accordingly).
* As mentioned earlier in this chapter, most agents do not bother with FSBOs (thus reducing your pool of eligible buyers).
* Real estate transactions require complicated legal agreements and contracts (if you do not know what you are doing, you could quickly find yourself in a legal bind).
* You will have to negotiate on your own behalf (never an easy task—think about professional athletes, entertainers and authors. If they could do it themselves, they probably would. Most

however have learned for best results to have an agent negotiate and handle the details in their stead.)

The list of possible problems that can appear when selling on your own goes on, and the list of benefits to selling on your own can be a fairly short list. Put simply, unless you have experience in the market, a fair market price in mind, and a "sure thing" buyer who is going to purchase your home, then listing with a real estate agent is your best bet.

The All-Important Disclosures

We covered disclosures in depth in Chapter Nine, but it is important to note that you will be responsible for the same level of disclosure, even if you do not work with an agent. Please review Chapter Nine to find out exactly what needs to be disclosed and when. Ignoring this step as a FSBO could cause problems.

In the next chapter we will cover a topic that many homeowners across the U.S. are grappling with right now—how sellers can sell a home that is worth *less* than what is owed on their current mortgages.

Four Things to Remember from Chapter 16

* Selling a home as a FSBO (For Sale By Owner) is an option that all homeowners have.
* Without hands-on experience buying and selling homes, a homeowner will run into challenges trying to sell a home as a For Sale By Owner.
* FSBOs are not listed in the local MLS and generally do not have support of local real estate agents.
* The fact that nearly 95 percent of FSBOs *never* sell—and their owners wind up listing the home with a real estate agent—makes the 45-day mark we are striving for with this book improbable to attain.

CHAPTER 17

When My Home is Worth Less Than What I Owe

∾ Money is not the most important thing in life,
but it is reasonably close to oxygen on the
"gotta have it" scale.

ZIG ZIGLAR

WHEN THIS BOOK WENT TO PRESS, roughly 10 million or more homeowners across the country were either very late on their mortgage payments or owned homes that were already in foreclosure. If you are one of them, there are some remedies available to you. If it is early enough in the process, for example, you could ask for a loan modification or tap into one or more government programs. If you are further along and have not paid your mortgage in one or two months, then a short sale may be possible for you.

Regardless of the avenue you select, it is imperative that you make your move now. Do not wait until your home is auctioned off on the courthouse steps. Take a proactive stance, open dialogue with your lender and find a real estate agent who has successfully handled other short sales.

Loan Modifications

A loan modification is a permanent change in one or more of the terms of a borrower's loan, allows the loan to be reinstated and results in a payment the borrower can afford. If you experience difficulty paying your mortgage, you should immediately contact your lender or a housing counselor to try to work something out. If you just need a little time to get back on your feet, your lender may agree to a loan workout plan to temporarily reduce or suspend your payments, allow you to repay what is past due in monthly installments or provide some other type of relief.

The Home Affordable Modification Program (HAMP) is another option for homeowners who are in financial distress. If you wish to keep your home, the very first thing that you should do is check to see if you qualify for either HAMP or a standard loan modification. Through HAMP, the federal government offers borrowers with loans insured by Fannie Mae or Freddie Mac the opportunity to refinance into lower interest rate loans.

Deed in Lieu

Generally, if a borrower makes a good faith effort to sell the property but is not successful, a servicer may consider a deed-in-lieu of foreclosure. With a deed-in-lieu, the borrower voluntarily transfers ownership of the property to the lender—provided the title is free and clear of other mortgages, liens and encumbrances.

Deeding your property to someone else without paying off the loan is always a bad idea. In the first place, the lender still considers you primarily responsible for payment on the loan. If loan payments do not get paid, or if the lender ultimately forecloses, this will show on your credit.

Home Affordable Modification Program (HAMP)

Home Affordable Modification Program (HAMP) is a federal program of the U. S. to help eligible homeowners with loan modifications on their residential mortgage debt. The purpose is to help approximately 8 million Americans facing the risk of foreclosure and to help protect home values.

Secondly, when you deed your property to someone else, you give up control of the property. Along with the deed goes the ability to control the property. Do not deed your property to someone without paying off the loan unless you have consulted with an attorney.

Short Sales

The term "short sale" has been used in real estate and mortgage circles for decades, but it was not until the last few years that it became a part of the average person's vernacular. When the real estate market and credit markets began to slide in the mid-2000s across the country, more and more people learned about short sales and how to use them.

In a short sale, the amount owed to the lenders is more than the amount for which the home can be sold. In a typical sales situation, the homeowner would need to bring in the difference between the mortgage balance and the net proceeds from a contemplated sale in order to sell the property. A short sale is different. It offers relief to the homeowner by allowing them to sell the home at a price less than what they owe. As part of the deal, a short sale attorney or other licensed negotiator may negotiate with the lender to accept less than the full amount owed to satisfy the debt, allowing it to be paid off "short." The attorney of course will attempt to negotiate away any deficiency judgment. Thus in a perfect short sale, the seller walks away from the deal without the lien holder seeking further payment.

From the lender's perspective, a short sale is preferential to a foreclosure. In most instances, the lender will receive as much as 20 to 25 percent more in net dollars than they will receive if the property proceeds to a foreclosure. Furthermore, the lender will not have to manage the property or hire a management company, which is the case in the event of a foreclosure.

The number of short sales has increased exponentially as the num-

---

Short Sale

A short sale is a sale of real estate in which the proceeds from selling the home fall short of the amount that is owed to a lender on the home. The lien holders agree to release their lien on the property and to accept less than what is owed on the debt.

---

ber of homeowners in default on their mortgage payments has grown. The short sale is seen as a viable alternative to foreclosure in that it saves the homeowner money and stress and saves the bank from receiving even less in the event of foreclosure and from paying out excessive property management fees and attorney fees.

Here are the basic documents you will need for a short sale:

* Purchase and sale agreement. This is the accepted offer. This document is evidence that, under a certain set of conditions, the owner is willing to transfer ownership of the property to the buyer. Of this set of conditions, purchase price and possession date are the main focus. The Offer to Purchase and Contract agreement needs to be well executed. To be legally binding, it must be signed by all who claim ownership of the property.
* A short sale addendum must accompany any Offer to Purchase and Contract agreement. This addendum informs all parties that this short sale is contingent upon acceptance by the lender. If the lender does not accept, then there is no deal. Furthermore, in the short sale addendum, the buyer is given the right to cancel the contract at any time prior to lender acceptance. Therefore, it is incumbent upon all parties to recognize that short sales typically take a long time to complete, sometimes as long as three to six months and that the buyer must exercise patience.
* As a part of the package presented to the lender for review and possible acceptance the following must be included:
* Hardship Letter. This is a personal letter, from the homeowner to the lender, explaining the reasons for being unable to continue paying the mortgage. This is a critical document. To be effective, it must clearly state the situation, show concern, and

demonstrate that the homeowner is taking action for the problem to be resolved. It is best if this note is hand written and not very long.

* Homeowner's financial statement. This is a worksheet presenting all income, assets and liabilities. The homeowner and all co-borrowers must be included.
* Latest two bank statements. If the homeowner has more than one account, all the statements must be presented.
* Latest two pay stubs. If the homeowner has more than one job, all the stubs must be shown. Unemployed homeowners must present the latest pay stubs available. Self-employed individuals can provide a profit and loss report.
* Last two years tax returns. Often, homeowners in foreclosure have missed filing their taxes. In this case, present the latest tax returns available and write a personal note to the lender explaining the situation.
* Last two years W-2s. Employers provide W-2s to employees and the IRS every year. Provide the latest W-2s available.

Supplemental documents that you may or may not need to present include but are not limited to:

* Death certificate
* Divorce decree
* Incarceration decree
* Bankruptcy discharge letter
* Relief from stay
* Proof of disability
* Insurance claims
* Police reports
* Court approvals

Some or all of the forms listed above will comprise your "short sale package," which must be complete and accurate before being submitted to the lender for review.

The HAFA Short Sale

If your mortgage payment is unaffordable and you do not qualify for a modification, you may be eligible for a short sale or deed-in-lieu of foreclosure through HAFA, Home Affordable Foreclosure Alternatives. The benefit of a HAFA short sale is that you are no longer responsible for the difference between what you owe on your mortgage and the amount for which your home sells. You may also receive $3,000 in relocation assistance upon successful closing of your short sale.

In a short sale, the servicer allows you to list and sell the mortgaged property with the understanding that the net proceeds from the sale may be less than the total amount due on the first mortgage or deed-in-lieu of foreclosure. With a deed-in-lieu of foreclosure, you voluntarily transfer ownership of your property to the servicer— provided the title is free and clear of mortgages, liens, and encumbrances. Generally, if you make a good faith effort to sell your property but are not successful, a servicer may consider a deed-in-lieu of foreclosure.

You may be eligible to apply for HAFA if you meet all of the following:

* You live in the home or have lived there in the last 12 months.
* You have a documented financial hardship.
* You have not purchased a new house within the last 12 months.
* Your first mortgage is less than $729,750.00.
* You obtained your mortgage on or before January 1, 2009.
* You must not have been convicted within the last 10 years of felony larceny, theft, fraud or forgery, money laundering or tax evasion, in connection with a mortgage or real estate transaction.

HAFA is available for mortgages that are owned or guaranteed by Fannie Mae and Freddie Mac or serviced by over 100 HAMP participating servicers. If you have additional questions about getting mortgage help, contact a housing advisor at (888) 995-HOPE (4673). These HUD-approved housing counselors will help you understand your options, design a plan to suit your individual situation, and prepare your application.

In a short sale, all of the fees involved with selling a home are paid by the lien holder (bank) and there is no out of pocket expense for you (the seller). By accepting the short sale, the lender is able to avoid the lengthy and costly foreclosure process, and the homeowner is able to save their credit from a public record.

Foreclosures

Walking away from your home and your mortgage obligation should only be considered as a last resort. If you cannot refinance or modify your loan, if your bank will not agree to a short sale or deed-in-lieu of foreclosure, and if bankruptcy is not an option for you, foreclosure may be your only choice.

After missing several payments and exhausting any and all grace periods, your lender's attorneys will schedule a date for a Sheriff's or Public Trustee's Sale in order for the bank to recoup any or all of its investment. Note that the time frame between missed payments and actual foreclosure sale has lengthened over the last few years across most of the U.S., thanks to the sheer numbers of mortgages that are in delinquency.

Foreclosure will have the most impact on your credit and will be the most difficult from which to rebuild your credit. When a property goes to foreclosure, it will show up as a public record on your credit report, the same as a bankruptcy will show. The impact of a foreclosure can sometimes be as high as 300 points. A foreclosure will typically affect your score for a minimum of three years and will remain on the credit report for seven to ten years.

A short sale has less severe impact on your credit rating. When a short sale is completed successfully with the remaining balance waived, only the late payments on the mortgage will show on your

---

Know the Competition—Short Sales and Foreclosures

Otherwise known as distressed properties, these homes will have a negative pricing impact on the market. While short sales typically bring the bank about 85% of what they are owed, the time involved in purchasing one is many times between three and six months and may be longer. Try to have your agent show you any of these homes that compete with yours. Yes, the pricing may be good but many buyers cannot wait the time necessary to close. Also most buyers do not like the uncertainty of not knowing if the offer (after three to six months) will even be accepted.

---

credit report and affect your credit score. A short sale is nothing more than a closed/settled account. Once the short sale is completed, it will be reported as "settled for less than full amount due" (or similar verbiage).

Depending on the number of other trade lines you have, balances on credit card accounts, and if everything else is kept current, the impact can be as little as 50 points. A short sale's effect can be as brief as 12 to 18 months.

Deficiency Judgments

A deficiency judgment is a judgment lien against a debtor, defendant or borrower whose foreclosure sale did not produce sufficient funds to pay the mortgage in full. This option may or may not be available to the lender, depending on whether they have made a recourse or nonrecourse loan.

Deficiency Judgment

Any unpaid balance owed to a lender as the result of a short sale is known as a deficiency judgment. Any deficiency or unpaid balance is not necessarily forgiven but many times may be negotiated or forgiven during the process. Make sure to speak with your real estate advisor, agent or attorney about deficiency judgments and how they may affect you in the short sale process.

Depending on your state's laws, many loans give the lender the right to pursue the homeowner for a deficiency after the foreclosure has taken place. Typically, in a foreclosure, the final sales price of the property is lower than in a short sale and the fees involved in the foreclosure are higher. If the lender does have deficiency rights, this can result in a higher amount that they will be able to pursue.

During the short sale negotiations, in most cases we are able to have the lender agree in writing to release the homeowner from any future deficiency right after the close of escrow. This is not always guaranteed and is why it is so important to use an experienced professional and an attorney who will thoroughly review the terms of the short sale approval.

The good news is many lenders do not pursue deficiency judgments because someone that has lost a house to foreclosure is a poor candidate to collect on a deficiency judgment.

Handling the Details

On the surface, a short sale may seem like an easy process: you and your agent find a qualified buyer, the offer is presented to the bank, the bank accepts it, and everyone proceeds to the closing table. Unfortunately, the process is not as easy as it sounds. For one, it usually takes at least 90 days from the day of contract signing to closing for a short sale to be completed, basically doubling the time frame we have been working toward throughout this book. Many speed bumps will come up along the way and place that closing table further into the future. There are stacks of paper to sign, unqualified buyers to manage, intense pricing negotiations to handle, and so on.

Now is *not* the time to hire an agent who lacks experience in the distressed market. It is also *not* the time to lean on your agent for legal advice since agents are prohibited from dispensing legal advice. Hiring an attorney will pay off, as will working with an agent who can effectively work with the lenders to provide the extensive documentation they require initially and to keep providing regular documentation to keep the file updated as per the lenders requirements.

An attorney can also help you put together a solid short sale package, negotiate on your behalf against a deficiency judgment by the lender, and fill out all paperwork correctly. They will provide the lender with updates to those documents as needed and continue to negotiate on your behalf.

If you decide to take the short sale route, remember that many of the same lenders are also working with many other properties nationwide. Not only does the lender have to approve the short sale, it has to go to the underlying investor of the note for their approval as well. This is one more reason that the process takes as long as it does. Be sure to have a good attorney and agent on your side.

The Short Sale Disclosure

When you list your home as a short sale with a real estate agent you will be asked to read and sign a form that is known as a short sale disclosure. Here is an example of what the disclosure will contain:

HAFA Short Sale

The Home Affordable Foreclosure Alternatives program provides two options for transitioning out of your mortgage. These are either a short sale or a deed-in-lieu (DIL) of foreclosure. Unlike a conventional short sale, a HAFA short sale completely releases you from your mortgage debt after the property is sold. The mortgage servicer will guarantee to waive deficiency. A HAFA short sale has less of an effect on your credit than a foreclosure or a conventional short sale.

This disclosure will serve as an independent agreement and relates to the contract executed by the buyer and seller involved. It is expressly understood by all parties that the seller owes more than the amount of the contract and is unable to bring cash to closing, therefore the sale will require the approval of the lender and the underlying investor.

* Following are some potential issues that can affect a short sale:
* After the lender receives the short sale package, the lender may require at least 30–45 business days to approve the short sale. After approval, the sale must close within lender-approved time frame, typically 30 calendar days.
* The seller will receive no cash from this transaction. Any funds usually due to the seller will be paid to the lender.
* The seller has no additional cash and will be unable to pay for any closing costs, such as the buyer's appraisal or home warranty. Should the buyer desire a home warranty they are free to purchase one at closing. Lenders will typically not pay for a home warranty.
* The seller may be unable to pay for maintaining the property. The property will remain in the current condition through closing; the seller will not be able to make any repairs to the property. The lender may be hesitant to make repairs as well.

Many times the seller's broker will agree to share with the buyer's broker any commission paid by the lender. If that commission has been reduced by the lender due to the short sale, then they will share it on a 50%/50% basis. Please note that since the lender is taking less than what is owed to them in a short sale, the lender in some cases may decide to pay a lower commission than what might be paid on other sales in the marketplace.

The seller's forgiven or cancelled debt may be taxable income. The seller should discuss this matter with a tax professional. This has no bearing whatsoever on the buyer. There is legislation in place currently that may protect the seller from any taxes that may be owed due to what the IRS views as a taxable event.

In some cases the lender may pursue a deficiency judgment against the seller for any funds not collected at closing. This has no bearing whatsoever on the buyer.

By signing a disclosure provided in the instance of a short sale, you acknowledge that you have read and understand that these situations may be applicable to you as a seller. Any changes to the commission rate will be provided by the lender at the time of the lender's final approval of this short sale. This however does not affect you as the seller since it is the lender that is paying the real estate commission.

Mortgage Debt Relief Act of 2007

The Mortgage Debt Relief Act of 2007 allows qualified taxpayers to exclude income from the discharge of debt on their principal residence. Debt reduced through mortgage restructuring and mortgage debt that is forgiven in connection with a short sale or foreclosure generally qualifies for the relief. For example, if you owe a debt to someone else and that person cancels or forgives that debt, the canceled amount of the debt may be taxable.

However, if the cancelled debt applied to your qualified principal residence, the indebtedness could be forgiven. This Act was originally set to expire in 2008, however it was extended through the end of 2012. Only cancelled debt that was used to buy, build or improve

---

Mortgage Debt Relief Act of 2007

The Mortgage Debt Relief Act of 2007 generally allows taxpayers to exclude income from the discharge of debt on their principal residence. This has been extended through 2012 and may be extended beyond.

---

your principal residence or refinance debt incurred for those purposes qualify under the Act.

On February 15, 2012, it was announced that Obama's fiscal year 2013 budget proposal includes an extension of the Mortgage Forgiveness Debt Relief Act of 2007 through the end of 2014. An extension of the act would ensure that homeowners who received principal reductions from loan modifications or other forms of debt forgiveness through short sales or foreclosure on their primary residences would not have to pay taxes on the amount forgiven. Under the Act, up to $2 million in debt elimination can be tax-free.

With the selling portion of the book behind you, it is time to set your sights on purchasing your new home. Planning, staging, marketing and finally understanding the forms, legalities and process of selling has set you on the road to having your home sold in 45 days or less.

Four things to remember from Chapter 17

* Many American homeowners are currently underwater in their mortgages.
* You have several ways to get relief from your mortgage debt without going into foreclosure.
* A short sale is a good way to deal with a mortgage that you cannot afford without inflicting too much damage on your credit.
* When conducting a short sale, always use a reputable attorney and an agent who have experience in the distressed property market.

CHAPTER 18

Owner Financing—Think of it as Your Secret Weapon

> ᴄ⸰⸱ One of the first rules of science is if somebody delivers a secret weapon to you, you better use it.
>
> —HERBERT SIMON

OWNER FINANCING is when you the seller become the lender on your property and provide the financing to the buyer. In order to provide owner financing, you must own the property outright without a mortgage lien against the property. Nearly every mortgage now has a "due-on-sale" clause. That means if you have a mortgage, it would need to be paid off before you could sell and offer financing to a potential buyer of your home. For that reason, if you have a mortgage, this section may be of little use to you. But if you own the home outright, it may make some sense to consider owner financing. The decision to do this should not be made without a good deal of deliberation. Usually I find that sellers are worried about what will happen if the buyer does not pay according to terms and if they are forced into a lawsuit to regain the property. This is certainly worth considering and asking the opinion of your real estate advisor or attorney.

The reasons for providing owner financing relate to three factors. These factors are the home and its attributes, the personality and needs of the seller and the market itself.

The Home and Its Attributes

One reason to owner finance a home is that its desirability may be less than average. Let's face it, there are properties that are dream homes. There are many homes that are very desirable for any number of reasons, i.e., features including location, layout of the home, size, amenities offered in the neighborhood, etc. There are also those homes that lack some or all of these characteristics and buyers tend look at these but then to move on to look at and buy a competitor home time and time again. A home that has some feature of undesirability is a great candidate for owner financing. Take an honest look at your home. If the neighborhood is nice and homes around you are selling and your home is in good condition, you probably do not need to offer owner financing. If the opposite is true and you are in an area where homes are moving very slowly, this may be the remedy you need to sell and sell quickly.

Needs and Personality of the Seller

The greatest determinant of whether a home may be offered for sale with owner financing relates to the needs and personality of the seller. The seller of a home may need the cash funds immediately for some other purpose; and, in this case, owner financing may not work unless the buyer has a lot of money to put down and will need the financing for a short time. Also the seller may have a risk-averse personality and will just say no, this is not for him. On the other hand there are those who will study and understand the risk involved and will make the decision to move forward under the right set of circumstances. There are some sellers of retirement age who find that a stable 5% return that they may get on the note may be preferable to the 1–2% return that they may be receiving from treasuries or the money market.

The Market

Prior to 2008, when the mortgage and real estate market melted down so to speak, this country was awash with "easy" money. Prices were artificially high, appraised values were inflated and lenders made millions of loans that today would not be made. Many of these loans were the no documentation loans that have come to be called "liar loans." These "no doc" loans allowed the borrower to simply make statements about income, assets and other loans that they had without providing any verification. Banks and lenders were all too eager to loan money. These mortgages were packaged and sold on Wall Street and the brokerage houses were screaming for more.

At the peak of lending in 2005 and 2006 an average of 13 million government-insured loans per year were written. In 2011 and 2012 only around half of that number were written.

The underwriting guidelines were greatly tightened. Ask anyone who has applied for a loan lately and it is likely they will tell you that the process was quite difficult if possible at all.

The Three "Cs"… Collateral, Capacity, Character

When lenders consider making a loan they consider the three areas of underwriting known as collateral, capacity and character. These are sometimes known in the lending industry as the three "Cs." They are the same things you would be considering of a buyer asking you for owner financing. If you decide to offer owner financing, think like a lender. Get as much information as possible on the buyer and make sure it all checks out.

Collateral

When reviewing the collateral, most lenders will examine the home's value and take a look at the down payment made by the borrower and examine the property type. The lender will have an experienced MAI (Member of the Appraisal Institute) appraiser take a look at the property and set an appraised value. The appraiser will look at the home, what it is currently worth and how the neighborhood may affect future value. The lender wants to insure that the value of the home will support the amount of the loan they are willing to extend. This should be exactly the way you look at the situation, just as the lender would. There is a reason why the borrower has come to you for the loan on the property and this probably relates to a lack of credit (or even a foreclosure on his part). If you are willing to take a chance, the borrower is at the least going to have to come up with a down payment that is acceptable to you. I have seen buyers put down as much as 25% but usually it is more in the range of 10%. Since a lender will require at least a 5% equity stake by the buyer and since there are many more closing costs a buyer would face with a traditional lender, it only makes sense for you to require at least a 10% down payment if not more. The other big cost you are saving the buyer is the private mortgage insurance. With either a conventional lender or a government insured lender the borrower would be facing paying the PMI with less than 20% down. On an FHA loan in the amount of $225,000, for example, a borrower would have to pay an upfront payment of $5,062 for mortgage insurance (MIP) and an additional $93.75 per month for at least five years. If you are saving the buyer this amount of money, require that they make a larger down payment or perhaps pay a higher interest rate. There is a balance that you should be able to find that saves the buyer some money and at the same time compensates you for the risk you are taking in providing the loan.

Capacity

When a lender looks at capacity it is verifying a borrower's income, overall debt and cash reserves. Lenders prefer that a borrower's housing expenses (including principal, interest, property taxes, homeowners insurance, private mortgage insurance and Homeowners Association [HOA] fees if any) do not exceed certain ratios (see Debt to Income Ratios, which follows The "Fourth C"—Credit). You, as the potential lender of the home, need to look at your borrower in the same manner. First of all, you are not going to turn over your home to someone about whom you know nothing. The buyer must provide you with an application that would show their financial details just as any lender would require. You or your agent will need to check these details as thoroughly as you are able. What you are doing here is performing the task that a loan underwriter would normally perform and you have to think like a lender would think. Ask questions and require explanations on anything that is hazy. If the buyer cannot provide satisfactory proof that he is able to afford the monthly payment to you, do not proceed. But if things check out and you are relatively comfortable with the risk, then move forward with checking out other details about the buyer.

Character

Character to a lender is defined as one's responsible handling of life. A lender who is loaning money to a buyer wants to know that the buyer has stability in keeping a residence and a job. Their ability to show "roots" is just as important to a lender as is their ability to show a past history of paying bills in a timely manner. You must think here like the lender and be prepared to check the employment and residence references of the buyer. There are services online that can be used to do this and it should be of great importance for you to understand the job history and personal and employment references of the potential buyer as well as references from landlords they may have had.

The "Fourth C"—Credit

Lenders review a borrower's credit when making loan decisions. The lender orders a credit report supplied by a credit-reporting agency. This report is supplied by one of the three major credit-reporting agencies, Experian, Trans Union or Equifax. These three own or control over one thousand regional credit bureaus that exist across the country.

The credit report may be an individual or a merged report. The merged report will include information from all three bureaus in an easy-to-read format with corresponding credit scores. Lenders may then simply compare the score to their minimum requirements to quickly decide if the loan may or may not be underwritten.

A government sponsored enterprise like Fannie Mae or Freddie Mac, for example, will lend to someone with a credit score of 620, the minimum, but would not lend to someone with a score of 619. In addition to increasing the minimum scores, these two agencies also charge higher fees for every 20 points that one's score drops below 740. There are many people in some stage of credit repair. Credit repair involves paying off old debt, restructuring and occasionally identifying mistakes on a report, and taking the necessary effort to have them rectified. There are services online that will allow you to pull the credit report (for a fee) of the buyer asking you to provide the owner financing. Be sure you have their written permission to do this. It is paramount that you read the report and understand how it rates the buyer. You can ask your real estate advisor for help here but consider that many lenders look for a minimum score of 620 and some will require higher. The lower the score the bigger the risk. Of course that risk might be lessened with a very large down payment. The important thing here is to gain a measure of comfort with and trust in the potential buyer.

Checking Your Buyer's Debt-to-Income Ratio

One item of great interest to any lender is the borrowers debt to income ratio. This ratio will compare the monthly bills and obligations of the borrower to his or her monthly gross income. The monthly bills and obligations would include his or her mortgage, credit card payments, car payments, alimony, and all other bills. In short, everything a borrower is expected to pay each month would form this number. The income would be the money he may expect from all sources and includes money received from bonuses, commissions, Social Security payments, pensions, and alimony or child support.

The debt to income ratio is also known by professional lenders as the back-end qualifying ratio and this ratio goes a long way toward determining whether the lender will loan the money the borrower needs for the home. It will also be a factor that the lender uses to decide how much will be loaned and at what interest rate the loan will be made. Sometimes the lender will recommend that the borrower pay off a debt such as a small credit card balance or a car that is nearly paid off in order to improve the ratio. Generally speaking, lenders consider debt to income ratios of 35% to be ideal, 36% to 42% to be manageable, 44% to 49% to be risky and over 50% they are not going to make a loan.

There is a second qualifying ratio used by lenders that is called the front-end ratio and it compares the total mortgage payment to the borrower's gross income. This will determine if he or she qualifies for certain mortgage loans. Traditionally lenders have looked at .28 as the ratio level that is at the top of being acceptable. In other words, 28% of his or her income before taxes could be used to make the payment on a home. Some lenders will exceed this amount but over time it has been shown that levels too much above this percentage are risky and often end in a default of the loan. You may have heard the term 28/36 if you have been around lenders. This refers to a front-end limit of 28% (housing expense) and a back-end limit of 36% (housing and other monthly debt). These limits are not hard and fast but do give a good indication of how someone will perform over time.

Most of the time a lender or a Realtor will be able help you understand how much home a buyer can afford. Look at this example:

* Total household income before taxes: $96,000
* All monthly debt besides housing: $1,500
* Assume a fixed interest rate of 4% on a 30-year loan
* The borrower has $20,000 down
* Assume that the seller pays closing costs for the buyer
* There is a Homeowners Association charge of $50 per month
* On the household income, dividing by 12 will give a monthly income of $8,000 and multiplying this by .28 will give a figure of $2,240
* The payment for the mortgage, which includes principal, interest, property taxes, homeowners insurance and HOA dues cannot exceed $2,240. This is the limit of the front-end ratio allowable for housing only.

$2,240	Total allowable for housing expense
−400	Property taxes (monthly)
−100	Homeowners insurance (monthly)
−100	Homeowners Association Fee (average monthly)
$1,640	can be used for principal and interest

This is the amount of money that this buyer could afford to pay you each month without getting behind with other payments.

On a 4% 30-year fixed loan this payment would allow for a loan of just under $344,000. Adding a $20,000 down payment would allow a borrower to qualify on the front-end ratio for a home costing $364,000.

This looks good until you look at the back-end ratio. Remember, the ratio of house payment and all long-term debt compared to income is also a consideration to the lender. When you add $1,500 in other monthly debt to the $2,240 housing expense, you get a total of $3,740 which compared to the $8000 in gross monthly produces a back-end ratio of 46.75% and that is in the risky category for a lender. To ratchet it back to 42%, which is at the top of the manageable range, a borrower would need to scale back on housing expense and it would look like this:

$8000 x .42 = $3,360	Allowable for housing and all other debt (monthly)
−1,500	All monthly debt besides housing
$1,860	Total allowable for housing expense
−400	Property taxes (monthly)
−100	Homeowners insurance (monthly)
−100	Homeowners Association Fee (average monthly)
$1,260	Can be used for principal and interest

Again, this is the amount of money the buyer could afford to pay you under FHA standards and not be in danger of falling behind on your payment or on his or her other bills.

On a 4% 30-year fixed loan this payment would allow for a loan of just under $264,000. Adding a $20,000 down payment would allow a borrower to qualify on the back-end ratio for a home costing $284,000.

The amount of money the borrower would be able to spend on a home would be governed by the back-end ratio and would be around $284,000. Of course, there are many factors that determine what a borrower may be able to buy but using the ratios above should at the very least put one in the right range.

Here again, if you are planning to provide owner financing, it pays to understand the ratios allowed by lenders and how they would affect you. Since it has been shown that borrowers that exceed these ratios usually end up in default, you probably do not want to make a loan to anyone whose ratios exceed these.

Your best course of action if you do not understand the above calculations is to have a lender or Realtor explain them to you. If you provide owner financing, you are taking a calculated risk just as any lender does. You want to make sure it is a wise decision, it is based on the best information at your disposal and that the borrower has the best chance of repaying the money he or she is borrowing from you.

Since the real estate downturn, there are a number of potential buyers that could qualify for a mortgage loan before that cannot qualify now. Many of these potential buyers truly have no business buying property anyway but that is not always the case. It is estimated that there are several million would-be buyers that for one reason or another no longer may qualify for what they want to buy (qualify, that is in the eyes of a traditional or government underwritten lender). There are potential buyers whose jobs have been down sized, those who have been laid off and then have found work elsewhere but have a short time on the job, and many whose credit has been negatively impacted. But I am here to tell you that there are some gems to be found in this group that may not qualify for a conventional or even government insured mortgage.

If you decide to be flexible on the financing terms for your home, you will be surprised at the increase in the number of potential buyers and the result is a higher level of demand for your home. Just look at retailers such as Best Buy and H.H. Gregg. These companies have offered attractive financing to sell their appliances and computers. The more attractive the financing terms that you set, the greater the number of people that will want to buy your home simply because they have no other way to buy. Offering owner financing or a lease-option on the home may help you sell the home for top dollar and depending on the situation should offer a viable alternative to get your home sold.

If it is a buyer's market and homes are not selling as quickly as they could, consider offering owner financing to attract more buyers to the property. It is always easier to sell a home with owner financing because of the layers of complexity involved with traditional lenders and banks and because you control the qualifications of your buyer. Just remember that the ratios are important. They give an excellent indication as to whether or not a buyer may live up to the terms of the agreement. And equally important is checking the references and assets and verifying employment

There are several advantages to owner financing.

You control the qualification standards. If your buyer has poor credit but has a good job, a sizeable down payment and an explanation that you believe as to why his credit was damaged, you may consider giving him a chance. There are also many investors in the market that have good credit but are maxed out on the number of properties on which they can have loans. A lender may be unable to write another loan or may be leery to do so. But there are many investors that may have a high level of interest in your home.

The closing costs are less for the buyer. Another advantage is that the closing costs will be much less for the buyer than what he would be facing on a conventional or government sponsored loan. A traditional financed deal requires points, origination fees, underwriting charges, credit report, appraisal, survey and a number of other charges. This allows the buyer to have more cash presumably to give to you the seller in the form of a down payment.

Quicker Closing. Usually an owner-financed deal can close in a few weeks. You do want to check the qualifications and references as mentioned above but checking these may be done in a few days, as opposed to waiting weeks on a lender. Theoretically to close, it just takes the attorney researching the title and preparing a deed and a promissory note. There may be more involved to close but usually not. A lender would ask for a survey, an appraisal and of course would have to go through the entire underwriting process.

Promissory Note

A promissory note is used for owner financing. This is a negotiable instrument that signifies a debt and is made when one party makes an unconditional promise in writing to pay a determined sum of money to another at a fixed future time under specific terms. Be sure to enlist the help of your real estate advisor or attorney when attempting to draft or complete a promissory note especially when it is used as the security for a home you are selling.

The surest and easiest method of owner financing is when you own the home or property outright. It is free and clear with no mortgages, no HELOCs or Home Equity Lines of Credit and no liens. In this instance the seller and the buyer must agree to the terms of the deal. Let us say for example that you agree to sell and the buyer agrees to buy your home for $250,000.00. You both further agree to the following:

Purchase price: $250,000

Due Diligence Fee: $1,000 (Non-refundable fee to you)

Due Diligence Period: Two weeks

Initial Earnest Money Deposit: $3,000 (Held by attorney in escrow)

Additional Non-refundable Down Payment at Closing: $21,000

Amount to be financed: $225,000

Interest Rate: 4.5%

Amortization Period: 25 years

Call with Balloon payment due for balance: 3 Years

Property Taxes and Homeowners insurance: To be paid by the buyer

Closing Date: 3 weeks from the date of signing by all parties

Let's look at this deal. The buyer is first putting up $1,000 non-refundable money to you and being granted a two-week period in order to inspect the home and come to an agreement with you on any repair items that may need to be performed. At 5 P.M. on the last day of the Due Diligence period, the buyer will inform the seller if he will not proceed forward with closing but in this example, he agrees to move forward. He has placed an additional $3,000 down as earnest money to be held by either an attorney or placed in a real estate broker's trust account and it is held for your benefit to ensure that the buyer goes through with the purchase as planned. This money is refundable if the deal is called off prior to the end of the Due Diligence period. At the closing, buyer agrees to pay an additional $21,000 giving him $25,000 in the deal as a down payment (the $1,000 DD fee + the $3,000 initial earnest money + the $21,000 additional down payment at closing). He is therefore asking for seller financing from you on the balance of $225,000 and he is asking for the agreed upon 4.5% with a 25-year amortization period. This produces a payment of $1250.62, which is due and payable on the first day of each month to you. Buyer further agrees that this loan will become due and the balance payable in full at the end of three years.

Also, the buyer agrees to pay the property taxes and homeowners insurance when due and to provide a paid receipt to you. There would also need to be a provision for late payments and of course there will be a provision for default, if one occurred. The property itself serves as the collateral and secures the loan.

The agreement can be as simple as this but must of course be reduced to writing and should be drawn by a real estate attorney. The point is this. It is simple, it can be done and it greatly enhances the chance of a sale. Be sure to let your real estate agent know if you are willing to finance the property since it opens many doors leading to a sale.

Balloon Payment Mortgage

A balloon payment mortgage is a mortgage that does not fully amortize over the term of the note and has a balance due at maturity. This is often the type of structure used in an owner finance situation. This allows that a seller may owner finance a property for a buyer for a specific negotiated period of time and at the end of that time receive a balloon payment from the buyer who has obtained other financing.

Lease with an Option

The lease with an option is another alternative way to finance the property and sell your home. This is an excellent way to move a property in a slow market or in a buyer's market.

A lease option is a combination of two transactions, a lease and an option on a sales contract to purchase the home. The option runs concurrent with the lease. The lease insures that the property will be leased through the agreed upon term but it is a unilateral or a one-way agreement. Just as in an offer to purchase and contract, you are obligated to sell the property to the buyer at a price to which you have both agreed. But the buyer has the option to complete the purchase or not to complete the purchase at the end of this time. The buyer gives you a non-refundable fee for this option and the fee is fully negotiable. I have seen option fees as high as 40% and as low as 3%. It is simply what both sides agree to accept. If you as the seller really desire to sell the home, you may agree to a lease option with a down payment amount in mind that you believe would keep the buyer committed and likely to close on the deal. Let us look at a lease option example:

Purchase price: $250,000

Due Diligence Fee: $500

Initial Earnest Money: $5,000

Due Diligence Period: Three weeks

Option Fee at lease signing: $19,500

Monthly lease fee: $1,800

Amount of monthly fee to be applied to the purchase: $400

Call with Balloon payment due: 3 Years

Property Taxes and Homeowners insurance: To be paid by the buyer (lessee)

Repairs and Maintenance: To be paid by buyer (lessee)

Closing Date: 30 days from the date of signing by all parties

In this deal the buyer (lessee) has put down a due diligence fee for the privilege of inspecting the property within a three-week time frame and again has the right to end the deal prior to 5 P.M. on that date and receive his earnest money back (but not the due diligence fee). The attorney that is drawing the lease option contract will likely hold the earnest money deposit. When the property goes to a closing in 30 days, an additional option fee of $19,500 will be given to the seller for a total now held by the seller of $25,000. This money is an option fee and the seller will retain this fee whether the buyer opts to go through with the purchase or not. If the buyer goes through as planned, the option fee is a credit to the buyer towards the purchase price at closing. Both parties have agreed that $400 out of the monthly rental amount will accrue towards the closing so at the end of the 36th month there will be an additional $14,400 credit to the buyer for a total of $39,400 toward the purchase of the property, $500 due diligence fee, $5,000 initial earnest money, $19,500 option fee and $14,400 accrued towards purchase from monthly rent payments. At the end of the 36 months, the closing for the sale and transfer of deed will occur if the buyer exercises the option to purchase and the buyer will need to bring $210,600 to closing in cash or loan proceeds or some combination of the two.

From your standpoint as one hoping to sell your property in 45 days, the lease option has a lower probability of being put into play. There are many variables to consider and many would-be buyers (and agents) use this term loosely and have no idea of the ramifications of some of the terms and options. It is however a viable alternative option that you may wish to consider after consulting your real estate advisor and/or attorney. These documents would always need to be drawn and reviewed by a real estate attorney.

A word of advice regarding the lease with an option is that it pays for you as the seller to require that all inspections are done and repairs agreed to and performed prior to the buyer occupying the home. It simply does not benefit you to allow someone to occupy your home for three years and then to perform repairs. That buyer (or renter as the case may be) would have less incentive to maintain things like the HVAC system for example, if he knew you would be taking care of everything after the lease period but prior to the closing. Be sure to have a written agreement to that effect if you enter into a lease option agreement with someone.

The promissory note is a negotiable instrument used in the owner-financing scenario. In this note the buyer makes an unconditional promise to pay a determined amount of money to you the seller at a set interest rate under precise terms and conditions. The note should include the principal amount, the interest rate, the dates on which payments will be made, the amount of the payment to be made on those dates, the parties involved, the date and the maturity date. Most of the time, provisions will be made in case of a default by the buyer, which may include foreclosure on the property. The maker of the note (who is the buyer) must sign the note. Be sure to have the note reviewed by an attorney and signed in the presence of an attorney or a notary.

The promissory note in the owner financing example above came due in three years but could just as easily have been extended to four years, five years or longer. All of that is negotiable. In fact, some owners are pleased to provide the owner financing for the entire term of the note as long as they are satisfied with the other conditions. There is a secondary market for seller-financed notes and this might be an option for a seller who agreed to finance the property for five years but then had a change in circumstances after two years and simply needed the money. These notes may be sold to various companies and individuals as investments but usually you would have to sell the note at a discount. Just remember that the more investigation of the buyer that you do the better off you will be. And the more security you have in the property by virtue of a larger down payment, the more likely the buyer will not go into default. Also if you are put into a position of selling the note later on the secondary market, it will be more valuable the more due diligence you have put into the deal making sure that you have set up a measured and acceptable risk/reward scenario.

Advantages to the Seller and Buyer with Owner Financing

1. Buyer and seller can negotiate interest rate, term, amount financed, repayment schedule and all other loan terms.
2. Buyer and seller can save substantially on the closing costs.
3. Buyer does not have to adhere to conventional loan underwriting guidelines.
4. There is no PMI required for the buyer.
5. Seller can receive a higher return than with many other investments.
6. Seller can often negotiate both a higher price than what he may otherwise have received.
7. Seller can often negotiate an above market interest rate.
8. Seller may be able to negotiate an as-is contract so there would be no need of repairs.

Disadvantages of Owner Financing:

1. The buyer could pay the loan in full but still not receive the title due to liens undisclosed or unknown by the seller. (For this reason it is always advisable to have an attorney research the title.)
2. The buyer may be overpaying for the home since he has not had the benefit of an appraisal.
3. Buyer may withhold true information about his or her employment, income or assets and this may make foreclosure more likely.

4. Foreclosure if necessary could be costly to and time consuming for the seller.

5. With a lease with option to purchase, the seller may have a current mortgage on the property and if the seller does not continue to pay the mortgage, the property may be subject to foreclosure thus jeopardizing the buyer's investment.

You will need to weigh the advantages and disadvantages carefully. Using owner financing can be your secret weapon in opening up your home to many buyers that could otherwise not qualify for the loan. Just be sure to take the appropriate safeguards and understand the risks involved.

Four Things to Remember from Chapter 18

* Most lenders have set higher standards for qualifying for a loan since the subprime mortgage crisis and financial crisis of the late 2000s.

* There are many buyers that have substantial down payment money available and good employment credentials that cannot qualify for a traditional loan.

* Owner financing when structured properly offers a way to capitalize on this group of potential buyers and may lead to a quick sale.

* A lease with an option to purchase has become a popular alternative method to sell a home while providing for cash flow until the sale is completed.

CHAPTER 19

Ready, Set, Go!

> ◠ Wisdom is the power to put our time and our
> knowledge to the proper use.

—THOMAS J. WATSON

I T REALLY IS POSSIBLE to have your home sold or under contract to a qualified buyer within 45 days. To achieve this goal, you must first have the desire to understand the selling process completely. That means gaining the proper knowledge (with help, of course) regarding the entire real estate process from start to finish.

It is also important to recognize the nuances of the selling process—a recognition that requires the help of a thoroughly trained and competent team of practicing home-selling professionals. Hiring the right real estate agent is paramount.

A home for sale should always have a pre-inspection done to point out any areas that will be of concern to a potential buyer and to deal with any shortcomings well in advance of a contract, which would lead to a closing.

You also have to prepare and then stage your home to show it at its very best and price the home within the parameters of its market value. The next step involves marketing the home to the widest array of buyers both in the geographic market and over the Internet to ensure that you reach individuals from other areas who are planning to move into your market.

I would like to conclude with some final thoughts on pricing and on selling motivations. Some sellers need to sell, some want to sell and some are just testing the waters. Real estate agents primarily want to work with sellers who absolutely need to sell and move onto the next chapter of their lives. Because of this, such clients receive the most marketing support, the highest level of attention, and usually the most showings and offers. Remember that the majority of real estate agents work on a contingency basis:

* If the home sells, the brokerage and the agent will earn a commission.
* If the home does not sell they will not earn a dime.

With these facts in mind, it is clear that the motivated seller is probably going to result in a sale so long as the agent exercises skill in the areas of marketing and constant communication with all other agents and with you, the seller.

Just as the agent wants to understand your motivation, you may also want to understand the agent's motivation. It goes without saying that all agents want to list your property and help you sell your home in hopes of earning a commission. Some agents may artificially price your home higher than it should be. This may be to make you, the seller, feel that they may be able to get you more than the home is really worth. They have given you a slightly (or more) inflated view of the home's value in order to obtain the listing and then hopefully have you reduce it later to its true market value. In the industry, this is called "buying a listing." The agent has made you feel your home is worth more than it is, in order to obtain the listing. If you have read and understood the concepts in this book and if you have looked at several CMAs and maybe an appraisal of your home, you will have a good idea of its value to start with and will not be mislead.

This is a competitive industry and a competitive world and not everyone will give a totally honest assessment of the value of your home. Recognize also that there is a level of skill involved in pricing and that not every agent has the experience necessary to make that judgment.

An agent's job should be:

"To obtain for you, the seller, the highest price in the shortest time with the least inconvenience."

To make that happen, the home must be priced at a competitive market value and in some instances may need to be reduced to ensure that it maintains that competitiveness. It is not about what you as the owner feel you may "need" from the sale of the home; it is what the market says the home is actually worth in comparison to what other buyers have paid for homes in the area with similar features.

For this reason it pays to talk to several agents to get a feel for the value of the home and, in some instances, to have an appraisal done. Finally, it is important to note that all of the education you achieve as a seller, and all of the marketing efforts made by the most talented team of professionals, will not sell an overpriced home. And by the same token, it takes no education and perhaps a much less talented team to sell a home that is priced way under its market value. The whole exercise is one of balance. You as the seller want and deserve the highest price the market will bear. Following the ideas in the book will get you there within the 45 days.

Glossary of Real Estate Terms

Acceptance: An offeree's consent to enter into a contract and be bound by the terms of the offer.

Adjustable-Rate Mortgage (ARM): A mortgage that permits the lender to adjust its interest rate periodically on the basis of changes in a specified index.

Agency: The relationship between a buyer or a seller and a broker or an agent and in this relationship, the broker or agent is authorized to represent the principal in certain limited transactions.

Amortization: The gradual repayment of a mortgage loan by installments.

Amortization schedule: A timetable for payment of a mortgage loan. An amortization schedule shows the amount of each payment applied to interest and principal and shows the remaining balance after each payment is made.

Amortization term: The amount of time required to amortize the mortgage loan. The amortization term is expressed as a number of months. For example, for a 30-year fixed-rate mortgage, the amortization term is 360 months.

Annual percentage rate (APR): The cost of a mortgage stated as a yearly rate; includes such items as interest, mortgage insurance, and loan origination fee (points).

Appraisal: A written analysis of the estimated value of a property prepared by a qualified appraiser.

Appraised value: An opinion of a property's fair market value, based on an appraiser's knowledge, experience, and analysis of the property.

Appreciation: An increase in the value of a property due to changes in market conditions or other causes; the opposite of depreciation.

Assessment: The process of placing a value on property for the strict purpose of taxation. May also refer to a levy against property for a special purpose, such as a sewer assessment.

Association fee: Amount of money required to be paid by the unit owner in a building for "common " areas in that building. For example, these common grounds could include elevators, swimming pools, or air conditioning systems.

Assumable mortgage: A mortgage that can be taken over ("assumed") by the buyer when a home is sold.

Auction: A form of selling property where written or oral bids are made and the property is sold to the highest bidder.

Back-up Offer: Secondary offer submitted to the property owner with the knowledge that it will only go into effect if the first offer is withdrawn or otherwise not able to be consummated.

Balloon mortgage: A mortgage that has level monthly payments which will amortize over a stated term but provides for a lump sum payment to be due at the end of an earlier specified term.

Bidding war: A multiple-bid situation where the seller may counter the best offers to see who will pay more.

Binder: The deposit paid to secure the right to purchase a property at agreed upon terms.

Bridge loan: A form of second trust that is collateralized by the borrower's present home (which is usually for sale) in a manner that allows the proceeds to be used for closing on a new house before the present home is sold; also known as "swing loan."

Broker-associate: A real estate agent who is employed by a real estate brokerage and licensed by the real estate commission as a broker-associate upon completing courses and passing examinations.

Building code: Any ordinance that defines minimum standards with the construction of buildings to protect public safety and health.

Buydown: A subsidy usually paid by a builder in order to reduce the monthly payment for the buyer.

Buyer's agent: A real estate professional. He or she is responsible for representing the buyer's interest in a real estate transaction.

Cap: A limit to the amount an interest rate or monthly payment can increase for an adjustable rate loan either during an adjustment period or during the life of the loan.

Cash-out refinance: A refinance transaction in which the amount of money received from the new loan exceeds the total of the money needed to repay the existing first mortgage, closing costs, points, and the amount required to satisfy any outstanding subordinate mortgage liens. In other words, a refinance transaction in which the borrower receives additional cash that can be used for any purpose. Cash-out refinance offers are sometimes used by predatory lenders to take advantage of vulnerable homeowners.

Certificate of Occupancy (CO): A document from a governmental agency stating that a property meets the requirements of local codes and regulations. Usually, upon issuance, a home may then be occupied.

Certificate of title: A statement provided by an abstract company, title company, or attorney stating that the title to real estate is legally held by the current owner.

Clear title: A title that is free of liens or legal questions as to ownership of the property.

Closing: A meeting at which a sale of a property is finalized by the buyer signing the mortgage documents and paying closing costs; also called "settlement."

Closing cost item: A fee or amount that a homebuyer must pay at closing for a single service, tax, or product. Closing costs are made up of individual closing cost items such as origination fees and attorney's fees. Many closing cost items are included as numbered items on the HUD-1 Settlement Statement.

Closing costs: Expenses (over and above the price of the property) incurred by buyers and sellers in transferring ownership of a property. Closing costs normally include an origination fee, an attorney's fee, taxes, an amount placed in escrow, and charges for obtaining title insurance and a survey. Closing costs percentage will vary according to the area of the country; lenders or Realtors® often provide estimates of closing costs to prospective homebuyers.

Closing statement: See HUD-1 Settlement Statement.

Commission: The fee charged by a broker or agent for negotiating a real estate sale. A commission is generally a percentage of the price of the property.

Commitment letter: See mortgage commitment.

Common areas: Those portions of a building, land, and amenities owned (or managed) by a planned unit development (PUD) or condominium project's homeowners association (or a cooperative project's cooperative corporation) that are used by all of the unit owners, who share in the common expenses of their operation and maintenance. Common areas include swimming pools, tennis courts, and other recreational facilities, as well as common corridors of buildings, parking areas, means of ingress and egress, etc.

Comparables: See Market comps.

Comparative Market Analysis (CMA): A study of properties currently on the market or recently sold to determine the fair market value of a home. These properties should be located within a certain distance of the home under consideration and should also have some similarities to that home. These properties should also have been sold within a reasonable time of the CMA.

Condominium: A real estate project in which each unit owner has title to a unit in a building, an undivided interest in the common areas of the project, and sometimes the exclusive use of certain limited common area. In a condominium the owner owns the air space within the unit.

Contingency: A condition that must be met before a contract is legally binding. For example, home purchasers often include a contingency that specifies that the contract is not binding until the purchaser obtains a satisfactory home inspection report from a qualified home inspector or perhaps until another property has sold and closed.

Conditions, Covenants and Restrictions (CC and Rs): The standards that define how a property may be used and the protections the developer has made for all owners in a subdivision or condominium.

Conventional mortgage: A mortgage that is not insured or guaranteed by the federal government; contrast with government mortgage.

Convertibility: The ability to change a loan from an adjustable rate schedule to a fixed rate schedule.

Cooperative (co-op): A type of multiple ownership in which the residents of a multiunit housing complex own shares in the cooperative corporation that owns the property, giving each resident the right to occupy a specific apartment or unit.

Counteroffer: An offer made by the buyer or seller that makes changes to the original or latest offer of the other party. A counteroffer has the effect of causing the first "offer" to be void. It is in itself a new offer given back to the original offeror.

Covenant: A clause in a mortgage that obligates or restricts the borrower and that, if violated, can result in a default of the terms and ultimately a foreclosure.

Credit report: A report of an individual's credit history prepared by a credit bureau and used by a lender in determining a loan applicant's creditworthiness. See merged credit report.

Deed: The legal document conveying title to a property.

Deed of trust: The document used in some states instead of a mortgage; title is conveyed to a trustee.

Default: A breach of a mortgage contract (usually not making the monthly payment).

Deposit: A sum of money given to bind the sale of real estate, or a sum of money given to ensure payment or an advance of funds in the processing of a loan. See earnest money deposit.

Depreciation: A decline in the value of property; the opposite of appreciation.

Designated Dual Agency: An agency option under dual agency that allows the firm to appoint an agent to exclusively represent one of the parties, either the buyer or the seller.

Detached property: A property standing apart; it is separate from other property.

Discount points: See point.

Down payment: The part of the purchase price of a property that the buyer pays in cash and does not finance with a mortgage.

Dual agent: Represents both the buyer and seller in a transaction. This agent is legally required to disclose the "dual" relationship to the parties involved. A dual agent must not disclose confidential information to either party.

Due Diligence: Buyers investigative process of inspecting the property, examining the title, and determining if the property meets the buyer's needs. Prior to the drop-dead date in the due diligence period, the buyer can terminate the Offer to Sell and Purchase agreement for any or no reason.

Due Diligence Fee: A fee that is offered for the privilege of placing a property under contract for a defined period of time, which is known as the due diligence period.

Due on sale clause: A clause in a mortgage contract requiring the borrower to pay the entire outstanding balance upon the sale or transfer of the property.

Easement: Right of way granted to a person or company authorizing access to the owner's land; for example, a utility company may be granted an easement to install wires or pipes.

Earnest money deposit: A deposit made by the potential homebuyer to show that he or she is serious about buying the house.

Endorsement: A provision added to a contract that alters the original contract in some way.

Equity: A homeowner's financial interest in a property. Equity is the difference between the fair market value of the property and the amount still owed on its mortgage.

Escrow: An item of value, money, or documents deposited with a third party to be delivered upon the fulfillment of a condition. For example, the deposit by a borrower with the lender of funds to pay taxes and insurance premiums when they become due, or the deposit of funds or documents with an attorney or escrow agent to be disbursed upon the closing of a sale of real estate.

Exclusive buyer's agent: An agent who does not ever take listings and who acts solely on behalf of the buyer. All agents of their brokerage firm do not take any listings.

Exclusive Right to Sell Listing: A listing contract where the owner hires a real estate broker as their exclusive agent to sell their real property for a designated period of time on the owner's stated terms for a negotiable commission.

Fannie Mae: Fannie Mae is a New York Stock Exchange company and the largest non-bank financial services company in the world. It operates pursuant to a federal charter and is the nation's largest source of financing for home mortgages. Over the past 30 years, Fannie Mae has provided nearly $2.5 trillion of mortgage financing for over 30 million families.

Federal Housing Administration (FHA): An agency of the U.S. Department of Housing and Urban Development (HUD). Its main activity is the insuring of residential mortgage loans made by private lenders. The FHA sets standards for construction and underwriting but does not lend money or plan or construct housing.

Fiduciary duties: A legal relationship between two or more parties, most commonly a "fiduciary" or "trustee" and a "principal" or "beneficiary." This relates most commonly to the handling of money or other financial transactions.

Firm commitment: A lender's agreement to make a loan to a specific borrower on a specific property.

Fixed-rate mortgage (FRM): A mortgage in which the interest rate does not change during the entire term of the loan.

Flood insurance: Insurance that compensates for physical property damage resulting from flooding. It is required for properties located in federally designated flood areas.

For Sale by Owner (FSBO): A property that is being sold directly by the owner. The owner has not retained the use of a real estate agent in selling the home.

Foreclosure: The legal process by which a borrower in default under a mortgage is deprived of his or her interest in the mortgaged property. This usually involves a forced sale of the property at public auction with the proceeds of the sale being applied to the mortgage debt.

Freddie Mac: A corporation chartered by Congress in 1970 to keep money flowing to mortgage lenders in support of homeownership.

It helps lower housing costs and provides better means to home financing.

Graduated Payment Mortgage: A fixed-rate, fixed-schedule loan which starts with lower payments than a level payment loan; the payments rise annually over the next several years and then stay constant for the remainder of the loan. These may cause negative equity.

Good Faith Estimate: An itemized approximation of the fees and costs (including the seller's costs) to close your mortgage loan. It is not an exact figure but rather an "estimate " of the amount of money you will need to bring to the closing table.

Gross Monthly Income (GMI): Consistent income that an individual receives each month, averaged over a period of time. It includes any bonuses, commissions, overtime pay, and income from interest or dividends.

Guarantee Certificate: A bond combined with an investment in an underlying value. The risk is limited with a Guaranteed Certificate because at the end of the lifetime of the Certificate you receive a part or all of the nominal value of your investment.

High-end home: High priced, expensive homes. Homes on the ultra-high end of the price scale. These are also referred to in the industry as luxury homes.

Home equity loan: A mortgage loan, which is usually in a subordinate position that allows the borrower to obtain multiple advances of the loan proceeds at his or her own discretion, up to an amount that represents a specified percentage of the borrower's equity in a property; also called a line of credit.

Home inspection: A thorough inspection that evaluates the structural and mechanical condition of a property. A satisfactory home inspection is often included as a contingency by the purchaser. A home inspection will often evaluate the electrical, plumbing and appliances as well as the condition of the roof, the crawl space and the presence or lack thereof of water in, around or beneath the home.

Home-loan underwriter: a trained professional who reviews all of the loan information, evaluates the creditworthiness of the borrower, and provides a decision on the loan request.

Homeowners association: A nonprofit association that manages the

common areas of a PUD (planned unit development) neighborhood or condominium project. In a condominium project, it has
no ownership interest in the common elements. In a PUD project
and in a neighborhood it holds title to the common elements.

Homeowner's insurance: An insurance policy that combines personal
liability insurance and hazard insurance coverage for a dwelling
and its contents.

Housing Finance Agency: A state agency that offers a limited amount
of below-market-rate home financing for low and moderate household incomes.

HUD-1 Settlement Statement: A document that provides an itemized
listing of the funds that are payable at closing. Items that appear
on the statement include real estate commissions, loan fees, points,
and initial escrow amounts. Each item on the statement is represented by a separate number within a standardized numbering
system. The totals at the bottom of the HUD-1 Settlement Statement define the seller's net proceeds (or net deficit) and the buyer's
net payment (or net proceeds) at closing. The blank form for the
statement is published by the Department of Housing and Urban
Development (HUD). The HUD-1 Settlement Statement is also
known as the "closing statement" or "settlement sheet."

Index: A number used to compute the interest rate for an adjustable-rate mortgage (ARM). The index is generally a published
number or percentage, such as the average interest rate or yield on
Treasury bills. A margin is added to the index to determine the interest rate that will be charged on the ARM. This interest rate is
subject to any caps that are associated with the mortgage.

Interest: The fee charged for borrowing money. The interest rate is the
rate of interest in effect for the monthly payment due.

Interest-only mortgages: A mortgage where the borrower only repays
the interest accumulated on the principal amount borrowed. The
principal amount of the mortgage is repaid at the end of the term
of the loan.

Interest rate lock-In: A written agreement in which the lender guarantees a specified interest rate if a mortgage goes to closing within a
set period of time. The lock-in also usually specifies the number of
points to be paid at closing.

Joint tenancy: A form of co-ownership that gives each tenant equal interest and equal rights in the property, including the right of survivorship.

Lien: A claim of monetary value against a property before the sale is finalized. Liens must be settled before the property title can be legally transferred to the new owner.

Listing: An agreement between a property owner and a real estate broker. The broker agrees to offer to sell the specific property at a certain price and certain terms in return for a fee or commission.

Loan commitment: See commitment letter.

Loan Default: Failure to make mortgage payments on a timely basis or to comply with other requirements of a mortgage.

Loan-to-value (LTV) percentage: The relationship between the principal balance of the mortgage and the appraised value (or sales price if it is lower) of the property. For example, a $100,000 home with an $80,000 mortgage has a LTV percentage of 80 percent.

Luxury home: See high-end home.

Margin: For an adjustable-rate mortgage (ARM), the amount that is added to the index to establish the interest rate on each adjustment date, subject to any limitations on the interest rate change.

Market comps: Also known as "comparables," an abbreviation for "comparable properties"; used for comparative purposes in the appraisal process. Comparables are properties like the property under consideration; they are reasonably the same size and location, and they have reasonably the same amenities and have recently been sold. Comparables help the appraiser determine the approximate fair market value of the subject property.

Mortgage: A legal document that pledges a property to the lender as security for payment of a debt.

Mortgagee: The lender who makes the mortgage loan.

Mortgage banker: A company that originates mortgages exclusively for resale in the secondary mortgage market.

Mortgage broker: An individual or company that brings borrowers and lenders together for the purpose of loan origination. Mortgage brokers typically require a fee or a commission for their services.

Mortgage commitment: A formal offer by a lender stating the terms under which it agrees to lend money to a homebuyer. Also known as a "loan commitment," a "commitment letter" or a "mortgage commitment."

Mortgagor: The buyer who pledges to keep the terms of the mortgage document.

Multifamily home: Properties that provide separate housing units for more than one family, although they secure only a single mortgage.

Multiple Listing Service (MLS): A marketing organization composed of member brokers agreeing to share their listing agreements with one another in the hope of finding ready, willing and able buyers for their properties.

Negative amortization: A gradual increase in mortgage debt that occurs when the monthly payment is not large enough to cover the entire principal and interest due. The amount of the shortfall is added to the remaining balance to create "negative" amortization.

Note: A formal document showing the existence of a debt and stating the terms of repayment.

Offer: A promise by one party to act in a certain manner if the other party agrees to act as requested. An offer shows an intention to enter into a contract.

PITI: See principal, interest, taxes, and insurance (PITI).

Point: A one-time fee or charge by the lender for originating a loan. One point represents 1 percent of the amount of the loan principal. If the lender charges one origination point on a $200,000 loan, the fee is $2,000, paid at closing or settlement.

Prepayment: Payment of all or part of a debt prior to its maturity.

Prepayment penalty: A fee that may be charged to a borrower who pays off a loan before it is due.

Preapproval: A guaranteed mortgage approval secured by a potential homebuyer before he or she makes an offer on a house. A lending institution guarantees, in writing, to approve a loan for a specified amount.

Predatory lending practices: Methods used by predatory lenders, appraisers, or mortgage brokers to sell, for example, properties beyond their worth by using false appraisals. These practices also include lending more money than a borrower can afford to repay or encouraging buyers to lie about their income.

Prequalification: The process of determining how much money a prospective homebuyer will be eligible to borrow before he or she applies for a loan.

Principal: The amount borrowed originally (excluding interest) or remaining unpaid; the part of the monthly payment that reduces the remaining balance of a mortgage.

Principal, interest, taxes, and insurance (PITI): The four components of a monthly mortgage payment. Principal refers to the part of the monthly payment that reduces the remaining balance of the mortgage. Interest is the fee charged for borrowing money. Taxes and insurance refer to the amounts that are paid into an escrow account each month for property taxes and mortgage and hazard insurance.

Private mortgage insurance (PMI): Mortgage insurance that is provided by a private mortgage insurance company to protect lenders against loss if a borrower defaults. Most lenders generally require MI for a loan with a loan-to-value (LTV) percentage in excess of 80 percent.

Property deed: A document that transfers ownership of real estate. It contains the names of the old and new owners and a legal description of the property. The individual transferring the property signs the deed and has it notarized. To complete the transfer, the deed must be recorded in the office of the Register of Deeds where the property is located.

Property disclosure: Makes known material facts, which are defined as the details about the condition or legal status, about the house that is being sold.

Property Survey: A drawing or map that shows the boundaries of the property. It may also show any easements or encroachments to or from the property and other existing conditions about the property.

Purchase price: The sales price or the amount that is paid for anything that is bought; the price paid for a home.

Purchase and sale agreement: A written contract signed by the buyer and seller stating the terms and conditions under which a property will be sold.

Qualifying ratios: Calculations that are used in determining whether a borrower can qualify for a mortgage. They consist of two separate calculations: (1) the total housing expense compared to the borrower's gross monthly income as a percent of income ratio and (2) the total housing expense and other total debt obligations compared to the borrower's gross monthly income as a percent of income ratio.

Real estate agent: A person licensed to negotiate and transact the sale of real estate on behalf of the property owner.

Real estate broker: A person who, for a commission or a fee, brings parties together and assists in negotiating contracts between them. The real estate broker is the person who handles (or "brokers") the transaction between buyers and sellers.

Real Estate Settlement Procedures Act (RESPA): A federal law requiring lenders to provide homebuyers with information about known or estimated settlement costs. The act also regulates other various aspects of the settlement procedures.

REALTOR®: A real estate broker or an associate who holds active membership in a local real estate board that is affiliated with the NATIONAL ASSOCIATION OF REALTORS®.

Recording Fee: A fee charged for recording the transfer of a property, paid to a city, county or other branch of government.

Refinance: The process of paying off one loan with the proceeds from a new loan using the same property as security.

Repayment mortgage: Involves the repayment of both capital and interest in monthly installments within a specified term of years.

Reverse mortgage: A financial tool that provides homeowners who are of retirement age (62 in the U.S.) and occupying the property as their principal residence with money from the equity in their homes. Usually, no payments are made on a reverse mortgage until the property is sold or the buyer moves.

Sales Contract: A contract between a buyer and seller which explains in detail exactly what the purchase includes, what guarantees there are, the price, when the closing will occur and other various details about the transfer of the property.

Seller's agent: An agent who represents the seller. Usually referred to as the listing agent, this agent is empowered by a property owner to find a buyer for the property.

Servicer: An organization that collects principal and interest payments from borrowers and manages borrowers' escrow accounts. The servicer often services mortgages that have been purchased by an investor in the secondary mortgage market.

Settlement: Closing.

Settlement sheet: See HUD-1 Settlement Statement.

Showing: Permitting potential buyers access to a home for sale.

Single-family home: Home that sits on its own piece of land. It is not attached to anyone else's residence.

Spec home: A house built before it is sold. The builder speculates that he can sell it.

Subagency: An agency whose broker brings the buyer to a property. Subagents are paid by the seller and have a financial responsibility to the seller.

Subprime lender: Charges a finance rate that is higher than the "prime" rate offered by conventional lenders. This type of lender approves loans for individuals who may have poor or no credit history.

Tenancy in Common: A form of ownership in which the tenants have equal ownership interests in a property. Each owner has the right to leave his or her share of the property to any beneficiary of the owner's choosing.

Term: A length of time assigned to something such as a payment.

Time is of the Essence: Phrase in a contract requiring the performance of a certain act no later than the stated time. Should this certain act not be completed by the prescribed time, the non-compliant party is in breach of the contract, which may be voidable.

Title: A legal document evidencing a person's right to or ownership of a property.

Title company: A company that specializes in examining and insuring titles to real estate.

Title insurance: Insurance that protects the lender (lender's policy) or the buyer (owner's policy) against loss arising from disputes over ownership of a property.

Title search: A check of the title records to ensure that the seller is the legal owner of the property and that there are no liens or other claims outstanding.

Townhouse: A single-family dwelling unit built in a group of attached units in which each unit extends from foundation to roof with open space on at least two sides. Townhouse ownership does include individual ownership of the land.

Transactional brokerage: Limited agency that represents neither the buyer nor the seller. This brokerage only facilitates or conducts the sale.

Transfer taxes: Taxes levied on the transfer of property by state or local government.

Valuation: The estimated worth or value of something.

Veterans Administration: A federal agency that insures mortgage loans with very liberal down payment requirements for honorably discharged veterans and their surviving spouses.

Walk-through: A visit to the house to be purchased before the closing and property ownership is transferred. It is an opportunity to make sure that the house has been left in the expected condition and that negotiated repairs have been made.

Warranty: A promise either written or implied that the material and workmanship of a product is defect-free or will meet a certain level of performance over a specific period of time.

Zoning: Regulations established by local government regarding the usage of a piece of property within a specific area.